TEMPTED
Women

T E M P T E D

Women

❧

The Passions, Perils, and Agonies of Female Infidelity

C A R O L   B O T W I N

WILLIAM MORROW AND COMPANY, INC.
New York

It is the policy of William Morrow and Company, Inc., and its imprints and affiliates, recognizing the importance of preserving what has been written, to print the books we publish on acid-free paper, and we exert our best efforts to that end.

Library of Congress Cataloging-in-Publication Data

Botwin, Carol.
    Tempted Women : the passions, perils, and agonies of female
infidelity / Carol Botwin.
        p.   cm.
    Includes bibliographical references and index.
    ISBN 0-688-11646-9
    1. Adultery.   2. Married women—Sexual behavior.   3. Husbands—
Sexual behavior.   I. Title.
HQ806.B673   1994
306.73'6—dc20
                                                                                93-28822
                                                                                CIP

Printed in the United States of America

First Edition

1 2 3 4 5 6 7 8 9 10

BOOK DESIGN BY PATRICE FODERO

TO ALEXANDRA AND WILLIAM,
AS ALWAYS

ACKNOWLEDGMENTS

My very special thanks go to all the brave and candid women who revealed the passions, pleasures, and agonies of their extramarital love affairs either in letters or in person. Without the contributions of this necessarily anonymous group, this book could not exist.

I am also grateful to Liza Dawson for her editorial support, enthusiasm, and suggestions. Finally, Barbara Lowenstein, my agent, brought this book into being through her brilliant determination and initiative. I am indebted to her for that, and for her continued support over the years.

TABLE OF CONTENTS

Chapter 1

❦

THE GROWING WORLD OF
UNFAITHFUL WIVES

Linda is going about her usual morning routine. A sweet-looking, tall blonde, Linda at age forty is a successful interior designer. After seeing her husband, a lawyer, off to work she bundles her seven-year-old daughter into warm clothing and, in the brisk wind of the winter morning, walks her to school. She drops her child off, then strolls to a fashionable shopping area nearby where she stops to see a few antique dealers in search of some tables and mirrors for her clients.

When she finishes her business, Linda doesn't return to her own apartment. Instead, she walks to a building a few blocks away, takes the elevator to an apartment on the eighth floor, rings the bell, and is greeted at the door by an older, charming European art dealer she met while lunching with a client. He has been eagerly awaiting her.

Linda has been having an affair with this man for the past two years, seeing him three afternoons a week. She is part of a large group of daring women who have swollen the population of unfaithful wives in our society to an all-time high.

Husbands have always been known to cheat in large numbers—in 1948, Alfred Kinsey, in his first landmark study of human sexuality, pegged the rate of male infidelity at 50 percent. Other, more recent estimates place the contemporary figure at anywhere from 60 to as much as 70 percent for men in the upper income brackets.

Although it has taken a while for women to embrace the playing-around game, statistics from many sources indicate that wives increasingly have been taking lovers of their own. The rise in female infidelity is evident once you look at the results of these surveys:

In 1953, Kinsey reported that 26 percent of wives had been unfaithful.

By 1970, the number had risen to 36 percent, according to a poll done for *Psychology Today* magazine.

In 1975, a survey of the readers of *Redbook* magazine (considered to be a conservative population of women) uncovered the fact that 39 percent of them had been unfaithful.

In 1980, Paul Gebhard, a coauthor of the first original Kinsey report, estimated that 40 percent of married women would have an affair by the age of forty. That same year, a survey conducted by *Cosmopolitan* magazine came up with the startling fact that 51 percent of its readers had committed adultery.

In 1982, a survey by *Playboy* that included fifteen thousand females found that 38 percent of the wives had been unfaithful.

In 1984, *Playgirl* magazine sponsored a survey that revealed one out of every two wives among 1,207 women had played around.

In 1986, a survey of thirty-four thousand women by *New Woman* magazine found that 41 percent of the wives had actually had extramarital sex, while 44 percent admitted being tempted.

In 1989, *New York Woman* magazine polled its readers and reported that almost one out of every two wives surveyed had cheated.

In that same year *Woman* magazine revealed (in a report I wrote for the magazine) that half the women who had responded to its survey about office affairs were wives carrying on with men they had met in the workplace.

Of course, men still are having more affairs than women, but based on cumulative data, the evidence is quite clear: Women are catching up to men, and both sexes are indulging in a lot more extramarital hanky-panky.

The high rates of female infidelity uncovered by the more recent surveys jibe with earlier predictions by many respected sex researchers. Looking at the greater number of unfaithful wives among younger women (a finding of all surveys since Kinsey's), and figuring that these younger women would be moving through the life cycle, researchers Morton Hunt; James Ramey; and Gilbert Nass, Roger Libby, and Mary Fisher all made an educated guess that in the last years of this century—just about now—45 to 55 percent of all married women would be unfaithful by age forty.

As I report later in this book, two surveys reveal that in the youngest age groups, under the age of thirty, wives may even be outstripping husbands by a small margin.

No one knows how the fear of AIDS may be cutting into the infidelity rates of both sexes, but, according to recent reports, heterosexual women and men are still by and large continuing to practice sex as they did before it became so potentially deadly. Only two among the 250 letters in my files from women having affairs mentioned AIDS.

The statistics alone warrant a serious consideration of infidelity—a significant proportion of the female population is involved. Using a conservative estimate backed by the majority of the surveys cited, if approximately 40 percent of wives in the United States have had extramarital relationships, that means more than twenty-one million wives in this country alone have sampled the joys and sorrows of a secret love life.

Women as a group don't cheat lightly, and don't have quick or casual flings. Because most have serious, lengthy affairs that engage their emotions, unfaithful wives tend to be troubled in one way or another. They are afloat in uncharted waters, in which they often flounder.

WOMEN IN THE DARK

There are no guidelines for women in affairs, no models except soap operas and steamy novels, which serve up glamorized and inaccurate portraits. In more serious works of fiction suicide, social ostracism, and other disasters, unlikely for contemporary women, befall possible models like Anna Karenina and Madame Bovary.

Women are further hampered in understanding the female experience of adultery by the secrecy that surrounds their liaisons. Wives are extremely furtive about their extramarital activities. As a result, many of them have no idea how other women act and react in similar situations. With no confidantes, they have no place to unload their feelings. They are unable to seek solace or insight into their dilemmas. They often feel very alone.

As I have discovered, an illicit relationship is not all glamour, romance, or joy for the woman involved. Romance and joy may, indeed, be there, but wives involved with other men are also often conflicted, confused, subject to incredible highs and devastating lows.

I am quite certain, from the 250 letters written in response to the office affair survey I authored, and from the other case histories of unfaithful wives that form the basis of this book, that in the end wives are not liberated as women by their affairs, as Dalma Heyn suggested in her recent book, *The Erotic Silence of the American Wife*. Instead, there is a tendency for wives to become obsessed with their lovers and emotionally dependent upon their relationships. They are unable to break off their affairs even when they want to.

Here is an example of the kind of helpless dependency that too often sets in:

Dear Carol,

I am a thirty-three-year-old woman. I have been married for fifteen years to a man who is gentle, kind, and a very good provider. In the first three years of our marriage we were very much in love and our sex life was excellent. Twelve years ago we moved to the town we live in at present. I met this man twenty-one years older than I am. We began an affair. He was also married. Gradually I grew apart from my husband, although I believe he still loves me. I love this other man more than I ever believed possible.

Four years ago he was divorced from his wife. Just prior to his divorce I had a son. I do not know which man is the father. Since his divorce, this other man started to date other women in the open while continuing to see me secretly. Three months ago I decided I couldn't take his seeing other women, so I told him we should stop seeing each other. He agreed, mainly because of my intense jealousy. He says he has to get on with his life and he never promised me any future with him. I still see him about twice a week. I know for both our sakes I need to let him go, but I can't. Each time I see him I fall apart. I can't help myself and I don't know what to do.

Another wife wrote:

I still love my husband and I never want to hurt him. I hope to God he never finds out. I also know I cannot stop this affair. I need it. My greatest fear is that my lover will want to call it quits.

My own conclusion about the way wives ultimately lapse into dependency upon their lovers is echoed by sociologist Annette Lawson's observations about a population of unfaithful women in Great Britain. What we have here, then, is a large group of women still, in many ways, at the mercy of men they care for, even in an outlaw situation.

Why women get involved and what happens to them when they do are the subjects of this book. Although there are some wives who get sexually involved with other women, that is another story for another time. This book is about heterosexual affairs. There is a heavy concentration on *real* affairs—the ones that seem to go on for years—because they seem to be what most women have. That was certainly true among the 250 women who wrote letters about their extramarital liaisons, among those seeking my counsel as an advice columnist, among the women whose case histories are in my files, and among participants in my workshops. It is also serious, emotional affairs that tend to get women into the most trouble.

In addition to wives already embroiled with other men, this book is for the uncounted but considerable number of women consumed by temptation, who fantasize about extramarital partners and wonder what it would be like to have an affair.

Studies show that sex with a different partner is the favorite fantasy of married women. This fantasy generally arises while they are making love to their husbands, but I have found it haunts a lot of wives outside the bedroom as well. Here are two examples, drawn from the many letters about extramarital fantasies I received during my years as an advice columnist for *New Woman* and *Woman* magazines:

Dear Carol,

I am very happy with my married life of five years, but I catch myself daydreaming about one of my co-workers. We have been friends since I started working here three years ago. We find it very easy to talk to one another. I can tell he finds me intriguing and I like the attention he gives me! He says, "Boy, if you weren't married." I only want to have a platonic friendship with him and have told him so. But we both get a feeling of excitement when we are with each other. I know if I wanted him sexually he would hop to it. I like the fantasizing I do about him, but I have become so obsessed. . . .

Dear Carol,

I'm going crazy. I find myself extremely attracted to a man I work with. I think about him all the time and find little excuses to go in his office and talk to him. The trouble is I am married and have been for fifteen years. I love my husband and don't know why I am having these fantasies about someone else. I am anxious at the thought of a possible romance and all the wonderful feelings associated with it, coupled with guilt for even thinking about such a thing. My mind is always wandering to this man.

INCREASING TEMPTATION

I believe we are currently living in a world of tempted women. What draws wives into actual affairs is explored in the heart of this book. However, our culture contributes to the temptation that women everywhere are experiencing—often to their own discomfort, as the letters above indicate.

Soap operas, best-selling novels, the lyrics of country and rock music, and the movies all portray wives in affairs, often in appealing, glamorous ways. Subliminally these images pave the path to adultery. When an opportunity presents itself (as it does increasingly among working wives, who constitute the majority these days) women are more likely to want to try extramarital romance.

The media are also full of real-life illicit affairs. Royal princesses are accused of having lovers on the front pages of tabloids. Royal princes are accused of having affairs with women married to other men. Married movie and television stars are, thanks to the press, having "secret" affairs publicly. Biographies and autobiographies of film stars like Ingrid Bergman and Joan Crawford reveal lives dotted with extramarital affairs. Maria Callas, the opera star, carried on her liaison with Aristotle Onassis quite openly, even though she was married at the time. What all this public exposure of the love lives of the high and mighty does is create a climate of acceptance for extramarital affairs for others.

We are in an era of quick fixes as well. When something goes wrong we look for a fast remedy. If there is trouble in a marriage, it often seems easier to seek solace with another man than to confront the problem and go to work on the marriage.

The philosophy of me-first selfishness holds sway in our culture and contributes to adultery, too. The idea that you have a right to whatever you think will give you pleasure or happiness makes it easier to give in to temptation when it arises.

Finally, there is a less obvious but intriguing factor at work. Adultery has always been associated with dominance on the part of the adulterer. Men have been able to institutionalize it as their right and get away with it so freely in the past because they were the ones with the power and the control of financial resources within the family. Historically, women with power and resources of their own have always indulged in more adultery than others. Queens like Catherine the Great of Russia took lovers rather openly. In the upper classes generally, women with their own wealth and influence have always had more lovers than their middle-class sisters, and have silently been permitted to do so in their own circles.

If there is a relationship between rates of adultery and dominance, and I believe there is, then we must look at the increasing number of dominant women in our society today. As I point out in other parts of this book, higher education, larger paychecks, the power to make decisions in the family, sexual aggressiveness—all have been shown to be linked with increased rates of female infidelity. Since, in our culture, there are more college-educated women, more women earning higher salaries, more women who are able to make the first move in the bedroom, and more women involved in making family decisions than ever before, females may simply be seizing the prerogative that has always gone along with dominance.

In my last book, *Men Who Can't Be Faithful,* I gave women insight into the extramarital excursions of their husbands—something they sorely needed, according to the response of readers. With this book, *Tempted Women,* I am rounding out the subject of infidelity and giving women information they need to understand themselves or other women in the most secret part of female life.

I have found out, in the writing of this book, just how curious men are about women's infidelity as well. So, I say welcome, too, to any male readers who want to understand more about what tempts wives to stray and what they think and feel when they do. A lot of what you will be hearing will be in the unfaithful women's own voices.

Chapter 2

❀

How to Predict
Whether a Woman
Will Have an Affair

What makes a woman a prime candidate for a steamy affair? Novelists have drawn memorable portraits of Anna Karenina, Madame Bovary, Hester Prynne in *The Scarlet Letter*, Isadora Wing in *Fear of Flying*—unforgettable women drawn into forbidden, overwhelming passion. The *Odyssey* gave us their opposite—Penelope, who remained faithful despite the long absence of her wandering husband, Odysseus, and plenty of suitors clamoring at her door. Tales of King Arthur and the Knights of the Round Table told us of Arthur's wife, Guinevere, lusting after Lancelot. Isolde letched after Tristan. The movies gave us Mrs. Robinson seducing Dustin Hoffman, as a very young man, in *The Graduate*.

Always the stuff of fiction, adultery in real life has only more recently come under the professional scrutiny of social scientists and professionals in the field of psychology, who have been pondering the question of who commits adultery and why. Ever since Alfred Kinsey first made the study of human sexuality a respectable pursuit with the publication of his first groundbreaking Kinsey Report in 1948, there has been a stream of professional and scientific papers, studies, and surveys on the subject. They have given us clues as to why a wife who, like most young brides, originally believed in fidelity, turns around and risks all—her marriage, her home, her children, her security, her social standing, and sometimes her job—for the forbidden: the anxiety-provoking but incomparable excitement of a secret love.

Here is what has been uncovered about factors that could predict whether you, your wife, or a woman you know might play with fire and take a lover:

1. ***You have the chance to do it.***   It seems that virtue is not always behind monogamy—the lack of an amorous male in the vicinity may be more to the point for some wives. Ralph Johnson, who examined the background causes of extramarital sex in the *Journal of Marriage and the Family,* came to the conclusion that opportunity was one of the prime reasons it took place. When the subjects of his study perceived the opportunity for a liaison, it occurred 40 percent of the time.

A woman, married for twenty-five years, explained in a letter how she seized her chance: "After my children were grown and had left the house, I went to work. Little did I know I would be pursued and so taken by the owner of the company who is ten years my junior. I had always fantasized about sex with other men because my husband was my one and only lover. When this man made *extreme* advances I decided to try it out.

"What a trip! Our sex is fantastic and it has made my sex life with my husband even better. Everything is so *intense!* I can't imagine giving up either one as they both satisfy me on different levels. I hope this situation continues forever."

2. ***You are a working wife.***   What better place is there for opportunity to present itself than an office, where, like the woman above, you find yourself in close proximity to attractive men? More than half the wives in the United States are working today, and if you are one of them you stand a better chance of having an affair than if you stay at home.

The link between employment and infidelity showed up clearly long ago. In 1977 Carol Tavris and Susan Sadd, reporting on the sex lives of one hundred thousand women, found that 47 percent of wives employed full-time had been unfaithful by the age of forty. This was true for significantly fewer (33 percent) of the women who remained housewives. In 1989, half the respondents to *Woman* magazine's office affairs survey confessed that they were married. One out of three wives had found a lover in the place where she worked in sociologist Annette Lawson's 1988 study, *Adultery.* Among younger women the number increased to 44 percent. The overall total was still higher because an additional group of working wives had found the men they were carrying on with not in their own places of employment, but in meetings connected to work. In a 1986 sex survey by *New Woman* magazine, 57 percent of employed wives had met their lovers at work.

The workplace, it seems, is a sexy place. Here, from a woman involved with her boss, is a glimpse of what can go on: "I really enjoy teasing my lover at work. Sometimes I won't wear any underwear and then I will tell him that we are the only people who know this fact. Sometimes I will brush up against him, with no underwear on, and it drives him wild! It is also very exciting to know that we are having an affair about which the other office help don't know, especially if we have a roll in the hay at lunchtime and then come back to the office and act very professional and businesslike."

3. *You are in a formerly male profession.* Doctor, lawyer, movie producer, trucker, business owner, engineer, architect, scientist, ad space salesperson, manager, construction worker—Annette Lawson found the number of affairs increased for women working in what used to be typical men's jobs. Interestingly, for men in typical female occupations such as teaching, the number of affairs decreased.

4. *One of your parents cheated.* According to psychiatrists, psychologists, family therapists, and other mental health professionals, there is a great tendency to repeat a family pattern. If your mother had an affair, you may believe, based on your earlier experience, that infidelity in marriage is normal. Or if your mother suffered from the cheating of your father, rather than become a victim of male infidelity like her, you may become the doer and start to philander yourself.

5. *You make sexual overtures to your husband.* In a study analyzing factors connected to female infidelity, sociologist Robert Bell found that almost half of 172 unfaithful wives were also sexual initiators at home more than 16 percent of the time. This connection may account, at least in part, for the contemporary increase in female infidelity.

Women under about the age of forty are more likely to make sexual overtures than older women who were trained to wait to be asked. As they go through the life cycle, these younger women continue to be more aggressive about their sexual desires and, if their marriages persist, are therefore more likely to cheat.

A study in the August 1992 issue of the *Journal of Sex Research* confirmed, through a comparison of groups born between 1900 and 1970, that an increasing proportion of women are initiating sex.

6. *You believe that infidelity is justified under certain circum-stances.*   Although, basically, you may believe monogamy is best, you may have more liberal attitudes when certain conditions prevail—for example, if a woman feels unhappy with her mate, if a couple are separated for a period of time, if a wife falls in love with someone else, if a woman doesn't receive sexual fulfillment in her marriage. Whatever the reasons, psychologist Shirley Glass has concluded from her studies of extramarital relations that people are more likely to cheat at some time themselves when they believe that there are some legitimate excuses for adultery.

7. *You know someone who has had an affair.*   After examining the cases of forty unfaithful wives, sociologist Lynn Atwater found this was a powerful factor leading up to a woman's decision to try it out herself. The same was true of women who had talked to someone about extramarital sex. Annette Lawson discovered that the more liaisons people had, the more friends they had who also were adulterous.

A woman involved in a fifteen-year relationship with a man in her own profession revealed this sequence of events: "Before I started my affair, I knew one woman who had a lover. And then in an organization to which I belonged I discovered, after I got to know them, that a couple of women who are my best friends now were also having affairs. Then after I got involved with Sam there was another couple, both married to other people—the four of us would do things together. It was like a little club outside of marriage, you know?"

8. *You live in a large city.*   A paper investigating the relationship between community size and infidelity published in the *Journal of Marriage and the Family* in 1985 found that residents of rural areas disapprove of extramarital sex much more than city dwellers. The study concluded that the size of the community in which you reside has a lot to do with infidelity.

9. *You dominate decisions made in your family.*   John Edwards and Alan Booth, investigating sexual behavior in and out of marriage, discovered that the woman who rules the roost is more likely to have an affair.

10. *Your husband loves you more than you love him.*   In their study *American Couples,* Philip Blumstein and Pepper Schwartz concluded that if you are the partner who loves less, you are less committed, less needy, and more apt to take risks in the relationship. Based on their data these sociologists said, "When a partner was the less committed person, he or she was also more likely to be non-monogamous. On the

other hand, the more committed partner is too much in love and prizes the relationship too highly to look at other people."

Approximately 20 percent of the adulterous wives in Annette Lawson's study said they had not been in love when they married—less than 10 percent of the faithful wives made this claim.

A woman in her forties, involved in an affair with a co-worker for more than a year, said, "I don't feel guilty because I have never told my husband I loved him. Not even once. I married him for financial security. We have been married for fifteen years. With my lover I am finally able to feel lust and all the things that go with being in love."

A thirty-six-year-old wife confessed, "I married a man I didn't love. My parents said, 'Marry him, he will be good to you.' I was young and I did marry him. My mistake." She went on to describe the affair she is now having: "It didn't happen overnight. It took four years for us to be even alone together. We made love for the first time this summer. We spent seven hours together. It was the most beautiful day of my life—the first time I had been in the arms of a man I loved. I was faithful to my husband for sixteen years. I am good to him as he is to me, but now I know what it is to make love to a man I am in love with and it's incredible."

11. *You are a young woman.* Ever since Kinsey's days, women in younger age groups have been having more affairs than older women. In 1975, for example, Robert Bell's study of female infidelity found the highest rates of extramarital sex in the twenty-six-to-thirty age group. The *American Couples* survey in 1983 also found that young wives were more likely to have sex outside marriage.

In recent times there are reports that wives are having even *more* affairs than men at young ages. A *Playboy* survey of one hundred thousand people in 1982 found that women in their twenties had 10 percent more affairs than their youthful husbands.

Annette Lawson's study of adultery in 1988 contained similar findings—10 percent more adultery by young wives than husbands. She also discovered that younger women start affairs much earlier in their marriages than women used to, moving from the previous average waiting period of fourteen and a half years for a first liaison for those married before 1960, to just a little more than five years for the modern bride.

12. *You are in your thirties or early forties.* Another surge of infidelity in the lifespan of married women occurs in this age group,

according to the surveys of Alfred Kinsey, Robert Levin, and Robert Bell. Despite the fact that younger women start their affairs at an earlier stage, and outstrip young husbands in adulterous encounters, in sheer numbers it is women in their thirties and early forties who have the most affairs.

This may be because the adulterous younger women's marriages are of shorter duration. According to the findings of Morton Hunt, women who had affairs within the first two years after they wed were also likely to end up divorced early in the marriage. In general, divorce rates for young women who have extramarital adventures are higher than for unfaithful older wives.

In Robert Bell's survey of more than two thousand women, the mean age for women in affairs was thirty-five, a finding pretty much duplicated by a survey of members of the American Association of Marriage and Family Counselors, which pinpointed thirty-six as the average age of danger for women.

13. **You have had a lot of premarital sexual experience.** Since Kinsey's original sex surveys, researchers have consistently found a link between sex before marriage and extramarital sex—the more you have of the first, the greater the likelihood of the second.

If this connection is still as strong as it has been in the past, then there should indeed be a lot of adultery today: The number of females who are sexually experienced before marriage has increased from about 50 percent in the 1940s to 90 percent in the 1990s, according to Dr. June Reinisch, director emeritus of the Kinsey Institute for Sex Research.

Not only do contemporary unmarried women give up their virginity, but once they do, they have more sex partners than nonvirgins used to. A study by Dr. Gail Wyatt and others in the *Archives of Sexual Behavior* pointed out the dramatic increase: In the Kinsey sample, 42 percent of the women had had only one premarital partner. However, just 11 percent of contemporary women limited themselves to a single premarital lover. The proportion reporting eleven or more partners rose from 7 percent among Kinsey's subjects to 52 percent among today's women.

14. **You are better educated than your husband.** Annette Lawson discovered that women whose education exceeded their partners' had higher-than-average rates of infidelity and a greater number of extramarital partners.

Kinsey found that before the age of twenty-five education made little difference in the rate of infidelity; however, after the age of twenty-five there was more adultery among better-educated women.

Gail Wyatt found that less-educated women are currently catching up to those with higher educations. The greatest increase in extramarital sex in recent times is among women with a high school education or less. However, whatever your educational level—if you went to school longer than your partner, you are more at risk for an affair.

15. *You are at a transition or crisis point in your life.* It may be that you are at or near a birthday with a zero at the end of it—30, 40, 50—and feel uncertain about the direction in which your life is going or that time is slipping away.

Perhaps you have gone back to school or returned to work and found your horizons changing. Maybe you have been unsettled by an illness and are more aware of the fragility of life. Possibly your children have all left home or you have lost a great deal of weight.

Events that make you change your viewpoint about yourself or life, that exhilarate and expand you or throw you a little off balance, can lead to seizing a new love or trying another man on for size.

A woman who went back to college in her forties wrote, "I never intended to have an affair. My lover is my former college professor who shares my love of literature. We started this relationship very innocently, by having lunch after class and discussing the class. I found him to be caring, sensitive, understanding, and very sexy."

16. *You have just moved to a new community.* According to research, moving is one of the twenty most stressful events in life. It is often accompanied by a sense of loss—of familiar surrounding, friends, sometimes family. Some women unconsciously react to the upset in their lives by finding a lover, often to their own surprise, as in the case of this twenty-seven-year-old woman who was forced to move to another part of the country: "I started my affair two and a half years ago when my husband was transferred here. My lover was one of the first people I met, and it was like an explosion, an electrical charge. Love at first sight, and I don't believe in that stuff!"

Another woman explained, "I was married for twenty-nine years and *never* had an affair. We recently moved from Boston to Vermont. I met this man at my new job. There were no marital problems. I don't know why I got involved other than a sudden very strong attraction."

17. ***A parent has recently died.*** Sometimes this makes a woman feel free to do things she knows her mother or father would have disapproved of, like involve herself in an extramarital affair. Sometimes she doesn't feel her husband is supportive enough at this needy time in her life. Other women, according to leading sex and marital therapist Dr. Harold Lief, are unconsciously trying to compensate for the loss they have suffered.

A woman who started an affair at a time of mourning explained, "I was trying to adjust to the death of my father and remarriage of my mother. My boss understood my feelings of confusion and readjustment. He listened. He showed me he cared by doing little 'romantic' things for me—flowers, tapes, notes. I responded although I am married. No one had ever done these things for me before, and things like that mean *everything* to me. I didn't mean to fall in love with him, but I did."

A woman in her thirties in New England told of meeting a man at work who first impressed her because he was sympathetic and listened to her problems there. "About three months later," she explained, "my father passed away and that was very difficult and traumatic. My husband was not too consoling. He and my father did not get along very well. Again Chuck was there for me when I needed someone. That was when the affair started. I was quite vulnerable at that time and had no resistance."

18. ***You and your husband spend a lot of time apart.*** You work inordinately long hours and are apart from each other practically from the moment you leave for work till the time you crawl into bed. Or you work different shifts and one sleeps while the other is awake. Or one of you travels a lot on business. Or you spend a large part of your leisure time pursuing individual interests.

The *American Couples* survey found that partners who lead "separate" lives have more of a tendency to engage in extramarital sex. Researchers Graham Spanier and Randie Margolis found 20 percent more extramarital sex among spouses who took separate vacations.

A thirty-seven-year-old woman in the Midwest explained her circumstances: "I work forty hours a week. My husband has two jobs, and when I am off work he is still at one of them. This doesn't leave time for a relationship. I met my lover at my place of employment. We have known each other for ten years, but two years ago he kissed me a couple of times over a cup of coffee and that was the beginning of a love affair."

28

A woman in her early thirties said, "My affair began three years ago at a time when I was very vulnerable. I am the mother of two children. My husband works the night shift at his job and I spend a great deal of time with the children or alone."

19. *You feel sexually deprived.* Anthony Thompson, examining the body of research about infidelity, found a pervasive theme and pinpointed it in the *Journal of Sex Research*: the lower the frequency and quality of marital intercourse, the more likely the occurrence of extramarital sex. For wives, sexual deprivation as a reason for adultery has increased along with sexual liberation and the feeling among women that they are *entitled* to certain things, among them a good sex life.

A redheaded woman in the South told of meeting her lover at a time of sexual need: "My husband decided to go back to school and we left the city we were in to go to a university in another town. I think in that year maybe we had sex four times. He said he was too busy with schoolwork. I began to feel more like his mother than anything else. I was neglected and sexually starved. Then I took a class at the college and I met Frank. He was very attentive to me and I knew right away I wanted it to be sexual. I felt that he was a gift from heaven."

20. *You are dissatisfied with your marriage.* Anthony Thompson, in his review of the research literature about extramarital sex, concluded that a negative rating of one's marriage is another of the strongest antecedents to an affair. Shirley Glass and Thomas Wright, investigating the relationship of marital satisfaction to infidelity, found that unhappiness contributed greatly in general, but was even more strongly correlated with extramarital sex for women married more than twelve years. Older wives try to compensate for the deficits in the marriage with a lover, while these days young wives who are really unhappy tend to divorce early in the marriage instead.

"At the time my affair started," explained a wife in Florida, "my husband was drinking too much, not coming home, or coming home late and falling asleep immediately in front of the TV. I began to wonder if, at age forty-four, I was still desirable to anyone. I'm not bad-looking, am not overweight, have a college degree and a good job, but I felt underappreciated, undesirable, and lonely. On a business trip I was having a drink with my boss. He very tentatively leaned forward to kiss me. I kissed him back."

21. ***You are content with your marriage.***   This may sound like a contradiction of the above; however, it describes a significant minority of women having affairs—20 percent of the wives in Robert Bell's study of female infidelity, and 34 percent of the unfaithful wives in a study of three hundred people by Shirley Glass and Thomas Wright published in 1985 in the journal *Sex Roles.*

Analyzing the phenomenon of adulterous happy wives in the *Journal of Marriage and the Family,* Glass and Wright found that these women were, for the most part, young and married two years or less (the unhappy ones divorced, as mentioned above). These young wives, who often entered marriage with a lot of premarital sexual experience, seem to be having a hard time adjusting to monogamy. They are just looking for a new sexual thrill. (See Chapter 4.)

A twenty-seven-year-old woman from the Midwest explained, "Why do I get involved with other men? Mainly for the excitement. Just seeing that special person makes my heart race. Those knowing glances, stolen kisses, or quick touches are incredible! This is the first real affair I've had with a co-worker. I've had lots of one-night stands for fun. I don't want to marry any of these guys. My husband means too much to me. I have all the love and security I need right here at home. The difference between me and a lot of people I've come in contact with is that I see love and sex as two *totally* different things. Sex is fun. Love is forever."

22. ***You have fantasized about having an affair for a long time.***
According to Lynn Atwater's study, women often pave the way to an affair by spending time thinking about it.

Watching sexy soap operas or reading novels that feature adulterous affairs, or simply wondering persistently what it would be like with another man, mulling over whether you really want outside sex, figuring out whether it would be good or bad for you and your marriage, can plant a mental seed that grows with time.

Thinking about infidelity persisted from several weeks to several years for three quarters of the unfaithful wives in Atwater's study, who were, as a result, ready for an excursion into extramarital sex.

23. ***Romance has disappeared from your marriage.***   If you long for the lost feeling of romance in your relationship and your husband isn't interested in restoring it, you may be ripe for an extramarital liaison that will bring back the thrills, excitement, and charged emotions you remember so well. The search for romance motivated many of the subjects

in John Cuber and Peggy Harroff's study *Sex and the Significant Americans,* as well as in a survey conducted by *Playboy.*

"The thrill of romance" was what 21 percent of the wives in *New Woman* magazine's infidelity survey were after as they entered affairs—more than twice the percentage that got involved initially because of lust or love.

24. ***There have been threats to leave home.***   John Edwards and Alan Booth, reporting on a study involving 294 women in the *Journal of Marriage and the Family,* found that this kind of outburst often predicts an extramarital excursion on the part of a spouse.

25. ***You have a special friendship with a man.***   Shirley Glass and Thomas Wright, analyzing the way people enter extramarital liaisons, concluded that women start by having an intimate friendship with a male, which gradually gets them emotionally involved. Then, if this special relationship continues, it very often leads to sex. An overwhelming majority—82 percent of those who responded to *Woman* magazine's office affairs survey—stressed the friendship they had found with their lovers. It was the starting point and the glue of the affair.

"I got involved with someone at work," wrote a forty-eight-year-old woman in Seattle, "through our daily telephone contact. We found out that we had a lot in common and we liked each other's personalities. We were good friends over the phone before we ever met each other. After we met it was many, many months before anything of a sexual nature occurred. I became more and more attracted to him over time, until finally the emotional attachment and physical attraction became so strong it was too difficult not to get involved sexually."

For men, the sequence is reversed. It is sex first and emotional entanglement later—if at all. This is but one of the many differences in the ways men and women conduct extramarital affairs.

Chapter 3

❦

THE DIFFERENCES
BETWEEN WOMEN'S AND
MEN'S AFFAIRS

Barbara, a professional educator, is preparing to leave the small southern community where she lives for a conference with fellow educators. Her husband watches her as she packs. Since Barbara attends similar business meetings one weekend a month, he doesn't feel anything out of the ordinary is going on. But if he could read Barbara's mind her husband might feel alarmed, outraged, betrayed. Barbara is thinking of what will take place at the conference. Of course she will be attending meetings and working, but she will also be spending her nights in the bed of another man. Barbara has been having an affair—spending a whole weekend once a month for sixteen years—with a colleague at these conferences.

Barbara is one of the large underground population of women leading secret lives in this country—wives who are enjoying the passion and risking the perils of infidelity.

Barbara was attracted to her lover, Bruce, because she felt they had a lot in common. They originally met when they worked on the same professional committee. "We spent a great deal of time together. Having the same work makes it real, real interesting," says Barbara. "We had lots to talk about. We were friends first, then the friendship developed into a sexual relationship. It was just something I slid into. We always ended up together and one day we decided to go a little bit further with this relationship."

When Barbara first met Bruce she was feeling disenchanted in her marriage. "Real differences had started developing between my husband and myself. We even had different friends," she explained.

Although female extramarital relationships have many individual variations (as do men's), Barbara's affair illustrates two of the primary factors that lead to infidelity for women.

Like Barbara, *most unfaithful wives suffer from the Double D's—they are Discontented and Disillusioned in their marriages.* Feeling that something is wrong or missing, they try to compensate for it by taking a lover.

Although there are men who are dissatisfied with their marriages, too, *most unfaithful husbands in our society are not trying to compensate for something they feel is intrinsically wrong or emotionally missing.* In a study of affairs by Morton Hunt, the majority of straying husbands considered their marriages to be happy, while the majority of cheating wives thought they were unhappy. More recently psychologists Shirley Glass and Thomas Wright came up with the same findings in their study of the differences between unfaithful men and women.

What the largest number of men are seeking is a sexual adventure for its own sake. They are after novelty, a fresh body, someone to excite their senses again.

Most women are also led into an affair through the pull of the Double F's—Feelings and Friendship. Women have affairs when they find someone they can relate to *emotionally*, a man who seems to understand and accept them just as they are. Of the 250 wives who responded to the survey of office romances, the vast majority revealed in their letters that the initial attraction to the other man was more emotional than physical. What lured these and other wives into a strange bed was the ability to talk to and confide in their lovers, and feel that they were being heard and understood.

A wife in the South, involved with another man for over a year, explained how her extramarital relationship had evolved: "I became attracted to my boss for his gentleness, kindness, and thoughtfulness. We started to go out after work to talk and have a few drinks, and we first became very good friends before we had sex. I consider him my best friend and he considers me his."

A woman in her twenties in New England remembered, "I met my lover at a lifesaving class at our place of employment. We became friendly. He went out of his way to talk to me and listen. He showed interest and I needed a friend and someone to talk to. I was feeling lonely in my marriage—I work evenings, my husband works days. One night a group was going out together after work. This man asked me to go along and I did. When I started to leave, he said he would walk me to my car. It was then he kissed me and came right out and asked me if I wanted to have an affair. I was frightened. I had been married six years and never had done anything like this before."

From an initial need for someone to confide in grew a full-blown affair and a passion that this woman admits presently controls her inner life: "I think about him all the time now. It's almost like an obsession. How many days has it been? When can we be together again?"

Although the sharing of intimate thoughts is foreplay preceding intercourse for women, it works the opposite way for men.

For husbands, an extramarital involvement generally starts with physical attraction—something about the woman ignites their lust. They are responding from the beginning to a body, while women fall for someone they think is a soulmate.

Often a man will strike up a friendship with a woman because he finds her physically attractive. If she is having problems with her job, he may listen sympathetically. If she is married and having trouble with her husband, he consoles her, often recognizing either consciously or instinctively a vulnerability—something that might turn the woman into a sexual partner.

It isn't that all men feign friendship to get a woman to succumb to sex (although some experienced seducers do just that). Sometimes men fall into a genuine friendship with a woman, but almost simultaneously it becomes eroticized and they start thinking about getting her into bed. In or out of marriage, men tend to sexualize their relationships with women.

So, along the most typical male path to infidelity, sex comes first. Friendship or a sense of emotional intimacy may follow—or it may not. An erotic itch is both the instigator and the binding factor in most men's liaisons. For women, however, feeling close to a man is the most important thing before, during, and after the affair, although they may also become more hooked on the sex as the affair progresses.

Annette Lawson in her study of adultery found that men put sexual fulfillment at the top of the list of what they got from extramarital relations. Women placed much more importance upon friendship and love.

Eighty-one percent of the married women in the office affair survey rated friendship and companionship as the most important factor among the things that kept them interested in their lovers, with sex coming in second.

The disparity that can exist between what is on a woman's mind and on a man's is illustrated in this letter from a twenty-seven-year-old California woman describing her boss and lover: "We actually became very good friends. We talked about our families, friends. When I was down he lifted me, and vice versa. He complimented me all the time. We took walks. He bought me trivial things. I was aware that there was sexual electricity between us, but we would only hold hands and hug each other when a hug was needed. One day we were sitting together laughing and teasing each other when he looked at me, pulled me towards him, and gave me the most passionate kiss I had ever had. Nothing else happened for two more months. Then one night I went out of town on business, and when I got to my hotel there were a dozen roses in my room from my boss. A half hour later there was a knock on my door. It was him. We talked for hours, went to dinner, and came back. He went to his room. I went to mine. An hour later he came back and no talk was needed. We went straight to bed."

Although this woman thought she had found a true friend in her lover, her next sentence revealed that, for him, the friendship may have been merely a prelude to sex: "Things changed after that night. He cooled off and we are back to being boss/secretary now." This wife ended her letter ruefully: "If I had to do it over again I would have remained friends and not gotten sexually involved. It wasn't worth it."

This doesn't mean that all men quickly lose interest after a seduction as this one did, but this woman's story illustrates the intrinsic differences in the ways the two genders approach extramarital sex—a difference that is well documented. The research studies of Shirley Glass and Thomas Wright, as well as Gurgul, point out that not only are men's extramarital adventures primarily sexual and women's basically emotional, but married men think there's nothing wrong with having a fling if it's mainly for sex without emotional entanglement, while for a surprising number of wives the exact opposite is true: Even in this time of sexual freedom, an emotional affair is okay as long as it isn't sexual. (See Chapter 5 for more about this.)

Numerous studies report the end result of the different approaches of the genders:

Men have many more extramarital partners than women, and more short and casual affairs—sex without involvement. One-night stands, common among husbands, are quite rare among wives (if they have a choice).

It takes longer for wives than husbands to start having extramarital sex. In every age group except the youngest (below thirty), men have their first affair before wives do. It frequently occurs within the first five years of marriage, as the sex simmers down and babies are born. It is common for husbands to react to the emotions and pressures connected to fatherhood with an extramarital adventure. On the other hand, women with young children are known as the least likely group to commit adultery.

Wives don't jump into strange beds as quickly as husbands even when they have met someone who interests them. Sixty-two percent of the wives in the office affairs survey knew their lovers for *more than six months* before they had sex with them. Most husbands are ready for sex in an extramarital relationship much sooner, although they are willing to wait for a woman they really want.

Wives have more serious affairs than husbands do. Because "sex and run" is not satisfying for most women, wives' affairs generally last a lot longer than men's, and they become more emotionally attached to their partners. The *American Couples* survey found that half the wives who were unfaithful had *serious* affairs, compared to only a little over a third of the husbands. Gurgul reported that 37 percent of the wives in his study cited love as the reason for their extramarital liaisons, while this was true of only 16 percent of the husbands.

LOVE AND SEX

For the most part, sex and love remain two separate things for straying husbands. Many divide it up neatly. Affairs are for sex; wives are for love. One well-known study of male infidelity was centered on a cocktail lounge where married men who were regulars came to pick up single women for casual sexual encounters. This kind of institutionalized meeting place for wives eternally on the prowl simply doesn't exist in our society.

Traditionally, women don't share the male ability to compartmentalize.

Wives can't separate their feelings from sex. Caring creates the desire for intercourse; sex produces emotional bonds. Even when they start out thinking that they will keep an affair casual or within bounds, sooner or later most wives find themselves more involved than they ever intended to be and often deeply in love with their extramarital partners.

A Colorado wife in her late thirties talked about how this happened to her: "I was immensely attracted to one of my customers and secretly harbored the wish to go to bed with him. There was nothing wrong with my marriage and I thought a good roll in the hay would satisfy my curiosity about being with another man (this is the first time in my eighteen-year marriage that I have ever cheated on my husband), but that is not what happened. Somehow I haven't been able to keep the emotional part of the relationship separate from the physical."

Several months into the affair this woman found herself deeply attached to her lover, and she described her distress: "I can't see or talk to him at all on the weekend, and every Monday morning I tell myself that I don't need all the pain that this is causing me, and I'm not going to see him again. Of course, that resolve lasts just about as long as it takes me to get to work. I have lied, connived, deceived, done virtually everything Mama taught me was wrong just so I could continue this affair. I can only see him once a week and the days in between are agony. Some days I just want to die from hurting so much. I want to see him and I can't. I want to be with him and I can't be. I'd be happy just to talk to him, but I can't do that either.

"Sometimes I just drive by his apartment, and simply seeing his car in the driveway makes me feel better. I know a lot of what I'm dealing with here is obsession, pure and simple, but I can't stop . . . don't even want to.

"Do I still love my husband? I don't know."

"Having an affair isn't easy," began an administrative assistant in her thirties. You're telling one lie to cover another; you're sneaking around all the time. All the while hoping you don't get caught. I don't like to do these things to my husband—I love him. In his own way he's good to me and a good father. Sometimes I panic when I think about him finding out—I know he'd divorce me. But at the same time, I'm not ready to break off my affair—I love him also. I've shed many tears over my situation."

As these letters illustrate, *women ponder their extramarital liaisons endlessly, and emotionally—much more so than most men.* If your marriage wasn't so terrific to begin with, you may obsess less about your husband's deficiencies as you concentrate more on what's happening or not happening with your lover. You may wonder about whether the other man really loves you, where this is all leading, what would happen if your husband found out. Indeed, as these ongoing ruminations fill your head, they dilute the pleasure from your affair with anxiety, frustration, and dread about the outcome.

Men don't want to be caught any more than women do, but they worry less about it, as a group. There is one important reason for this. Many women, even when they are working, depend at least in part on their husbands for security and financial support for themselves and their children. They don't feel they could manage on their own. This makes women's fear about being found out more urgent and panicky.

No matter what state the marriage was in as an affair started, studies reveal that *men get happier while women become unhappier once a lover is on the scene.*

Why? Because for women discontent with their marriages increases once they are in an affair. Another important reason is that women generally don't end up getting what they want from their extramarital relationships, while men do.

For men the sexual variety is enough. It makes them feel less restless, bored, tense, or trapped in their marriages.

But since sex and love are so entangled in the female psyche, even when a woman is aware that her married state (and usually her lover's) makes what she wants impossible, she starts desiring more contact, more time, more love, sometimes more of a commitment to her personally from the lover, who may be unwilling or unable to give enough of these things. Under the circumstances she may not even verbalize her wishes to her lover, but she feels her frustrations acutely and these negative emotions vie with the pleasures she is experiencing. The conflict can cause an ongoing inner struggle—with pleasure winning out one day, pain the next.

"There are times when I want more out of this affair," wrote one wife, "but deep in my soul I know that there isn't going to be anything more with us than there is. Sometimes I find it very hard. Then there are times I love it so much that I don't care about the hard times."

The shift in focus from the marriage to the affair that occurs among women was subtly revealed in a large number of the letters in the office affairs survey. Woman after woman kept referring to the misery of being in the "other woman" role with their married lovers, ignoring the fact that they themselves were married. And although they were wives, many cautioned other women not to get involved with a married man.

"I keep reevaluating the situation and I keep hanging in there because I love this man too much to give him up," wrote one wife in her forties, involved with her lover for two years. "But if I had to do it all over again, I would advise anyone thinking about getting into a relationship with a married man not to do it, because it is a no-win situation. Someone is bound to get hurt and the chances are it will be you, the other woman."

However, wives may also think their lovers are providing them with whatever their husbands aren't. Although for some this may make an unhappy marriage more bearable, for others it tends to increase overall unease as the wife sees what could be, if only her husband were more like what she imagines her lover to be.

GUILT AND SECRECY

Women find themselves in greater conflict than men over the transgression itself. Studies show that cheating women are more burdened by guilt.

They also show that *husbands feel more entitled to a little extra sex on the side.* They assume it is built into the male nature. Women don't feel similarly "entitled" and, therefore, are more bothered by the idea of cheating and lying.

There are some women, of course, who feel less guilty than others. How rotten you feel is often a question of how bad you think your husband is to you.

If your husband is either verbally or physically abusive, or is very negligent and uncaring, you may feel justified—at least somewhat and sometimes—in going to bed with someone else.

"I was at a vulnerable point in my marriage when I got involved with my lover," explained a thirty-four-year-old woman from the Midwest. "My husband and I weren't getting along. I was getting a lot of negative things thrown at me and my lover kept giving me positives. He was always complimenting me and seemed to understand when my husband did not.

"I don't know what my hopes for the future are," she said sadly. "When my husband and I are getting along I feel a tremendous amount of guilt. When we don't get along I then understand why I am doing what I am doing."

Men have a better support system. They know they can rely on one another to understand what they consider to be a masculine need—something that is lacking from either sex for women. For males, adultery is like an open sport: They know another man will not blow the whistle on them. Husbands may even take part in extramarital adventures together, for example going to bars to pick up women.

One executive on a prolonged job project in Europe introduced another married co-worker, also there without his wife, to the attractive friend of the woman with whom he was having an affair. These husbands then both carried on their sexual liaisons quite openly, as did other men on this same assignment, for the nine months it lasted. This kind of introduction for purposes of sex, and openness about extramarital carrying on, would never occur among wives.

By sometimes wearing their affairs proudly before other men, husbands are, in a sense, showing how masculine or sexy they are.

Women have to live in secrecy. They don't flaunt. They hide, afraid they will be condemned by those around them—male and female—no matter what the extenuating circumstances behind the extramarital alliance. Studies verify that wives are more secretive than men about their affairs. Since women, in general, find it harder to justify their infidelity to themselves as well as others, hidden shame may compound the need for secrecy. As a result, wives often feel more isolated than husbands by their adultery. There is no one they can confide in. Letters poured into the office affairs survey from women who explained how happy they were to be able to finally tell someone—even in the mail—about their secret lives.

"It has been eighteen months now since my affair began," wrote a woman in her forties in the Southwest. "I only wish I could confide in a girlfriend, but I don't think my friends would understand. I feel so alone."

"Absolutely no one has been told about us," wrote a thirty-five-year-old woman involved with her fifty-year-old boss. "The love I have for him is something I never knew existed. He's my friend, adviser, lover, teacher, and boss. I'd like to share this with a girlfriend, but you really can't trust anyone."

Of course there are, increasingly, pockets of women friends who have affairs and talk about them among themselves, but it is still far from the rule in our society.

Despite the typical conflicts that arise, according to the findings of Annette Lawson, women are generally happier in first affairs than if they go on to subsequent ones.

The reason? The same one that makes a lot of women fall out of love with their husbands as they fall more in love with their extramarital partners. The very thing that makes it more difficult for women than men to sleep with a spouse after being with a lover: Unlike men, who thrive on variety, women are basically monogamous creatures. Non-monogamy—having a series of lovers—is simply not a congenial lifestyle for women, as it is for a sizable population of men.

WHY WOMEN LIKE MONOGAMY AND MEN DON'T: THE ORIGIN OF DIFFERENCES

Women prefer familiarity and bonding over what men find so thrilling—the excitement of a new body. Not that there aren't some women who are more like men. But, at this moment in history, they are still a small minority (see Chapter 4).

The contrast in the basic nature of male and female sexuality may very well be programmed by nature. It is a difference that holds true in dating patterns as well, and has been strikingly demonstrated in laboratory experiments.

Two researchers, R. P. Michael and D. Zumpe, studying the mating habits of rhesus monkeys, paired a male with a female for three and a half years. During each year of this period with the same female, the male's interest declined, and there was less and less sex. However, when the familiar female was removed and a new mate introduced, copulation increased dramatically. When the new mate was replaced with the old one, sexual activity fell precipitously again. Similar results, pointing to an innate male response to novelty, were found in experiments with dogs and rodents.

In the rat experiments, the female nature showed itself. Females tended to return to sexual mates with whom they had experience, and even preferred spending more time near the odor of familiar males.

One can argue that these were, after all, monkeys, dogs, and rats, not us. But similar differences between males and females showed up in an experiment with human beings.

In 1986, researchers in the Department of Psychology at the State University of New York at Albany tested the ways in which males and females responded to repeated exposure to the same sexually titillating film, and then to new films of this genre. Sexual arousal that occurred during initial viewings declined after repeated exposure to the same film

41

for men and women alike. However, when new erotic material was introduced in the form of two fresh films, one showing the same actors from the first movie performing different sexual acts, the other featuring different actors, a marked gender disparity showed up. Men responded with greater excitement to the *new* partners, while women's excitement escalated when they saw the same, by now *familiar* actors in the films.

This kind of biologically programmed mating behavior may be nature's way of ensuring the continuation of the species. Men can easily have sex with many different women without becoming bonded to them the way women do, because this behavior originally encouraged the impregnation of more than one woman, leading to more offspring and future generations.

On the other hand, females who were impregnated were essentially out of commission for the next nine months, so they couldn't be as casual about sex as men. They also had to identify, with certainty, the father of their offspring to ensure food and protection for themselves and their young children from a male with a vested interest in their well-being. This programmed them to bond with the male upon whom their survival depended.

When a woman has sex with a man this ancient formula, originally designed to guarantee survival of the female, her young, and the species, goes into effect and she bonds emotionally with the man—even an extramarital partner—causing confusion and conflict over whom and what she really wants. Of course, this primitive urge is augmented by the conditioning of women in our society, who were historically always censured, and still are, for sleeping around.

The fact that the wife in an affair finds herself emotionally enmeshed with her lover doesn't mean that she necessarily wants to marry him, however. The office romance survey revealed that a little less than 40 percent—a minority (albeit a hefty one)—of the unfaithful wives would wed their lovers if they were available. In a survey by *New Woman* magazine, only 13 percent of the women wanted to marry their lovers. Thirty-two percent, however, were undecided, indicating some of the confusion, the push and pull, in the minds of wives who are involved with other men. This leaves more than half who definitely did not want to leave their marriages for their lovers.

The majority of unfaithful women, then, are in a position that is essentially the same as that of men involved in extramarital sex: They may have different motivations, and they may have different kinds of attachments, but in the end husbands and wives alike want the same thing—both security at home and a lover on the side.

Another result of the office romance survey reinforced this notion: 61 percent of the wives said they did not want to end their affairs.

The majority of unfaithful wives are obviously getting enough from their love affairs to offset whatever they suffer in the way of confusion, pain, self-reproach, fear, and guilt. However, although the majority of women wrestle with real and troubling conflicts, there is a new group of women emerging on the contemporary scene for whom adultery is a lighter game.

Chapter 4

☙

THE GROUNDBREAKERS:
THE NEW UNFAITHFUL
WOMEN

There are females who operate quite differently from other women in their extramarital affairs. These untraditional females are what I call the Groundbreakers, women able to defy custom, even the way they were brought up. They think or act as *they* think fit, or they are reacting ahead of other women to new conditions in society. In some ways they act more like men.

Here are some of the differences that distinguish Groundbreakers in their affairs:

1. ***These women may have basically happy marriages.*** They aren't, like most traditional women, propelled into an affair through some great lack in their married lives. For many of the Groundbreakers an outside relationship is just a plus in their lives, not the compensation it is for other wives.

"My lover is quite different from my husband, but I really do love them both," wrote one woman in her twenties. "My husband is gentle, patient, and a great husband and father. He takes pride in my being his wife and is protective of me. My lover is my closest confidant and encourages my education and my career. My husband offers me stability and security, while my lover challenges me and offers the other side of life. My husband is not suspicious because our relationship is sound."

"My husband and I were getting along fine," explained a woman in her thirties, describing what led to her affair. "I just needed a change."

"I love my husband and would never leave him—and yet I have no regrets. Being involved with this other person has added so much to my life. The kind of relationship we have happens only once in a lifetime," explained a hospital worker in Utah.

Although many of the Groundbreakers fall in love with their outside sex partners just as other women do, they don't fall out of love with their husbands as a result. These are females who are able to love two men at the same time, and, like men, to separate what they get in their domestic lives from the rewards of their secret, private worlds.

2. *They are able to compartmentalize.* Many go one step further than women who are able to keep love for the extramarital partner and love for the husband going at the same time. For them, love and sex are *not* the same thing, and one does not necessarily lead to the other as it does for most other wives. These women can have gratifying affairs without emotional attachment. In this respect they operate more like typical males.

"My marriage is great and I have a wonderful husband," explained an administrative assistant in her forties. "I have had many affairs before and probably will after this one ends. I just feel I need the extra relationship and I have no problem with it. I don't take my affair all that seriously. We get together for fun, friendship, and conversation. He is a terrific lover! We enjoy what we have at the moment and don't worry about when it will end."

An office worker in the Midwest said, "I'm an attractive woman and I like being chased. I don't expect the affair to go any further than an 'affair.' I don't want it to. Just because the sex is good or the companionship is good, you don't need to get emotionally involved."

3. *Their initial reaction to an extramarital partner may be based on a strong sexual attraction, rather than on the man's character, personality, or a friendship, as it is for the majority of women.* Groundbreakers are not shy about describing the sparks, tingles, and internal jolts that set them aflame.

"He had to accompany me to a research site," said a professional woman in her forties. "After we left, we were crossing the street to the parking garage, sharing an umbrella in the rain. He put his arm around my waist to pull me closer under the umbrella and it was like we both received an electric shock. We started having lunch together once a week, and one evening he asked me to go to the beach to talk about a work problem. I went. We were sitting on a bench, people were all around us, and he gently reached out and pulled my face to his and kissed me very softly. The electricity again was incredible!"

A woman in Arizona, in her late twenties, explained the start of her liaison: "I took a leave of absence from work when my son was ill. When I went back to work we had a new store manager. About two weeks after we met, he leaned over my shoulder to whisper something to me, and wow! My body was tingling all over. My face felt flushed and my heart started to flutter."

"Fireworks just set off all over," said one factory worker describing her reaction to a first accidental touch from the man who was to become her lover.

"I felt all tingly the first time I saw my new boss," said a woman in her twenties.

"He bent over in front of me to fix my typewriter, and I couldn't resist his body," confessed a thirty-three-year-old secretary in New England.

"From the start we knew it was only a physical thing. We enjoy each other's company and the sex is wild. I love my husband but the sex is much better with my lover than him," explained a saleswoman in Texas.

4. *These women are willing to experiment with age differences in their extramarital relationships—not only with men much older than their husbands, but—and here's the big news—with younger men, as well.* In this respect the groundbreaking woman reflects a growing trend in our society. The office affairs survey uncovered a noticeable number of liaisons with younger men, relationships that provided a particularly daring thrill and extra ego boost to the women involved.

"I got into this affair," said a West Coast woman in her forties, "because he would not give up. It started when he came into my place of business and told me he liked my blouse, that it was sexy. I said, 'Thank you.' He said, 'I'd like to take you to lunch.' I said, 'No, I'm married and don't do those things.' He said, 'How about coffee?' I said no again. He finally left but was back in two hours. After about a month of his pursuing, I couldn't wait. He is nineteen years younger than I am and, undeniably, I am flattered. It's been almost a year and I still love it!"

A bookkeeper in Texas told of her affair, which started overseas: "I had been attracted to Glenn for a long time and had fantasies but never thought about acting on them. At the office we flirted a lot, but most of it was not serious. There was 'unintentional' touching, friendly lunches. Then, because of my husband's career we had to move back to the United States. My husband returned three months before I did. I invited Glenn to a farewell lunch at my apartment about two months before my departure date. When it was time for him to leave, he said, 'I just want to hug you.' This led to eyes meeting and the first kiss.

"Oddly enough, my marriage is better than ever since meeting my lover. Sex is great! My husband is very sensitive and loving. Yet I want Glenn's 'love.' Perhaps it's being wanted by a younger man. He's twenty-eight, I'm forty-three. My lover is thousands of miles away now. Yet I eagerly await his letters, his calls, and him telling me he misses me. If he were here I'd continue my affair. But I wouldn't trade my husband for Glenn who, in comparison, pales on every count when placed beside my husband of twenty-two years."

"My lover is ten years my junior," wrote a restaurant chef in California. "He is extremely attractive and desirable. I'm not attractive but have beautiful eyes. When this began to happen I found his attention so surprising. He is so young, vital, and educated. Such flattery! I loved it then and I still love it. I would recommend a younger lover, if only for sex a few times, to every woman in the world. They can really give a boost of morale and energy to you."

The differences in age when the lover was younger—ranging anywhere from five to twenty years—made most of the women who wrote about these affairs cautious with their feelings. It is the rare man who stops himself from falling in love with a younger woman. In fact, he may fall in love simply because she is much younger. Women, however, in assessing their affairs keep the age difference clearly in mind.

Said a secretary on the East Coast in a liaison with a man twelve years younger, "I don't want to marry my lover. He is too young. However, I would like to keep him in my life for maybe a year. It's best not to get too emotional or attached to a younger lover—just enjoy the relationship for what it's worth."

Her lover's age allowed another woman to be very generous: "While I know my affair won't last forever, maybe not even the year, I'm happy I had the chance to share my life with this man. I love him very much, enough to let him go and live his young life with his dreams and hopefully a woman who loves and appreciates him as I do."

On the opposite end of the spectrum from the growing number of women having affairs with younger men is this woman of forty involved with a much older man of seventy-six. "I like this affair too much to stop it," she wrote. "My lover can give me the most wonderful orgasms. Sex three or four times a week with orgasm has been keeping me healthier. I have had less colds, no flu, etc. There is nothing wrong with my marriage; my lover just satisfies me more."

5. *Among the groundbreaking women are a growing number of wives in their fifties, and sometimes even their sixties—a group that was small enough to be considered insignificant in the female infidelity research of previous decades.* No longer thinking of themselves as old and undesirable, often zooming along in careers started late in life, with children gone from the home and free of the burdens of child rearing, still looking and feeling good, the fifty-plus woman is reexploring her sexual potential in extramarital affairs. As one magazine survey of infidelity in 1986 reported, "Apparently some women in their fifties—like some men in their fifties—are taking a return trip to the wild party days of youth." The conclusion: Women in their fifties are in lust in a way similar to women in their twenties.

6. *These groundbreaking women can be aggressive about going after what they want: Unlike most women, who generally wait for the man to make sexual overtures, they may make the first move.* A woman in her thirties said, "It was the second time we met alone and we sat in a park in the car talking. The first time nothing happened. This time we talked for a long time. Then I got brave and unzipped his pants. He nearly fainted. From then on we have met in that same park once a week. Once we even got locked in. The cop who is supposed to check out the grounds before closing the gates didn't that night. When we arrived at the gate it was locked. We had to use some tools in the back of the car to break out of the park."

Another woman in her forties found herself at a wedding where her boss was also a guest. "His birthday was coming up so I asked him what he wanted as a present—coffee, tea, or a blow job. Of course, he chose the sex. That's how it started."

"I initiated the affair," confessed an office worker on the West Coast. "He didn't want to hurt me. He told me he was not going to leave his wife and two small children. I didn't care. I just wanted him."

A woman of forty-seven confessed, "The affair began mostly on my part. I began flirting and saw his interest. I lost several pounds, began exercising, and became interested in myself, and then he became interested in me. It began with a kiss and a lot of forethought on my part. He left town for two weeks and when he came back it happened."

Karen, a successful woman in her early forties, explained how she set out to seduce the third of her lovers, a man five years younger than she is (the first was also a younger man):

> He was someone I worked with. We just had so much fun together. He made me laugh constantly and was a very nice guy. I definitely made a move on him. He did not want to sleep with me at all.
>
> I invited him over for dinner while my husband was in the hospital. He lived far away from where we worked and had to take a lot of buses to get home. He came to the house for dinner and I asked him to spend the night, because it would take forever for him to get home. I sounded innocent, but I had actually planned that we would sleep together.
>
> He was hesitant. I think he knew what I was up to. But he agreed to spend the night. I showed him around the house, and when we got to my bedroom, I sat down on the bed and asked if he would join me there. He said, "No." I said, "Okay," and we went downstairs to wash the dishes. I told him I would still like him to spend the night and asked him not to feel uncomfortable. I said that I was sorry if I offended him.
>
> I showed him to the bedroom that was to be his. Then I went downstairs and turned the heat way up in his bedroom. We lived in a very hot area and I knew it was going to be really warm and uncomfortable in there and he would have to take off all his clothes.
>
> I was in my separate bedroom. I had the door unlocked and he just came in. It was a lot of fun.

7. *These women are capable of one-night stands and quick, casual affairs as well as the longer, deeper affairs that are more common among traditional women.* Karen, the woman quoted above, explained what happened with this man whom she had so adeptly engineered into her bed: "We never did it again. I never wanted to. But we remained friends and he became engaged to another woman and now, I don't know—I've lost contact with him."

Karen's second lover, whom she also deliberately seduced after meeting him just once on her job, was a one-night stand as well. In contrast, the affair with her first lover had lasted about nine months, during which time she constantly obsessed about him.

The woman who unzipped her lover's pants explained that for her, "When you get in too deep, it's time to jump on a new boat, 'cause you just sank that one." She has had many casual affairs where this was indeed her attitude, but she is serious enough about this man to have left her husband and is now waiting to see if her lover will divorce his wife for her.

A professional woman described her first affair—a quickie: "It was the first big professional conference I had gone to. The people I had gone with were real busy. I ended up sitting with this guy at dinner. We just went in and danced and had a few drinks and decided to go to bed. It was that quick. It was a physical attraction. The next time I saw him we had nothing to talk about."

8. *These women don't feel as much guilt as other women—most often, none at all.* "I do not regret it for an instant," wrote a nurse in Maine. "My lover made me feel alive and exciting again. If another opportunity like this comes my way, I will seize it and enjoy it for as long as it lasts! I thought of myself as a bee. I enjoyed the nectar of this affair for as long as it lasted and was good. Now it's time to move on to the next flower!"

A forty-six-year-old woman involved with her thirty-three-year-old boss said, "We promise each other nothing except that when we are alone together it will be only *us* for those few precious hours. It has been heaven and I will never feel guilty about the joy we have shared with each other! Sometimes it is difficult to be so near each other in the office and not be able to touch and talk, but that, too, seems to just add to our excitement and anticipation of what we *know* happens when we *can* meet again. Yummy!"

Still another woman, who had had three affairs, said she never regretted any of her escapades and never felt guilty despite the fact that she didn't want anyone to know, to protect her husband's dignity. "The secrecy and lying were necessary," she said, "but it never bothered me. I feel there are separate parts of me that I don't have to share with anybody."

9. *Many of these women have a more than average need for the excitement that comes with new relationships.* Having grown up during the era of sexual liberation from the late 1960s on, they have become

accustomed to the heady highs and peak sexual excitement of new romances, and find it hard to adjust to the simmering-down stage inevitable
in all marriages. These are women who have no big complaints but just
feel vaguely restless at home. They may talk of the routine or boredom,
but what they are really missing is that special feeling, the intensity and
passion they remember from the love relationships of their single years.
An affair is their attempt to recapture it. This was certainly true of a
wife in her thirties:

"I was a faithful wife for ten years. There have been many men I
was attracted to over the years. Recently I gave in for all the typical
reasons—the attraction; he's kind, attentive, etc. But the biggest reason
is I miss the newness of a relationship. Discovering a new mind, a
new body—it's a wonderful feeling. No matter what you do or try,
after being married for a while you can't get that new feeling back
with your husband.

"Don't get me wrong. Love is also wonderful, but I missed that feeling
in my guts. I missed the excitement of a new touch. I realize it's a
dangerous game, but I need to take the chance. I realize now I can't
trust myself to be faithful in any relationship."

Another wife recounted, "I was remarried for two years when I met
Tom. My marriage was already routine. I got involved with him for
excitement. My greatest wish for this affair is *not* having my husband
find out. I have no desire to break up our marriage, but a secret affair
gives me the thrill I need."

"The reason I got involved with my boss," said a wife in her early
twenties, "was because I was bored and needed some excitement. It was
Christmastime and everyone was exchanging gifts at the office party. He
got me under the mistletoe and kissed me. From then on I daydreamed
about his body. I would think about how his hands would feel on me
and how it would feel to have him make love to me. Then one day we
went out to lunch and it happened. I do not want to continue this affair
forever, but right now it is fun being with each other."

10. ***Many act out of a sense of financial independence.*** The feeling that she can take care of herself seems to liberate a wife. The more
a wife earns, the more likely it is that she will commit adultery. A survey
sponsored by *Playboy* magazine found that 41 percent of women earning
more than sixty thousand dollars a year had been unfaithful to their
husbands. *New Woman* magazine's infidelity survey also found that the
women with the highest paychecks were more likely to initiate an affair—

top income in this poll meant earnings of twenty-five thousand dollars a year or more.

Patricia McBroom, in a book based on a study of successful professional women, found more than half had taken lovers. Dr. Ethel Person, in *Dreams of Love and Fateful Encounters,* noted an unpublished study by a therapist friend who had discovered that all her married professional women patients had been unfaithful.

It is assumed that most of these professional women make a good living. However, I discovered among the letters I perused that a sense of financial independence can exist in women with all kinds of jobs, and with all kinds of salaries—for example, factory workers, nurses, small-business owners. The idea is having money of your own. Not only are the practical issues eased—the woman, from her own earnings, can hire more baby-sitters, take cabs, buy fancy lingerie or new clothes to look more physically attractive—there is also the general feeling of independence from her husband that makes a wife more liable to take risks with her marriage.

One woman wrote, "Something snapped inside me. I thought, why be emotionally dependent on my husband when I'm financially independent? It was then I noticed a co-worker paying attention to me. He was very well built, always seems to have money, and is a kind of happy-go-lucky guy. We started slow and have been going strong for nine months now."

11. *Many of these women are reacting to the pressures of their multiple roles as working women, wives, and mothers.* Groundbreakers are sick of all the responsibilities they are managing, often single-handedly, at home and also on the job. They feel as if they are overworked and always giving to others. The affair, for them, is a way of reclaiming themselves.

"I feel like the weight of the world is on my shoulders," complained a thirty-five-year-old woman. "My husband works sometimes ten hours a day, but that is all he does—I get no help from him in the house, with the kids, or running our two stores. I also work fifty or sixty hours a week as a nurse. It is very stressful at times. My affair makes me feel like I'm somebody besides wife, mother, or charge nurse. I don't think it will last forever, but right now it's exactly what I need."

"The time with my lover is time to get away from the rest of the world," said a woman in her late twenties in the Midwest. "It is time that is just mine. I don't have to tell anyone else what I'm doing. I don't have to do anything for anybody else. I still love my husband and never want to hurt him. I hope to God he never finds out. I also know I cannot stop this affair. I need it."

A woman in her thirties remarked, "Not that I am trying to justify what happened, but I spend an incredible amount of time tending to other people's needs. Now suddenly someone was actually interested in *me.*"

"I wanted the affair just to spend some time with someone without having to do the duties of wife and mother on top of my full-time job. I needed someone who didn't expect me to be Superwoman, just to be intimate," wrote a thirty-year-old woman involved with a twenty-four-year-old co-worker in a kissing, petting relationship that, at least as yet, does not include intercourse.

And this brings us to that odd but not rare form of infidelity, the "everything but" affair.

Chapter 5

※

THE "EVERYTHING BUT"

AFFAIR

You love a man with all your heart, feel as close to him as you can—but you keep the relationship in check. For one reason or another you refuse to consummate your attachment. Other things may be in, but intercourse itself is out. You are having an "everything but" affair—the most underexplored kind of female infidelity.

"Everything but" affairs come in three forms. The first resembles the way teenagers used to act together before the sexual revolution took hold at ever younger age levels.

YOU CAN'T GO ANY FURTHER

In the good old days, when people were still trying to preserve virginity, teens would often grope and grab each other. They would stroke and touch with hands, kiss with mouths and tongues, and often pet each other's genitals (frequently to orgasm). What they wouldn't do, however, was go all the way. Penises never made it into vaginas.

Well, I have discovered that the same is now true for a group of married folk, even in our sexually liberated age.

Their affairs—and wives call them that—include varying amounts of hanky-panky but, even after years of intercourse in marriage, these women won't go all the way with their lovers.

A forty-four-year-old wife in the Midwest, involved with a younger co-worker, described how her "everything but" relationship had evolved:

There was an attraction, but we ignored it and concentrated on our friendship and working relationship. We spent hundreds of hours together working in the office and in the field. We even had many overnight stays alone in motels far from home. We always got separate rooms, spent the evenings together walking, talking, watching TV, then said good night. After about a year we found ourselves sometimes touching while talking or during long drives. One day he suddenly grabbed my hand and held it while we were discussing something. We never seemed to run out of things to talk about.

Once when I thanked him for something especially sweet he had done, I kissed him on the cheek. Weeks later, during an overnight stay, as we sat side by side on his bed watching TV, he just wrapped his arms around me and held me for a very long time. It felt absolutely wonderful. My husband is not at all affectionate. He has not held my hand, kissed, or hugged me in years, no matter how often I tell him I need this.

This man and I were already best friends. When I finally looked up at him, he kissed me so tenderly, I nearly cried. Then we couldn't stop kissing—all the sexual attraction we had been ignoring for a year exploded. We are both disciplined people, so nothing happened that night, but after that we gradually got closer and closer.

Once in a while, I would meet him in the evening for a drink, then we would sit in the car and hold each other. Each time we touched was more exciting than the last. After several more months it felt right for both of us to meet at his motel room. He never pushed or pressured me in the slightest. And I never, never knew sex could be this fantastic. He is the most amazingly wonderful lover. I should mention that we have never had intercourse in all our times together. I won't take the slightest chance on pregnancy and my lover and I are good Christians and believe that only intercourse constitutes infidelity. Though I have always had orgasms with my husband, they in no way compare in intensity or number to the ones he gives me.

Intercourse or not, this woman has not entirely avoided conflict over what she is doing. She concluded her letter with this thought: "I never knew two people could feel such passion. But I will always carry guilt, and my only hope and prayer is that no one will suffer pain because of it."

A twenty-six-year-old woman on the East Coast explained her relationship of three years: "Even though this affair has not involved sexual intercourse, there has been a great deal of intimacy—kissing and touching each other—between us. It isn't that intercourse has not been thought about by both of us, it's just that we respect one another immensely and do not want to ruin each other's marriages and our friendship."

Some "everything but" affairs are limited to just kissing and hand-holding and they stay that way, while others, after a while, go a little further, with some touching or fondling of body parts. Still others involve bringing each other to orgasm in any and every way except through penile insertion. Even oral sex is not considered real sex by a lot of these people.

In the original Kinsey surveys, 16 to 20 percent of wives had engaged in petting without intercourse, with men other than their husbands. Almost a half a century later, in 1983, Graham Spanier and Randie Margolis, in a study published in the *Journal of Sex Research,* reported that 25 percent of separated women among their subjects had had at least one relationship during their marriages that involved kissing or petting but not coitus.

Like the two wives whose letters I quoted above, people who stop short of intercourse generally rationalize their involvement. They may feel some guilt—and many do. They may call what they are having an affair—and many do. But, by setting limits on the kind of physical contact, a percentage of spouses preserve the feeling (rightly or wrongly) that what they are engaging in is not really adultery, because a penis has not entered a vagina.

The decision not to go all the way may be mutual, but sometimes the choice is one-sided. One wants to really "do it"; the other doesn't.

A wife in the Midwest told me, "He keeps after me to have real sex with him, but I know I wouldn't feel right about it. A little playing around is okay—I can live with that. But intercourse? I would feel so guilty it would ruin everything."

Interestingly, although traditionally it has been women who have drawn the line in their entanglements with men, today one occasionally finds women who are willing to have intercourse, but men who aren't.

A letter from a wife of twenty years illustrates this turnaround: "I have been romantically but not sexually involved with a single man for four years. I have a happy marriage and a good career. I would like to have sex with this man, but he doesn't want to do anything to harm my relationship with my husband—and, in a way, I think I am grateful for that, but I think of him all the time."

It may not be out of choice, but this woman is involved in the next category of "everything but" affair.

No Touchy, No Feely

In addition to relationships ranging from just kissing to heavy petting or oral sex, there is a form of "everything but" affair that is more pristine. In these relationships there is a sense of closeness and emotional caring. You confide in one another. You may or may not flirt but, in any case, overt sexual gestures or physical contact of any kind is considered off limits. The relationship is bonded through talk and feelings rather than touch.

In one extraordinary case, a thirty-five-year-old married woman in the Southwest told of an "everything but" affair that precluded even meeting. "I consider what we have an affair," she explained, "because we have been having *terrific* 'telephone sex' for two and a half years now. We have exchanged Polaroids of ourselves, so that all that is missing is the actual person-to-person contact the typical affair has."

More usual is the case of Selma and Harold.

They met originally when Selma arrived on the West Coast to edit a magazine. It was a job she didn't want, but had to take. It meant leaving her children and her husband at home on the East Coast. She took the position because her husband was out of a job, the magazine she had worked for had just folded, there was a recession going on, jobs were hard to get, and the only one offered her at a substantial salary was this one, which took her far from home. It made her lonely but helped pay the family bills.

Soon after settling into an apartment in San Francisco, she looked up a couple that a friend back home had told her were nice. One member of that couple turned out to be Harold. From the beginning there was a special chemistry between Harold and Selma. He made her feel extra bright, attractive, and special; she made him laugh. They talked to each other with ease about a myriad of subjects that interested them both.

Although Selma socialized a lot with both Harold and his wife, the real friendship that developed was with Harold. He would invite her out for drinks after work; she would take him to lunch on her expense account since he was a writer who might contribute to her magazine.

Selma confided in Harold about how much she missed her kids, the problems on her new job. He confessed the unhappiness that was plaguing his marriage of many years. There was some flirtation—neither of them denied it. Once Harold tried to make it go further. He placed his hand on Selma's thigh beneath the table while they were having a drink together. Selma lifted his hand and placed it on the table.

Selma was tempted, but she was not about to have an affair at this moment in her life. Her marriage was strained enough because of the separation without adding that to it. She talked it over with Harold and they both decided to exercise restraint, despite their mutual attraction. Sex was to be kept out of the great relationship they had. The friendship deepened and lasted. Although Selma, after a year, returned to the East Coast and Harold remained in the West, they stayed in regular contact. They talked at least once every week by phone and visited in person for weeks at a stretch a couple of times a year.

Today, twenty years later, Harold and Selma still endure. They have never lost that special "thing" for one another and still find themselves verbally flirting in their phone conversations. However, when they meet in person, they behave themselves. They both understand the boundaries of their relationship.

Harold is now divorced from his wife and he confides in Selma about his love life as a single man. Selma remains married to her husband.

"I cherish my relationship with Harold," she says. "We are the closest of friends and there still is that little extra edge we have with one another, a special kind of chemistry that is attraction in every sense of the word. Not acting on it in a sexual way, I believe, is what has allowed us to continue this way for so long. There are none of the complications that would have developed if we slept together. And yet I experience a special kind of thrill with him. It's like having a lover without the danger."

Although many women agree with Selma that intercourse would inevitably destroy a valued friendship, others abstain from sex because of the threat it would pose to a marriage they like. For still others, it's religion that creates restrictions—adultery is a sin.

However, for some the decision not to have intercourse is less shadowed by temptation. Deep caring and strong emotional bonds exist but sexual attraction does not. This is true of a forty-five-year-old woman in the South who has had a special relationship with a man her own age since they were both in high school. It has lasted through the two marriages they've each had. They are in constant touch, confide their deepest secrets to one another, are ready and willing to fly to each other's aid when it is needed. "But from the beginning, even in high school, we loved each other but dated others," this woman explained. It isn't that either of these two lack physical charms. The woman was a beauty queen in her earlier years; the man is considered quite good-looking. What does or doesn't make for sexual chemistry between two people who adore each other is sometimes mysterious and, as this case illustrates, more than skin deep.

It Just Disappeared

For some women in "everything but" affairs, sexual tension existed originally, but eventually petered out.

This was true for Charlene, who encountered Dan when she was thirty-three and married just a year. She met Dan at work.

Recent research points to the workplace as the starting point for the majority of affairs that are emotional but not sexual. Sharon Lobel, an assistant professor of management at Seattle University who has studied these new personally intimate work relationships, finds they generally evolve through a lot of contact—the couple may share assignments, work overtime, sometimes even travel together. Work talk is interspersed with long private conversations about personal matters. The relationship is characterized by genuine affection and concern for one another, shared attitudes, a sense of trust, mutual admiration of each other's worth.

Charlene's no-touch affair started in a rather typical way. "We had to work on some projects together," she said. "Our rapport was terrific from the beginning. I also thought he was very cute. My initial reaction to him upset me because I was still a bride and in love with my husband. I would blush in his presence, lose my train of thought in an uncharacteristic sort of way."

Despite the signs of obvious attraction, Charlene explained that nothing came of it. "Dan was also newly married, so there was never a hint of anything besides a blooming friendship between us. We talked about lots of things but trading information about our careers was very important to us. He has been enormously helpful to me over the years. I don't know anybody I trust more.

"I've known Dan now for five years. We have lunch regularly. If we are working late we have dinner. We phone each other at home. I speak to his wife. He talks to my husband. I feel he is one of the people I depend on most in my life. The initial sexual attraction, which really was strong, has just about gone now. I used to have sexy dreams about him in the beginning. They have stopped and so has the chemical reaction that made me feel like a dumb teenager with a crush. Dan is an important part of my life. I love—really love—him, but no longer in any sexy kind of way."

Although women in no-touch affairs often rule out intercourse for the same reasons as those in relationships that involve kissing or petting— strong religious convictions or loyalty to the spouse—others are swayed by career considerations. They feel it is dangerous to mix sex with business, or they are afraid to violate company policies.

WHY DOES IT HAPPEN AND HOW OFTEN?

Why do women form these "everything but" attachments in the first place?

Experts agree that, mainly, it is for the same reason that wives get embroiled in sexual liaisons. There is something missing in the marriage. These women are often fulfilling with other men an unmet need for emotional intimacy with their husbands.

You would think in this highly sexualized age that the "everything but" affair would be rare, but this turns out not to be the case. In recent years there has been research indicating that unconsummated relationships constitute a sizable minority of all cases of infidelity.

In 1985, psychologist Shirley Glass published a study of infidelity in which she found that one quarter of wives' affairs were emotional rather than physical.

In her 1989 study of more than one thousand corporate employees, Sharon Lobel came up with a similar figure—22 percent of office affairs were deeply emotional but not sexual.

Annette Lawson found in her study of a British population that 40 percent of her subjects reported relationships they considered adulterous even though they did not involve making love.

Experts like Dr. Glass feel that these unconsummated affairs are currently on the upswing for one simple reason: With more women working and exposed to an increasing number of men on the job, *all* kinds of affairs are on the rise.

There is the possibility, as well, that with the threat posed by AIDS, some people feel that it's safer to love in ways that do not include intercourse.

THE GENDER DIFFERENCES

Dr. Anthony Thompson, a renowned researcher of extramarital relationships, noted an additional reason why wives get involved in nonsexual affairs. In a paper published in the *Journal of Marriage and the Family* in 1984, he found that although women, more than men, thought *all* kinds of extramarital involvement detracted from their primary relationships, they considered emotional involvement without sex the least damaging and least wrong. Men, on the other hand, were more likely to consider sex without emotional involvement as the least damaging and most acceptable form of adultery.

This, of course, reflects the general traditional orientation of men and women in our society, with men placing the most importance on the sexual aspects of a relationship and women on the emotional ones (see Chapter 3).

THE EFFECT ON A MARRIAGE

Because the male comes at affairs differently, it is very hard for most husbands to understand that a wife's emotional attachment to another man may not lead to sex. Dr. Glass maintains that men tend to sexualize their friendships with women and, she says, "Most men feel that if they were sneaking around, or making excuses to see someone, they would certainly be having sex."

Of course, if you are having the kind of affair that includes petting and orgasms, your husband will consider it just as much a betrayal as if you had gone all the way. It will be difficult for him to see it your way— that it doesn't constitute genuine adultery because, although you included everything else, you managed to leave intercourse out of your relationship with your lover.

The advice that follows in other parts of this book (see chapters 13 to 16) can help you if you get caught. However, the best way to achieve damage control in emotional but nonsexual affairs is through preventive measures.

First, you must recognize certain dangers inherent in these relationships.

A good number of women start to obsess about the other man. They can't get him out of their heads. This may happen to you. If you are consumed by thoughts of another man, it takes energy and closeness away from your marital relationship.

In addition, if the other man gives you more of a sense of emotional satisfaction than you receive at home, you may end up wondering if you should stay with your husband, since you are capable of having so much more. You have to be aware that dissatisfaction with your marriage can increase.

You also have to keep in mind that if you are confiding in your emotional partner at work, you may also stop confiding in your husband. You may also quit trying to improve conditions in your marriage if what you lack is being satisfied with someone else.

Some women start to compare the husband unfavorably to the other man. This kind of negative comparison may be based on a false premise, since you have an unrealistic view of your partner in a no-touch relationship. In this respect an "everything but" affair is like other, more sexual ones: Your partner is idealized. You see him only in limited circumstances, often associated with work. You really have no idea how he would be in the everyday world of laundry, chores, tensions, babies, bills.

One woman found her illusions shattered when she became sexually involved with a man with whom she previously had only an emotional relationship.

When she and her husband separated, she called the man, who lived in another state, and discovered that his marriage was dissolving, too. After years of attraction, flirting, and sexual denial, these two finally decided to consummate their relationship. They arranged to go away together for a week.

"The sex was great, just as I imagined it would be," this woman confessed. "But nothing else was. I discovered just how limited he was and how little we had in common. He didn't like to read, he had no interest in politics, he never went to the theater. There wasn't enough to keep us together in the long run." The attraction to this man who had intrigued her for years fell apart when this couple entered the real world together.

The final danger to a woman, of course, is that after years of sexual restraint you may finally give in and have sex together, often in response to a problem at home.

According to experts, this often spells the end of the relationship. You may be overwhelmed by guilt, or you may feel that sex wasn't what your friendship was all about and now it is spoiled for good. Or you may be propelled into the troubling kind of full-scale affair you had been avoiding before.

ARE AFFAIRS WITHOUT SEX REALLY POSSIBLE?

Well, then, can a wife have an "everything but" lover and not jeopardize her marriage?

Yes, but I caution you again—your marriage *will* be endangered if you are physically intimate, even if your repertoire does not include actual intercourse. You have to draw the line very clearly—there can be no physical contact that is inappropriate or that can be misinterpreted.

The most important thing to do if you are involved in a no-touch affair is to be completely open about it. Experts agree that the greatest threat to a marriage is when there is a lot of secrecy about your relationship with the other man and you are keeping the depth of your emotional involvement with him from your husband. You have to let your spouse know all about the other man and, as much as possible, include him—and his wife—in your social life as a couple.

Once your husband is allowed to see that you care about this other man and your deep friendship with him, but that he, your husband, is your true love, marriage-threatening jealousy can be avoided.

THE MAN YOU CAN'T FORGET

Before leaving the world of affairs that preclude intercourse, I want to touch on a third phenomenon—mental preoccupation with and longing for a man you used to be involved with before you married. You can't forget him and you are carrying on an intense relationship with him in your head.

I found this type of obsession so common in the letters I received as an advice columnist that I created a special bulging file called "The Man You Can't Forget." Here is an example from it, written by a thirty-four-year-old married woman:

"I can't get over a crush I've had on someone since I was fifteen years old. I see him maybe two or three times a year. When we see each other I know something is there. We both have talked about it. But nothing has ever happened. Almost—but I always stopped it. And the last time he stopped it. I have tried to forget him, but I can't get him off my mind, and then when I see him—I melt."

Another troubled letter came from a woman married for three years: "My real problem is that I am in love with my high school sweetheart. When we broke up it was because of all the worry I was having about getting pregnant. It really hurt to think that he wouldn't marry me if I got pregnant. We never spoke for two years and said mean things about each other.

"Then, one day after I was married, he waved at me, and to my surprise my heart felt soft toward him. We talked and I slipped and told him that if I wasn't married I would kiss him. We didn't kiss but I could tell the feelings were there. Not a day goes by that I don't think about him. I even have dreams in my sleep about him."

Although these two wives occasionally see their old loves, which helps keep the flame alive, many of the women in my files have long since lost contact with the old boyfriend they think about constantly.

A romance with a man you can't forget is largely a fantasy affair fired by longings for someone you can't have. Similar to this is the no-contact affair that is wholly a product of the imagination. You obsess constantly about someone you may have seen, met casually, or work with, but with whom there has been little significant interaction or none at all.

Do such mental obsessions qualify as infidelity? In an important sense, yes, because there is another man living with you mentally. There is someone else with whom you are intensely involved emotionally. Even though the relationship may be all or almost all in your head, you have truly created a love triangle.

You may assume that these are harmless relationships because no sexual betrayal is involved, but, in terms of your marriage, they really aren't. As in all triangles, the emotions that should be going into your marriage are diverted elsewhere.

Indeed, to divide your attention may be the purpose. Mental obsession with one, while living in real life with another, is a way some women deal with their innate fear of too much intimacy. They can't be close to the man they long for because he simply isn't around, and they can't be close to the man who is around because they yearn for someone else.

In one sense, the obsession makes them uncomfortable because they can't control their thoughts; on the other hand, they may feel more emotionally comfortable than they would if they had all their love eggs in one basket.

A wife who imagines herself to be in love with an old boyfriend, because he seems more perfect in retrospect than her husband, also manages to keep herself suspended in a state of discontent. Instead of trying to solve problems with your husband, you retreat into a fantasy of a love you imagine would satisfy you more.

For some wives obsession with another man is an unconscious device to deal with a hidden fear of success in their lives. When you wish for someone else, you destroy full enjoyment of your marriage.

Some no-sex affairs, if handled carefully, can enrich a woman's life by providing her with a deep, caring, and nurturing friendship. Fantasy affairs simply don't work on any level—except perhaps to satisfy some hidden psychological agenda.

Now that we have looked at the various forms of affairs without intercourse, it's time to look at wives who *don't* set limits. What pushes a woman over the edge and into bed with another man?

Chapter 6

Situations That Drive Women into Affairs

"I was always the first person to condemn someone for having an affair," said a thirty-two-year-old woman, married seven years and involved with another man for three months.

Women almost always start out feeling like this, sure they will be monogamous in their marriages. Various polls and surveys show that fidelity is overwhelmingly still the ideal of brides.

However, life sometimes interferes with dreams, and like this woman, as their marriages progress, wives find themselves in situations that set the stage for the high-strung drama of a secret love.

The woman continued, "I still have a hard time realizing I am doing what I am doing. I fell in love with my lover and, horrified at myself, I went into counseling. I began to realize I had been suffering from emotional starvation with my husband."

This woman's case illustrates the first and most common situation that leads to infidelity. It is the affair that is, in essence, a reaction to the quality of a marriage. The cheating wife is someone who feels her husband let her down.

DISAPPOINTMENT

To judge by scientific literature on the subject of marital happiness, the disappointed wife is found in abundance in our culture. Studies show that, if you are a woman, the longer you are married, the more disenchanted you become.

The epidemic of disappointment among wives may, in general, be the result of expectations of marriage that are much higher for you than your forebears. At one time marriage was a practical arrangement. Basically, men expected sex and domestic services, care for their children, and maybe help around the farm. Wives expected economic support and protection. It was considered a fair deal if these conditions were met.

Then all kinds of other needs entered the picture, to the point where today your husband, in addition to providing security, must also supply you with love. Then you want sex that is preceded by closeness and conversation, and is passionate, considerate, and tender. Your husband is expected to be helpful around the house, be a partner in child rearing, be empathic to your needs, be supportive of your work endeavors, and continue to admire your looks openly. He must remember to be romantic, and most important of all he should be able to talk to you, understand you, and be emotionally available. In all, women have come to be primarily concerned with the emotional aspects of their marriages.

Four different studies of how women and men view each other recently conducted by Dr. David Buss, a psychologist at the University of Michigan, confirmed this. Women offered these major complaints about men: They don't show and express their emotions. They ignore your feelings and opinions. They don't spend enough time with you. They don't express their love for you.

Since, as these and other studies show, women rate their marriages based on emotional fulfillment (men tend to base their judgments on sexual satisfaction)—and emotions are a tough act for men in our culture because they have been brought up not to show them—it stands to reason that there is a lot of disappointment in the world of the wife. When disappointment leads to despair, and you figure you are never going to get what you feel you need from your husband, you are apt to join the legion of wives who are currently attempting to fulfill emotional cravings with another man.

Letter after letter in my files reflects husbands who, in the eyes of their wives, failed in some crucial part of the contemporary equation for marital happiness.

A forty-five-year-old woman in Kansas explained the background to her affair: "My husband was so into himself. I was unable to get him to talk to me and work things out together. I became lonesome and needed someone to talk to. My boss was there for me. The affair began mostly on my part. I started flirting with him and he responded."

A woman in her forties in a town near Boston stated, "I can honestly say I feel my husband has driven me into an affair. I get no attention or affection from him at all. He doesn't know I'm alive most of the time. We have been married twenty-two years and my marriage has become very dull."

An administrative assistant in a relationship with a co-worker explained, "I became involved because after twenty years of marriage (I married at eighteen) I felt there was something missing. I had this feeling long before this man came into my life. At the time I met Bob there were no emotions left in my marriage. My husband constantly yells at me for no good reason at home and in public. I'm lucky to have my husband sleep with me once a month—and then it's roll over, get on, get off, no holding, no kissing, and dammit, no sharing."

A botanist in an affair for more than a year, in New York State, wrote, "My marriage of ten years was at an all-time low. For the past year my husband had been withdrawing emotionally. I was starved for affection. The guy I became involved with had already had brief affairs with a couple of my co-workers. I thought just one time with him might ease my emotional pain. I pictured him as the safest man to be involved with, sure he had frequent affairs. He was a close friend and I hoped the physical relationship wouldn't change that friendship because I needed it. I don't promote affairs. I dislike the lying and deceit necessitated by them. Otherwise I find this a healthy relationship because it's with a real friend who wants it to be a good element in my life. He treats me very well. If you are going to have an affair, choose someone who treats you well and is considerate of what your needs are."

A woman in her thirties in the Far West, involved with a man who works with her husband, explained that in her marriage of ten years, "My husband and I have had good times, but I feel like there is nothing left for us anymore. We no longer do anything together. We each have different interests, we never agree on anything. We have spent most of our life together arguing about things—sometimes simple things, sometimes about the children. So when I met someone I enjoy being with so much and having someone to talk to, it was great. Seemed like it filled an empty place in my life."

Many of the women who complain have legitimate gripes. They really are in great pain about their marriages, and regret having to turn to another man for consolation and for whatever is missing—attention, lovemaking, consideration, respect.

However, experts who have studied women in affairs have noted that unlike men, who feel justified in having extramarital sex simply because they are men, women need to feel that there is a reason for violating marriage vows and moral beliefs. Because of this, you may find fault with your marriage in hindsight. You may be among the women who first start an affair and only then say, "Oh, yes, now I realize what I was missing before."

Whichever way you arrived at a sense of discontent and deprivation, these emotions help to alleviate guilt. In the office affairs survey, more than half the wives reported very little guilt, because, for the most part, they felt strongly justified in finding with a third party the pleasure and acceptance they thought was absent from their marriages.

I FEEL ATTRACTIVE AGAIN

Women have been taught to judge themselves by their looks in our society. Most of us validate ourselves not from within but by how we are viewed by others—mainly men. In marriage husbands often forget to give the compliments they were so generous with during courtship. Or they may even feel free to criticize a wife's appearance. As a result, once you are a wife you often stop feeling attractive as a woman.

When a wife goes back to work and men start noticing her—or if she is singled out by some man somewhere and is suddenly being showered with a lot of flattering attention, is complimented, is made to feel pretty and wanted again—she responds like a plant to water. Perhaps this isn't the way it should be. Maybe a woman should be able to validate herself from within. But given the way we have been brought up as women—to judge our attractiveness by how men react to us—the pleasure of being noticed again as a desirable woman is a strong factor in making a wife receptive to an affair.

A woman in her thirties in the Midwest, who recently became involved in an extramarital liaison, said, "I went to work after my kids were all in school. I couldn't believe all the attention I got from the guys. It made me feel good and sexy."

Another woman in her thirties, married for six years, admitted, "When I transferred to this office I had a weight problem which my husband put me down about. My lover started out as a friend and mentor who encouraged me to begin running, although he thought I was attractive anyway. I now run four miles a day and have an excellent figure. But even after I lost weight my husband still found me too fat, while my lover was finding me more and more attractive and more than a friend. On a business trip together, because he knew the situation with my husband had deteriorated, my lover asked me to his room to discuss my problems. I eventually seduced him."

There is no doubt that, no matter what the original motivation, having a lover rejuvenates a woman and makes her feel more desirable and excited about herself than she has in years.

A forty-four-year-old accountant, unhappy in her marriage, went back to full-time employment for the first time in eighteen years and almost immediately fell into an affair with someone she met in the workplace. "I feel ten years younger, sexier, and prettier," she said. They had been lovers for about three months. "It has been one of the best experiences of my life."

He Sees Me the Way I Want to See Myself

For some women, the boost they are seeking and receive from a lover goes beyond feeling more alluring physically. They may be looking for more self-esteem or a firmer personal identity. They may be seeking an affirmation of themselves, a sense of who they are apart from the roles they have assumed in the past—daughter, wife, mother—roles in which they felt they belonged to someone else or were living up to the expectations and needs of others.

A woman who had a long affair with a co-worker who then died reminisced, "The time we had together was the best I've ever spent with anyone. He loved me for myself and didn't want to try to change me. What we had and felt was special and I may never feel that way again.

He gave me a time of acceptance, laughter, and the *real* feeling that I was loved for who I am."

Another woman, who took a lover after twenty years of marriage, found that constant criticism by her husband had made her feel unsure of herself. "The last three years of my life," she wrote of her affair, "have helped change me to a better woman. I now have self-confidence. Thank you, Fred!"

A woman in her mid-thirties on the East Coast wrote, "This man helped build my self-confidence. I'm much more assertive and outspoken now. My self-esteem has improved. He makes me feel important."

An office worker who met her lover of five months in motels, in the park, in the basement of her office, and "anywhere we can think of" wrote, "This man can just say something to me and set me on fire, something I haven't felt in years. For me this has been a huge ego boost, something I was very much in need of. If nothing else, this man has given me confidence in myself and has made me feel wonderful for whatever length of time we might be together."

For many contemporary women, a love affair may have been *preceded* by a new sense of self that had developed in the work world. Employed wives often achieve a feeling of competence different from and better than the one they have had in a domestic setting. Especially if you went back to work after some years at home, your husband, who does not see you in your role in the office setting, may treat you in the same old paternal, patronizing, or denigrating way. He does not view you as you now see yourself. The lover you meet in the outside world does. One of his lures is that he provides validation and admiration for this other, competent sense of yourself that your husband doesn't recognize or acknowledge.

A woman in her thirties wrote, "I feel important because my lover praises me for my gifts and raw talent. He coaches me, encourages me, and points out to me my weaknesses—all in a loving, helpful manner. All I get from my husband is belittling. My lover appreciates my intellect as well as my looks, neither of which my husband seems to notice."

A DECLARATION OF INDEPENDENCE

If you have been very dependent on a husband, or dominated by him, an affair may be a way of asserting yourself.

72

"My marriage started really going downhill two years ago when I got this job. I guess I realized I could be independent and didn't need a boss at home," exclaimed a woman of thirty-two who works on an assembly line in Michigan. "The man I'm involved with doesn't try to rule me or change me. He understands me."

For a few women adultery is a way of declaring independence from the double standard. A woman in her twenties, whose husband resisted her desire to go back to work, got a job anyway because she was sick of staying home and she wanted income of her own. She had also been bothered by her husband's constant remarks about other women's figures. When she arrived at work, she remembered, "It was instant attraction when I saw my new boss. He was very friendly and I started to talk about my problems. He seemed very understanding and asked me to go to lunch with him one day. We got along great and when lunch was over, and I was getting into my car, he asked if he could kiss me. We now see each other whenever we can. If it feels good you should stick with it," she advised other women in affairs, "because men have been doing it for years!"

THE SEARCH FOR SELF-FULFILLMENT

As a nation we are still affected by the philosophy that took hold in the sixties: Fulfilling yourself is more important than obligation or commitment to others. You were put on earth to take care of your own needs, not the needs of others, is the message people heard from oracles like Fritz Perls, a key figure in the human potential movement, which promoted the cult of self-fulfillment. The search for self-fulfillment is often involved in divorce these days. A study of women splitting from their husbands reported that 41 percent of them complained about internal struggles as wives that involved issues of self-growth and development.

The desire to fulfill yourself is also subtly involved in many affairs. "If it feels good, go for it" was the way this belief in the prime goal of self-fulfillment was expressed in many of the letters in my files. Here is one example from a thirty-six-year-old woman whose extramarital partner for five years had been her fifty-four-year-old boss: "You have to follow your own heart. To me, if you can have an affair and not feel guilty being with your lover and it feels right, then go for it. You can only depend on yourself for true happiness."

A thirty-two-year-old woman, also carrying on with her much older superior at work, said, "My lover is my boss, my friend, and now my lover. I married my high school sweetheart at the age of nineteen. I have a ten-year-old son, an affectionate, loving husband, and a good marriage. We get along well and have a lot of fun together. Why, then, am I involved with my lover? Because this is for me! I've spent most of my life following all the rules, being a good daughter, wife, and mother. I'm being selfish for a change. My lover is romantic, sensual, intelligent, and sophisticated. Our time together is limited and therefore special, intense, and very satisfying."

A woman of forty-six wrote that she was cheating on her husband of twenty-five years because "I decided one day I was tired of being so nice and wanted to do something for myself."

A California woman who had been married for twelve years expressed the search-for-self-fulfillment philosophy in the last sentence of this passage from her letter: "In May of this year I was at a business function and struck up a conversation with a co-worker. We both seemed attracted to one another. We went out after the business dinner with a group and danced until 2 A.M. It was wonderful. The feelings between us were so in tune. He called me at work the next day and we discussed what happened. *We decided we owed it to ourselves to act on our feelings*" (italics mine).

The idea that adultery is acceptable if it makes you happy, that your desires take precedence over obligation to others, has given a jumpstart to many affairs being conducted today.

THE MIDLIFE CRISIS

Penny looked at herself in the mirror. She noticed a new line forming on her forehead. Her hair, which had always been healthy and shiny, was looking dry and dull from the dye she had been using to cover the gray hairs that were coming in at a fast pace. Penny sighed and thought, *I'm getting old.* She did not look forward to her forty-fifth birthday in a few weeks.

When a customer came into the store where she worked and started flirting with her, Penny felt a sudden lift in her spirits. Her face came alive and to her own surprise she found herself flirting back. The customer kept coming back on one pretext or another. After several animated exchanges between them over a period of several weeks, he finally asked her to have lunch with him. Penny hesitated. She half-knew what she was getting into, but she heard herself saying "Yes."

Penny found this man sympathetic, attractive, and sexy over lunch, and over drinks, and finally over dinner. She had to lie to her husband about having to work overtime and that did not make her feel good, but she had such a good time with this man that she soon forgot the bad feelings. He took her to a romantic place with candlelight, good food, and great wine. Penny felt like she used to in her early twenties—pretty, desirable, young. She was obviously being courted by this married man, who managed to tell her in their conversations about how his wife had grown fat and sloppy. At the end of their dinner Penny and this man had decided to meet the following week at the best hotel in town. They were going to become lovers.

Penny had embarked on a midlife affair, an extramarital adventure that tucked away Penny's fears of aging and gave her a new sense of youth and adventure.

The midlife affair is generally thought of as occurring around age forty, when you realize that you are getting older and life is getting shorter, signs of aging are appearing, and a general malaise sets in about where your life has already taken you versus where you would like to go. However, its symptoms can and do occur at any age after thirty. Some people begin to feel the ending of youth as they enter their thirties; others don't experience it until age fifty looms.

Adding impetus to affairs at midlife is the presence of teenagers at home. The romance of a son or daughter may create a yearning for the thrill of new love again in your life. Or a sense of rivalry may exist, an unconscious desire to prove that you aren't washed up yet and are still in the running for romance.

The Nest Is Empty

Often the midlife affair begins when the kids reach a certain age of independence and you realize that without them as a buffer your marriage is dead: "My children are practically grown," wrote a woman in Canada, "and I don't seem to have anything in common with my husband now. I would like to have someone to share my interests with. The guy I became involved with does," she wrote, and then added sadly, "But he's married, too, so I still don't get to share those interests with him."

"I was immensely attracted to my boss from the first day I started to work for him," said a woman of forty-seven. "My children had all moved out of the house and I had just changed jobs after being on the last one for ten years. It was obvious that my husband and I had nothing in common but our children and now they were gone."

Outrunning the Blues

Depression, too, can play a part in the midlife affair. A study in the *Journal of Abnormal Psychology* found that women (and men) between the mid-forties and mid-fifties run the greatest risk of serious depression of any age group. At this time in life hopelessness may take over. You feel you are never going to realize early dreams. Or the sense of loss prevails: Your looks are going, parents die, various ailments begin to erode your health. An extramarital adventure is often an attempt to outrun the blues and cheer yourself up.

Different Sexual Needs

In addition, a disparity between the genders in sexual needs and performance often shows up in midlife. Men's sexuality peaks in their teens and may begin to decline in their middle years. In contrast women reach their sexual zenith in their late thirties or early forties, when their potential for orgasms has been proven to be at its highest. As a result, a wife in midlife may be very horny while her husband is less interested in sex with her. He may try to pep up his sex life by getting involved with another woman, and she may be tempted to take care of her sexual needs with another man if a likely prospect comes onto the scene.

Speaking Up and Taking Action

Adding to the likelihood of infidelity is the fact that women become more assertive in midlife, according to research by Dr. David Gutman, a psychologist at Northwestern University. This means that a wife may not only feel more independent but, with the idea that time is flying,

76

may actually initiate an affair at this time in life.

The midlife affair among men is a well-known phenomenon. We are just beginning to recognize that the same thing is occurring more and more among women—with one big difference. The man at this time in life generally chooses a much younger, single woman as his fountain of youth. The woman generally chooses a married man closer to her own age.

REVENGE

"I've been married five years," said a woman of twenty-eight. "Just a few months ago I got a letter from a woman who has been seeing my husband for five years. It is definitely true, so I decided what is good for him is good for me.

"The affair I am involved in began when I would go out with a bunch of people from work and always end up riding home with one particular man. Three months ago we ended up in bed together."

Welcome to the world of the payback affair, sex with another man undertaken as a way of evening the score by women who know their husbands have cheated on them.

Full of rage, another woman, who had met her husband when she was fourteen and married him nine years later, told her tale of betrayal:

> After ten years of marriage my husband cheated on me. I hired a private detective. I have pictures, tapes of phone calls. He used credit cards to entertain her and take her on trips. I confronted him about the young woman and he denied it. The hurt was unbearable. It just did something to me. Now it's ten years later and he's having another affair with another woman. They go on trips together, etc. I confronted him but again he denied it. He sounded so convincing, but he didn't fool me.
>
> When I first saw my boss five years ago I was attracted to him and he was attracted to me, but I tried to dismiss it from my mind. Last month, after I found out about another trip my husband had made with his girlfriend, I was so hurt—it's impossible to describe how bad I felt.

My boss and I went to lunch. He had been after me to go to bed. But because of my spiritual beliefs and love for my husband I wouldn't do it before. But this time we went to a hotel. I was scared at first, but I relaxed and it was wonderful. We met again the next week. I don't feel guilty about cheating on my husband. I have been a faithful wife for twenty-one years. All men cheat, I don't care if they are ministers, churchgoing men, doctors, lawyers, policemen, firemen, congressmen, mayors—they all cheat.

In many cases the need is for reassurance as much as revenge. You know your husband has had a fling with another woman. You feel this as an agonizing blow to your ego. You have a need to prove that you are desirable and so, almost like magic, you meet a man a few months after your husband's infidelity who suddenly seems very attractive to you. Since he is giving you a lot of complimentary attention, which you need at this juncture in your life, you start an affair with him.

The worst thing that can occur when revenge affairs take place is that the marriage becomes a game of tit for tat, with a never-ending round of extramarital sex on the part of each partner. Nothing gets solved and the marriage is in great danger of collapsing, because nobody's tending the home fires.

The case of this twenty-seven-year-old woman is a good example of nothing getting solved. She explained, "I have been married for three years. I began my affair three months into the marriage. My husband began his affair three weeks into the marriage—well, actually he had countless one-night stands for the first year we were together. We lived in separate cities for career reasons. My affair began in reaction to a hunch I had that he was fooling around. There were mysterious phone calls and earrings found in the apartment. So I began my affair. His mistress phoned me in an attempt to end the marriage. Since I was involved with a successful local man, it was much easier for me to accept my husband's infidelities. [She walked away from that phone call crying.] I love my husband deeply, although I will never trust him and never feel secure with him. But I'll never leave him either. Guilt? Not me. Will I ever be faithful? Not in this marriage."

Sometimes, of course, an extramarital sexual adventure takes place as retribution for sins that do not necessarily involve cheating. A husband who has been mean or abusive or has incurred the wrath of his wife in other ways may be paid back when she decides to have sex with another man.

"The reason I got involved with someone else," wrote one woman, "was that my husband was being very critical of the things I did. He made me feel as if I wasn't as smart or intelligent as he is. He made me feel as if the women he associated with were smarter and more his type. Along came this guy who thinks I'm beautiful, bright, and intelligent. He also gives me compliments I needed because of all the negative things my husband said to me."

Wives angry at a husband's workaholism, alcoholism, or drug abuse also commonly indulge in revenge affairs.

One wife, who had initiated her affair with a co-worker by sending him flowers in order to get back at her cheating husband, gave this piece of advice, based on her own experience: "If you have thoughts about doing this because of your husband's faults, whether it was unkindness, rejection, or extramarital affairs, then go for it! If you want to get even and you feel this will do it, then do it, just as long as it makes you feel special again, and your self-esteem comes back."

Many times, when a wife uses an affair to exact revenge for the sins of her husband, she manages to get caught. Because it isn't full revenge unless he knows.

Affairs that are acts of retribution, therefore, are fraught with danger. When both spouses have been unfaithful, the whole marriage often blows up and cannot be put together again.

Said one woman whose husband had had an affair for love, to which she had reacted by having an affair of her own "for sex and companionship": "I don't think an affair is right. I would not encourage any woman to have one. I believed in my marriage until my husband betrayed me." She finished ruefully, "Now that my marriage is over, my affair is no longer an affair."

Revenge as a motivation for a fling of your own may be quite unconscious. Many women, like this twenty-two-year-old wife, deny the connection that was probably there psychologically: "My husband cheated on me and was caught—by me. I tried to forgive and forget, but no dice! I know I didn't turn to my lover because of that. We didn't start our fling until four months after I caught my husband."

I have found, too, that you don't actually have to know consciously that a mate has been unfaithful. Often it is a subliminal knowledge. There were many women who reported that they had started an affair and only later discovered that their mate had been cheating before their own transgression. This works the other way around, as well. Your husband subliminally knows you've been fooling around and pays you back in kind.

One woman found her husband in her bed with another woman after she had been carrying on with her own lover for close to a year.

THE POWER AFFAIR

The desire for power is involved in a sneaky way in a lot of affairs. To begin with, an enormous benefit of an affair for the female is that it makes her feel powerful: She has proven that she has the ability to attract, which all by itself makes her feel strong and sexy. Second, in marriage a woman often stops feeling like she is the most important person in her husband's eyes. She is taken for granted. The lover, in contrast, singles her out and makes her feel special. The intense pleasure of being significant again was voiced in letter after letter in the office affairs survey.

"My husband constantly told me I was ugly and my job was meaningless and I did nothing all day long while he slaved the day out. I felt he was rejecting me in every way possible, while my lover made me feel very special and good. I made sure he was aware I would not be a one-night stand, that 'I was special.' I wrote him a note saying this after our first kiss when he continued to make advances. He tore out the part of the note that said 'special' and kept it on his desk in sight. I was flattered."

A love affair, then, makes a woman feel wonderfully important, but perhaps the primary hidden way that power enters the picture in adultery is when extramarital sex is used as a weapon in a power struggle between husband and wife. Generally the power play going on is unconscious, but desperately real.

For example, a wife who feels controlled or intensely put down by her husband, like the woman above, may seize power in the relationship by taking a lover: She is putting something over on her husband. This hidden knowledge is a key element in her affair. It gives her ongoing pleasure and a sense of secret triumph in her marital relationship.

Sometimes what a woman seeks is a sense of power in her lover that she feels is missing in her husband. This means responding to a man of more wealth or prestige, or the boss or head of a company. "Why did I get involved with my boss in the first place?" asked a woman in her mid-thirties, in an affair with her employer that had lasted more than five years. "I suppose I was drawn to his power and wealth and flattered that he would pick me out of the crowd." Sometimes a woman is simply responding to a more dominant man.

One wife, in telling me her story, admitted being obsessed by her first lover, whom she had met when she went back to college after being married for five years. It was the dominating sex, she intimated, that grabbed her in this relationship. "My husband was always very gentle and very affectionate and very loving. But what I really wanted was some very animal type of lovemaking.

"This other man would hold my waist down so I felt captured. It was like it was against my will. Of course it wasn't, but that was the feeling, and that was what was such a turn-on to me. I wanted someone to take me in a forceful and aggressive way. My husband has never been like that with me."

PROXIMITY

"How did my affair begin?" asked a thirty-three-year-old computer programmer. "It grew out of a two-year friendship working side by side in a very small, closed environment." This woman could not account for her affair in any way other than the forced intimacy of close proximity over a long period of time. "I wonder to this day why I got involved with him," she says, remarking that her marriage was fine. "I was pregnant with my second child. I weighed 180 pounds and did not feel like anyone could have sexual feelings towards me, but both my lover and my husband showered me with love, affection, and sex." This affair had been going strong for more than a year despite the fact that the woman constantly regretted her involvement. "Once it gets started, it's hard to end an affair," she said. "We can be driving in a car and all of a sudden out of nowhere the urge overtakes us."

Many of the letters in my possession showed a similar pattern: You fall into a friendship with a man with whom you work in close physical proximity simply because he is there, and after a period of time, sometimes several years, it turns into something you never expected—a romance. This proves a theory that many social scientists subscribe to—that the intimacy of working in tight proximity can, all by itself, lead to the desire for sexual closeness.

DELIVERING A MESSAGE

Sometimes an extramarital liaison is a way of telling a spouse that something is terribly wrong and must be addressed. It is a booby-trapped way to deliver your message, because in order to be effective you have to be found out. So you leave clues that are sure to make your husband suspicious, or you make sure you and your lover are seen together. You may even entertain him at home, and then—surprise—your husband walks in on the two of you!

The result, of course, is uproar, and sometimes you are stuck with the turmoil and ensuing disaster to your marriage—but sometimes you accomplish what you set out to do.

An example of this is a twenty-six-year-old woman who told her story: "My husband is thirty-one and an alcoholic. We have been married for over six years and have a four-year-old child. My husband drank heavily all through our marriage and occasionally has been abusive. I was always faithful to him until three months ago. I met a wonderful man at work. I think I am falling in love with him. He wants me to leave my husband and move in with him. He has a good job, loves kids, doesn't drink, and cares very much about me. Recently my husband found out about this affair. He was very hurt but decided to forgive me. He quit drinking and desperately wants to work things out between us. He is a new person now and doing everything to try and please me. My husband and I are presently in marriage counseling."

Of course, things don't always work out neatly or as planned consciously or unconsciously. You may get what you want but be faced with something you didn't count on—the fact that women act like women and don't easily separate sex from love. There was an unforeseen consequence of this woman's message affair. "I feel a new respect for my husband now and I care for him, but I don't know if I love him anymore.

I think about this other guy all the time even though I told him we couldn't see each other for a while. I am horribly torn between leaving my husband and taking a chance with this new man, or staying with my husband and hoping someday love will return."

A WAY TO THE TOP

Molly was always an ambitious girl. In grade school and high school she tried to be the best and brightest in her class and often succeeded. In college she was Phi Beta Kappa. When she entered the advertising business after graduating from college, she was already married to a man she had met in her sophomore year. In her new job she was always looking for opportunities to shine. She knew she wanted to become an account executive and eventually a leading player in her firm. She worked hard and was rewarded with raises, but things weren't going quick enough for her. So when one of the men who headed the company seemed to take a shine to her, she responded by making excuses to go into his office, by wearing her best and sexiest clothing when she knew she was going to see him, by touching him on the arm or hand to emphasize the points she was making.

Soon Molly and the much older company executive were having lunches together, and it wasn't long before some of those lunches turned into sexual matinees at a nearby posh hotel. Molly loved her husband but she also knew what she was doing.

Six months into this hot affair Molly became an account executive. She is now planning her next career move with the help of her lover, a key man in the company.

Molly is one of a breed of calculating, superambitious women who use affairs—extramarital or otherwise—to further their careers. They choose their lovers based more on what these men can do for them than on friendship or attraction, as other wives do. For them, love affairs are not matters of love or lust, liking or trust. These women are manipulators out for only one thing—advancement in their chosen fields. And very often, when they are good-looking and clever enough, they get what they want.

Other manipulators are actually looking to trade in an old husband for a richer, more prestigious one. They have affairs in order to try to marry such a man and live the rest of their lives in wealth and style.

One of these women, a broker in a real-estate firm, set out to seduce the head of the company she worked for. The man, thirty years older than she was, married his whole life to the same woman—a conservative, old-fashioned wife from the small town he'd grown up in—was bowled over by the sexual lure of this more sophisticated, glamorous female. She got him into bed, and he had his first experience of oral sex with her. It blew his mind. Her sexual expertise ensnared him. Here in his old age he was having sex as he never dreamed it could be. He divorced his old-fashioned wife. She divorced her less affluent husband, and now these two are living together in the luxury she had always dreamed of. Is he happy? Who knows? Is she? You bet!

I HAVE CHANGED

Perhaps what suited you about your husband and marriage when you started your life together no longer does, because of some fundamental growth in a different direction that altered your needs, attitudes, or tastes.

A young wife, in love with a fellow executive in the firm she worked for, explained how this had developed for her: "I feel my affair began because my husband and I had grown apart instead of together. I have changed a lot during our marriage. I went to college and worked my way up to a very high management position in my company. My husband likes to stay at home and putter around the house. I enjoy dressing up, going to restaurants, going to the city. He enjoys none of these things. Our social tastes are exactly opposite. Mine used to be like his. I am the one who has changed."

This woman of twenty-nine, married since she was eighteen, went on to explain another change that had come over her in recent years: "As much as I adore my children I would love to be free of the responsibilities, have no strings attached, be free to come and go and do as I please."

Often a mate who was selected originally because he provided stability and security can seem dull later on, causing some wives to turn to other men for drama and thrills.

IT'S SO BORING

Some couples settle into a very humdrum, totally predictable existence. It can seem very tedious after a while. An affair can be a way of creating some excitement in a boring environment.

"I got married when I was nineteen," said an office administrator in her late thirties in Wisconsin. "I had a good job and lots of friends then. When I was twenty-eight I had my daughter. I quit my job and stayed home with her for eight years. We lost contact with most of our friends after we bought our house thirty miles away. Our social life became nonexistent and I became very bored. My husband turned into a couch potato. I didn't realize how unhappy I was until I went to work part-time for a small family-owned retail business. I worked in the office. That's where I met Hank. He was interested in me and paid a lot of attention to me. He kept asking me out for a drink for almost a year before I finally went out with him. We used to meet at a quiet little bar for a few drinks and then sit and talk for hours, sometimes in the bar, sometimes in the car. He was also married and a lot older than me. I never planned on getting involved. I had been married for seventeen years and had never slept with anyone other than my husband.

"After seeing this man once or twice a week for a few months, I went to a motel with him. He was exciting, romantic, and made me feel very special." This woman's affair made her life interesting again and she thrived on the excitement it provided. "I was hooked on him," she admitted. "He became an addiction. I was having fun, living on a constant high." Her lover ended the relationship after two years and left this woman feeling a terrible void. She is now even more conscious of the boredom she feels in her marriage.

A BRIDGE OUT OF THE MARRIAGE

For some women, an extramarital affair may be a shopping expedition. You are truly unhappily married, but you can't envision life without a man and are afraid to divorce, so you see if you can find another marital partner through an affair. All of this may not be conscious, but below the surface that's the game plan. Even if you aren't shopping for a new husband, an affair may be a way to ease yourself out of a miserable marriage.

A woman in her mid-twenties understood this very well:

> I have had problems in my marriage from the beginning. I have been married over eight years and have two young children. I stayed in the marriage at first because I had made a commitment for a lifetime and I was going to carry it out. We had gone for counseling on and off for the past five years but it never changed anything. My husband needed a housekeeper, not a wife. I am not gorgeous but I'm not ugly by any means. It did not matter what I did, I could not turn him on. He would never talk intimately about his feelings, or about anything really. We just lived side by side in the same house. I worked two jobs partly to be away where it did not hurt so much.
>
> About two years ago I had an affair. It was with a man with whom I became friends. It didn't mean anything. I did not love him and he did not love me. So we cut it off. But after that I never quit looking or hoping. I knew I did not want an affair just for sex. I wanted someone to love me and I wanted to love him.
>
> Then I met Dan. He trained me at work. I was very attracted to him the first day we met. He was also a nice person. We work the swing shift and one night a group agreed to go out together after work. Everyone else copped out, but in the parking lot Dan and I decided we still wanted to go out. We went to a restaurant and talked for two hours. We went again the next night and then he kissed me. That's how it started. We are both getting divorced now and are talking about getting married when our divorces are final, but who knows? My marriage was a disaster before the affair. Dan just gave me the guts to get out.

A woman on the East Coast, now divorced, reminisced about her transition affair:

> It was ten years ago. I had no intention of becoming involved at the time. I was married with one child. He was single. We used to

have lunch frequently with other co-workers. We were both heads of our respective departments and had a lot of contact with each other. One evening there was a going-away party for a co-worker. He and I ended up seated next to each other. As the night went on he kept touching my shoulders, arms, and finally my leg. One of the people at the party had too much to drink and we offered to drive him home. On the way back to pick up my car he kissed me. I knew I shouldn't let him but we both had too much to drink. I told him the next day it was a mistake. He didn't feel that way. He continued to make advances until I gave in.

My marriage had been burdened at best. My husband was into drugs and alcohol and only worked three years of our nine-year marriage. I had very little self-esteem other than at work. I was very well respected there. I ended up leaving my husband and continuing to see my lover for two years. My lover was wonderful to me but such a change from how I had been treated that I couldn't adjust. I ended up quitting my job and moving to another state where I grew up. My affair was a means to end my unhappy marriage.

A woman in her forties who had met her lover "at the tail end of a bad marriage" said, "I had no family except for a senile mother and a teenage son to give me support during the time I decided to separate and then divorce. This man was my lifeline. He has since moved to another job, but we still keep in touch and occasionally get together after six years. I'm divorced now and not romantically involved with anyone. When I do meet someone else the sex with this other person will end, but that special something will still be there for him."

Finally, many affairs start because of hidden needs you may not be aware of.

Chapter 7

※

HIDDEN PSYCHOLOGICAL

REASONS FOR AFFAIRS

There are a host of psychological reasons why wives turn to other men. These are the reasons for affairs that are least understood by the women involved and their husbands. Many unfaithful wives assume, and indeed say, "It just happened," when in truth there were, unbeknownst to them, subterranean forces at work, compelling them to try an extramarital relationship.

The first of these psychological motivations is thought to be more common among men. But for many women, too, it's a hidden reality.

THE FEAR OF INTIMACY

Although most women are seeking with a lover the intimacy that is missing with their husbands, another group is drawn into affairs for reasons that are just the opposite. On a hidden level, these are women who are escaping intimacy. They share a discomfort with too much closeness in marriage.

Stacy is an example. She married right out of college. Her groom was her high school sweetheart, Ken.

They settled down in an apartment and all seemed to be going well on the surface. However, although the sex was good all through her courtship with Ken, soon after the marriage Stacy began to lose erotic interest in her husband. It reached the point where, when he tried to approach her, she found excuses not to have sex or she turned him down, saying "I'm not in the mood." Ken was puzzled and angry. Stacy was perturbed as well. She couldn't explain to Ken, or herself, why she didn't want to sleep with him. She just knew she didn't.

In the law firm where Stacy worked was a young attorney who started coming on to her. At first, she resisted his blandishments, but soon she was saying to herself, *I find him attractive physically. I'm not interested in sex with Ken. I don't want to live my life without sex. Why shouldn't I sleep with a man who appeals to me?* Soon Stacy was involved in a full-blown affair with the young lawyer, who was married also. Sex was terrific with her lover. Now, eight months later, her passion still runs high. Stacy wonders whether her sex life as a wife would be better if she were married to someone other than Ken.

Unfortunately, it wouldn't be. Stacy was turned off by Ken because she felt too close to him once they were married. Women like Stacy are more sexual in less committed relationships. If they decide to divorce and marry an extramarital partner, they find themselves losing sexual interest once more and, as a result, are drawn into another affair.

Some women with intimacy problems don't lose interest in their husbands as the preliminary step that leads them to an affair. Their method of relieving the discomfort of living closely as two is to go directly into an affair and add a third figure to the picture—a lover, who now, along with the husband, shares the wife's thoughts and emotions. These women feel more comfortable juggling two men than having to deal intimately with one.

Signs that you may suffer from an underground fear of intimacy?

You may not know it, but you have a "comfort zone"—everyone does. It is the amount of emotional space between you and someone else you need to feel comfortable. When that space is violated because another person has gotten too close, or when someone withdraws too much, you manipulate to return the relationship to the comfort zone. If you feel you have gotten too close for comfort, you pull back and do something to make the other person move away. If the relationship has become too cool and there is too much space, you try to move closer or attempt to draw the other person nearer.

Everybody's need for space is different. Some people like a lot of closeness; some, a lot of distance. When you are afraid of intimacy, you desire a substantial amount of emotional space.

Each time your husband draws closer, or when a commitment like marriage or having a baby together makes you feel more intimate, you begin to get kind of edgy, and in some manner you pull away.

Sometimes you will become too busy to be very available to him, or you may do something you know annoys your husband, or perhaps you pick a fight with him. Anger is used a lot by people trying to duck intimacy. So is workaholism, a social calendar that leaves you little time alone together, being tired, losing sexual interest—or taking a lover.

Behind the fear of intimacy is often the model of parents who were remote or cold, or the dread of engulfment. You are unconsciously afraid that you will be swallowed up by someone you feel too close to. When you take a lover and run back and forth between him and your husband, you are avoiding complete union with either one, thus removing this unconscious menace. This tactic ensures that you will not be smothered or swallowed up by either one. By adulterous love you are guarding against the loss of your sense of self.

THE SHE WHO'S A ME

You know her. She's the woman who places inordinate value on her looks, on status, perhaps on the external trappings of wealth. She is very concerned about how things appear to others. She may be arrogant. Her ego seems huge, but hidden from sight is a very fragile sense of self-esteem. That is why a woman like this needs so much admiration from others. It shores her up. If a person dares to criticize her, it makes her feel, on an unconscious level, so vulnerable that she may very well fly into a rage or turn icy cold.

Women like this have narcissistic personalities. Mental health professionals consider narcissism the psychological disorder of the age. Those who suffer from it—the extremely self-centered, shallow people all around us—seem to be proliferating in our society.

A woman with a narcissistic personality has very limited empathy. If you are this kind of person, it is hard for you to put yourself in other people's shoes and understand how they are feeling. All the narcissist basically cares or thinks about is how *she* is feeling. She is really all me, me, me. Children, husbands, lovers, are seen as extensions of herself rather than as individuals with cares and concerns of their own. They are there to serve her purposes. Husbands of narcissists are often seen as providers of services and material goods.

Women who are narcissists are prone to extramarital affairs. First of all, they think they are entitled to have whatever they want. Second, they need the admiration that lovers provide. Narcissistic women generally have affairs with men who reflect well upon them—powerful figures in society, very wealthy men, very handsome or younger men. Women like this tend to work with unusual zeal to preserve their youth. In midlife, frantic about losing the attractiveness that they have based so much of their sense of self-worth on, they may have a particular need for affairs to reaffirm their ability to capture the interest of men.

THE BORDERLINE SYNDROME WIFE

Like the narcissistic "me" people, women who suffer from what mental health professionals define as a borderline personality have an identity impairment. At their core they don't know who they are. Borderline women tend to be clingy in relationships and to take their identity from the other person. They often need a lot of touching and holding and feel lost without it. They may be drawn into affairs simply to get the holding, rather than the sex, especially if they feel a husband does not give them the affection they want. Since women like this tend to be emotional bottomless pits, it is almost impossible for any man to give them all the attention, affection, and loving they crave.

PSYCHOLOGICAL COLLUSIONS

Among the women who have affairs because of unhappy marriages, many are involved in a neurotic collusion with their husbands: The pair collaborate on a hidden level to maintain the unhappiness that the wife thinks is all the husband's fault. The reason for the affair is not a situation these wives find themselves in, but one they helped create and perpetuate because of unconscious needs.

Let's look at the case of Sandra. Sandra met her husband, Barry, when she was eighteen. Barry was thirteen years older. To Sandra, Barry seemed the answer to all her problems. Her mother had died when she was seven. She was brought up by her alcoholic father, who never re-married. He was a loving man, but undependable and careless. As a child, Sandra took on more and more responsibility for running the home.

In contrast to her father, Barry seemed like a tower of strength. She felt he was mature, a man who would take care of her instead of the other way around, as it was with her father. Feeling she could lean on Barry, she married him.

Today, two decades and two children later, her marriage is very different from what she imagined it would be originally. She soon found she was making all of the decisions about everything—the house, the kids, leisure activities. Barry didn't have an opinion about anything. According to Sandra, she turned out to be the stronger of the two.

A few years ago, Sandra went to work as a real-estate salesperson and became quite successful. Meanwhile, Barry's career as an archi-tect had stalled. Sandra knows now that Barry is a passive man—and she feels these days that he is a loser, too. Her unhappiness at home led her to start an affair with one of the partners of the firm she works for.

She blames Barry: If only he were a different man, she would be happy with him and she wouldn't be having her affair.

But that isn't the case at all. Sandra is married to exactly the kind of man she requires.

Although Sandra can't stand her husband's passivity, his refusal to make decisions or take charge can be seen as partly her doing, if you look at how she has interacted with Barry since the beginning of their marriage. Every time Barry tried to assert himself, Sandra cut him down. When, for example, he suggested a family activity, she told him precisely why his idea was a bad one. When he offered a solution to a problem, her withering looks and sarcasm let him know how dumb it was. Sandra helped stamp out Barry's assertiveness by her constant negative reac-tions. Why?

Sandra had to re-create in her marriage the role she had played with her father: She needs to run things. This is the only role she feels comfortable in with a man.

She is playing out another scenario that dates back to her growing-up years with her father as well. When she was little she discovered the way to win her father's approval was to be an achiever. She earned good grades in school while also keeping the house neat and clean, looking after her younger sister, and, once she was old enough, holding down a part-time job. As a married woman Sandra is still acting like an over-achiever—the star in the family. Chopping down Barry is an unconscious maneuver to protect herself in that role. Barry responded to Sandra's criticisms by becoming more and more passive both at home and on the job, which meant that Sandra had to shoulder more and more responsibility in the marriage.

Barry has his own agenda, as does each spouse in a marital collusion. He grew up with a critical, domineering mother. By acting incompetent, Barry makes sure that his wife will both criticize him and overshadow him as his mother once did. At home he bungles repairs. At the office he forgets to return important phone calls and comes late to meetings with clients. Neither of these marital partners recognizes what is really going on, that in fact they are collaborating with each other to keep their relationship just as it is, with its built-in unhappiness. In this way each can live out a familiar role from the past.

Collusions like this exist between spouses who want to preserve a myriad of other set roles in a marriage, and the one who appears to be the long-suffering victim may actually be a partner in maintaining the problems in the marriage. If you blame marital unhappiness for your infidelity, the reason for your affair may be more complicated and less obvious than you imagine. Think about it. Do you find yourself in a role with your husband that is similar to the one you had in the family while growing up?

THE PROJECTING WIFE

Another hidden factor behind marital discontent that seems on the surface to be the reason for a wife's affair is projection. You don't see your husband as he really is as a person but, instead, project onto him the characteristics of a parent—your father, or even your mother. It is common for you to first view your mate as the embodiment of everything you felt was missing in your parent. During courtship you see him as having the characteristics of an ideal father or mother—someone who would never, for example, neglect you, or be cruel or careless with you, or try to rule you like a tyrant.

Once you are married, however, your original idealized view gets chipped away by reality. Over time you begin to see faults in your husband. Many people adjust to reality gradually. The fantasy fades and is replaced by a more realistic view of the partner. However, for some mates, the tactic is to switch fantasies. The "perfect parent" image is abandoned and now the spouse is seen as acting like the "bad parent"— like the father, for example, who was distant, or who rejected or criticized or frustrated or disapproved of you, or who made you feel overcontrolled, suffocated, or inadequate. However a woman felt wronged as a child is how she sees the husband now, through the haze of her projected fantasy. Your emotional reactions to this image are the same as those from childhood. You feel enraged, frustrated, frightened, rebellious, anxious, or saddened as you did in the past.

It is your distorted view of your husband and your emotional reactions culled from the past that have propelled you to seek refuge in an extramarital affair.

TRIANGLE LOVERS

For some unfaithful wives the name of the game is not love, romance, or sex, although on the surface it may seem to be any one or all of these. What really makes the woman's passion boil is the triangle she is in once an affair begins. Often a woman who comes to life in triangles has lived her formative years in one.

Her mother and father may have vied to show their daughter that each loved her more than the other, or perhaps during childhood she became adept at playing one parent off against the other. In this early-life triangle she achieved power over both mother and father. In adult life the woman marries, eventually takes a lover, and plays out her old role in the new family constellation, thus elevating herself to the powerful position of being fought over again by pitting her adulterous lover against her lawfully wedded husband.

A woman who is habituated to triangles needs to be in one. If one lover leaves, she takes another. If a husband takes off, she marries again and once more gets involved in an extramarital affair.

BLACK-AND-WHITE THINKERS

Some wives are unable to sustain love because they lack an essential ingredient in their psychological makeup. All lovers, married or not, have to be able to tolerate some ambivalence in their relationships—to realize that sometimes you may love your partner, at other times hate him for something he has said or done. Someone who can keep love going realizes that people have good characteristics and bad, lovable moments and dislikable ones. She can accept a husband as a combination of both good and bad and is able to live with some passing hostile feelings toward a mate along with loving ones. A great number of people in our world, however, don't get this. They are unable to see gray areas in their relationships. They live in a black-and-white universe. You are either good or bad. Anger or frustration, to them, is a sign that you have fallen into the bad camp.

Men who get involved with women like this become the containers of their black-and-white thinking. For example, the lover becomes the all-good one and, since these women have to split things up dramatically, the husband becomes the all-bad one. Or vice versa—since the husband is first seen as all bad, the lover has to be regarded as all good. Black-and-white thinkers tend to fall madly in love with their lovers, perhaps with the same passion they expended on their husbands in the period when they were considered all good, too.

Over the long haul, women who split people into good or bad cannot continue loving the same man if they live with him, since no one is ever all good. Hence the need for a lover.

HIGH-DRAMA WIVES

Colorful, lively, given to scenes, high-drama wives have hysterical personalities. They live to be the center of attention, and are at their best when emotions are at the boiling point. Women like this are drawn to extramarital affairs because of the drama involved. They also are romance junkies and get off on the feeling of being swept away by love. Since hysterical women tend to choose sturdy, methodical, logical, orderly husbands as an antidote to their own messy, unfocused personalities, they often complain that their husbands are *soooo* boring, *so* unemotional! They are tempted into an affair to liven things up, they think, not realizing that it is their own particular high-strung personality type that is sweeping them away as much as their lovers.

THE HOSTILE PAIR

Some wives are hostile people married to partners who share their love of war. Hate is what keeps a marriage like this together. Hostile people are mates from hell and do whatever they can to make each other's lives torture. This includes having affairs and being found out or flaunting them. If one spouse has an affair, the other then has to have one to "show" the first. Generally, even when an affair is discovered the attacks may escalate, but one mate won't throw the other out. It's part of their game of "Let's make each other miserable" and is yet another opportunity to attack and counterattack. Women and men in hostile marriages are happy only when they are miserable, and affairs are ideal vehicles to express the hate, spite, and venom that keep them together.

SAINTS AND SINNERS

There is a kind of wife who divides the males in her love life into saints and sinners. This is the female equivalent of the Whore/Madonna Syndrome in men in which the man elevates his wife into a madonna—someone so pure and good that he dare not touch her carnally. He therefore loses sexual interest in her. His sexual desire is alive and strong for someone he regards as a whore—someone who has sex with him outside of marriage—a lover.

For the female, the husband—her protector and the father of her children—becomes the saint in whom she loses sexual interest, and so she seeks sexual thrills with a man she unconsciously regards as a sinner—the guy who is willing to take her, another man's wife, to bed.

THE COMPULSIVES

A small number of women are compulsive about sex. For them, even when they know it is not in their best interests, playing around is something they *must* do. Their extramarital behavior is out of their control. It is addictive behavior—sex is used compulsively the way others use alcohol or drugs.

"I've been married for five years," a young woman explained. "For three and one half of those years I've been having affairs, and I don't know why. I would stop one, saying 'No more,' but go right back to it again." This woman lived in a web of lies, deceit, self-castigation, and the fear that her husband would find out.

An older woman of forty-eight, who was sorry about the toll her sexual addiction had taken on her life, confessed, "I've had many affairs and am known as a sleep-around. I've been married four times already and have always fallen for a best friend or neighbor or any man who wasn't my husband." This woman, too, dreaded her latest husband's discovery of her extracurricular love life—an outcome that seemed imminent since the wife of her most recent lover was threatening to call this woman's husband and tell all.

Both of the above women, realizing that they were involved in behavior that they would prefer to stop, stated that they knew they needed help.

The marks of sex addiction are the feeling that you are indulging in affairs because you have to, rather than really want to, and the desire to end your extramarital behavior with an inability to do so.

Sex addiction often runs in families—the woman whose sexual behavior is out of control often had a parent for whom this was true as well, a mother or father who also indulged in affair after affair. Other addictions, like alcohol or drug abuse, are often common in families of sex addicts, too.

Another common theme in cases of sexual compulsiveness is sexual abuse in childhood. If a woman was sexually abused as a child, she may learn to sexualize all her relationships as an adult. Current estimates indicate that a third of the female population of North America are sexually victimized before their mid-teens.

Although most wives are not compulsive about sex, large numbers of them find themselves enchanted by it when sex soars to new heights with their lovers. Let's find out more about why sex can be so terrific in affairs.

Chapter 8

※

PASSION AND ECSTASY: WHY THEY IGNITE

The majority of wives may not enter into affairs for sexual reasons. They may start out looking for someone to give them what they miss in their marriages—intimate communication, approval, a sense that they are valued or respected, the feeling that they are still a knockout.

However, once they find a special buddy who becomes their lover, judging from letters and case histories, they generally are swept up in very exciting sex. Their reaction is one of wonder and delight—almost of disbelief that they are capable of such incredible erotic feelings. It is often the best sex in their lives, and wives may discover depths of passion with their lovers they didn't know existed before.

Great sex then becomes one reason why women *stay* in an illicit relationship, even when it may be causing them emotional pain or conflict in other ways. Three quarters of the wives in the office affairs survey placed the lovemaking second—right after friendship—on the list of things that kept them interested in their lovers.

There are three categories of women, however, for whom sex plays a larger-than-usual role in creating the *initial* climate for an affair.

WHAT'S IT LIKE WITH SOMEONE ELSE?

Among them are perhaps the last of a disappearing breed in our sexually permissive society—the women who have known only one male sexually: the man they married. Generally these are women who became brides very early in life, often while still in their teens, or women who came from very strict, conservative backgrounds. With sex all around them—in movies, novels, television, song lyrics, with friends having a lot of different sexual relationships, and perhaps their own children acting freer than they ever were—these women often feel that they have missed something in life. They begin to wonder: What would it be like with another man?

"I married when I was eighteen," wrote a young woman in Maryland. "My husband is the only man I have ever been sexually involved with. I had my first child at twenty, my second six years later. I have a husband who adores me, does more than 50 percent of the housework, shares in child care responsibilities, and is very supportive of me. He encouraged me to go to college after our first child turned two, which I did, full-time. He enjoys seeing me do things I want to without him, like going shopping or visiting girlfriends. He's the perfect husband. So what is my problem? Why am I having my first affair in my ten-year marriage?

"I think a big part of it is that I got married too young. I feel like I missed out on many things. I feel there is so much I want to experience. Before my affair started I had a great curiosity about what it would be like to have sex with someone besides my husband."

Another woman explained, "I was a virgin when I married seventeen years ago. I'm now thirty-nine years old, considered young-looking and very attractive. I have a fabulous husband, four wonderful children, a lovely home, an exciting job, but . . .

"I feel this is my last chance before I get too old, so I want to have an affair just to be with somebody else who finds me irresistible."

When women have affairs to satisfy their curiosity, they often overlook the possible consequences. Many find they have bitten off more than they can comfortably chew.

"I thought I could remain emotionally detached and just enjoy the sex and friendship, but I could not," said one woman originally out just to satisfy her curiosity about being with another man. Her affair was more than a year old. She admitted it had mixed her up, and that although she got a lot of pleasure from her lover she also experienced a lot of anguish about her situation. She was caught emotionally between her lover and her husband, a common occurrence for wives.

Sometimes the sexual experience with another man is an eye-opener, as it was for this inexperienced wife who took a lover after sixteen years of marriage:

> I felt the least satisfactory part of my marriage was the sexual relationship. However, never having been with anyone else besides my husband I assumed "this is all there is."
>
> I was not looking for an affair, but at a group dinner after an out-of-town sales meeting this man sat across the table from me and catered to my every wish. When we all went out dancing later, I found him constantly at my side. His room was also the hospitality suite, and when I left that night he kissed me good night and asked me to come back when the others had gone. I did not.
>
> Four months passed and there was another sales meeting. This is when the sexual part of our relationship began. From making love with this new man I found out that the sex I had at home should have been much better. I started to realize that I love my husband because he is my husband, because he is the father of my children, because he is a good provider, but I am not in love with him as a lover. I was forty-six years old when I found how good sex was, how much fun it was, and how much better it is with someone who makes you feel good when he makes love to you.

This woman's marriage will never be the same again.

My Husband Isn't Interested in Sex

The second group of wives who are propelled by sex are those who feel physically starved. Either they have a higher sex drive than their husbands or their spouses stopped making love to them. They have sex infrequently or sometimes not at all.

A wife in her late forties complained, "Both my lover and I have been married for over twenty years. I am an attractive woman and the last few years my husband became less interested in sex. I have always enjoyed it. When I tried to interest my husband he was always too busy. At the time I started this affair I was sexually deprived and my lover was in the same situation. We decided to give each other the intimacy and passion we both missed very much. The sex we share is incredible. We have no inhibitions with each other. We are open and very loving. We share a wonderful bond and we are good friends and lovers. That is all I want. We have given a lot of enjoyment to each other."

A forty-six-year-old woman in an extramarital liaison with her thirty-three-year-old boss explained:

> I have been married for close to eighteen years. It was not long after we married that it became obvious that my husband and I were worlds apart sexually. When he saw that he could not (would not?) be able to keep up with me, it was easier for him to withdraw from me instead of trying to improve our lovemaking. I have always had a robust carnal appetite. I enjoy sex and know I am a good and loving sex partner. Although I have tried many times to discuss the matter with my husband and let him know how hungry and frustrated I am, my husband (to whom sex is unimportant) prefers to think we have no problem. I happen to think that having sex less than six to eight times a year for a maximum of ten minutes each time *is* a problem.

> I recognized a like spirit in my boss some time ago but never let on that I did. We decided to go to lunch one day, and over Chinese food we both finally talked about what turned out to be a mutual chemical attraction. Four days later we were at a motel after work. What an *amazing* experience we had, and have had since that first time together. From the beginning we were totally free with each other. We know what the other is thinking and feeling, and blend together so beautifully it is frightening. It is the most intense physical union I have ever had. We make love four to six hours easily and thoroughly enjoy every moment.

A woman in her thirties, in a six-month-old affair with her boss, said, "My husband had not made love to me for about a year when I got involved with my lover. It started when he was leaving the office for another job. We hugged each other. Mutual feelings that had never surfaced before suddenly did.

"It is great to have someone touch you, really care, send you a card now and then, hug you when he can, share special moments, talk, understand."

To be rejected or ignored sexually is devastating to the modern woman's self-esteem. The lover not only gives her the sex she craves but restores her sense of desirability as well.

"My husband and I had become like brother and sister," a thirty-eight-year-old wife confessed. "He was a workaholic and didn't seem to have time for me. He would stay up late looking at and then hiding *Penthouse* magazines from me. I went to bed alone a lot. He made me feel that I wasn't attractive enough for him. Why else would he want to look at pictures of other women instead of making love to me?

"The guy I became involved with is always telling me how beautiful I am and how I turn him on. He has restored some self-confidence in me. For that I will always be grateful."

I AM TURNED OFF

Sometimes it is the other way around. A wife finds she has lost sexual interest in her husband and so she looks to another man to turn her on.

A twenty-four-year-old woman confided, "From the day I got married I lost all sexual urges for my husband. I was only married six months when my boss and I started sleeping together. I thought maybe having this affair, seeing this man just once, might help restore feelings for my husband, but instead I keep seeing my lover, and it has made my sex life with my husband worse. I can't stop thinking of my boss, but I love my husband very much and plan to stay with him."

A twenty-three-year-old woman on the verge of an affair confided, "I have been married over five years and have two children, four and two. I'm having problems with sexual interest in my husband. I can't get aroused by him. Although I try hard, the problem isn't getting any better. I now make love three or four times a week without being turned on.

"I met a man at work who is making advances. He is almost thirty years older than I am but I'm seriously thinking about having an affair with him. I wonder if I will regain interest in my husband if I get out of my rut and have the affair."

WHY MATES LOSE DESIRE

The answer, of course, is no, because the loss of interest in a spouse has hidden psychological origins that are rarely understood by married people. Lack of desire is the number one sex problem being treated by sex therapists today. It is considered a sexual dysfunction and even has an official name: inhibited sexual desire. To find out more about the subject of why husbands and wives become turned off, I suggest you read my book on the subject, *Is There Sex After Marriage?* But, in brief, here is a rundown of some major causes.

If you rule out depression, certain illnesses like diabetes, and some medications, all of which can decrease libido, leading reasons why a wife turns off to a husband and vice versa include:

1. *Hidden anger.* You are mad at your mate for something. For example, you resent the fact that your husband doesn't give you the help with housework or kids that you feel you deserve, or you are hurt and angry that a spouse has turned full attention on the kids and not enough on you, or a mate spends too much time at work or belittles you. You don't express your anger, or you stop trying to work it out, or you deny it to yourself, so it festers inwardly and ultimately turns into loss of libido.

2. *A covert power struggle.* The husband or wife who turns a spouse down is controlling the spouse and therefore accruing power in the relationship. This underground way of getting back some power is quite common in relationships with a very domineering spouse.

3. *Fear of success.* Everything is going great in your life, so great that you think you don't deserve it or that the gods will exact payment for such good fortune. Unconsciously you feel you have to screw things up somewhere in order to placate the gods. One fine way of doing this is to lose sexual interest in a spouse.

4. *A problem with intimacy.* Some spouses become very uncomfortable when they feel too close to or emotionally dependent on a spouse.

They need to create some distance to counteract the discomfort. Losing desire for their mates accomplishes this.

5. *Identification of the spouse as a parent.* This is generally a subterranean dynamic outside your conscious awareness, but it is a very, very common phenomenon in marriage. Sex may have been great before the wedding ceremony, but once vows are exchanged and you are in a domestic situation similar to the one you were brought up in, the husband gradually begins to feel like a father, or the wife starts to become a motherly figure. Sometimes this happens because a husband acts in a paternal manner (or a wife acts like a mother). Frequently the parental image is projected onto one spouse by the other. Sometimes the identification of a spouse as a parent doesn't start to occur until after a child is born and the spouse is, indeed, a parent.

A twenty-seven-year-old woman wrote, "I am married for three years and have a two-and-a-half-year-old daughter. I was happily married for a year and a half, but my sex life went down the tubes after having a baby. While staying at home being a mother, I got bored so I did something I shouldn't have. I contacted my old lover."

No matter when in the marriage it begins, once you start to see a husband as Dad or a wife as Mom, the incest taboo is raised, or the spouse is seen as a restrictive, perhaps punitive, figure, and your libido erodes. When this happens, both men and women may look to an affair as the answer. And since sex in an affair often is so much more exciting than sex in marriage, it may indeed seem like the answer, at first.

HOT SEX WITH A LOVER

There is no doubt about it. Judging from the letters in my files and the women I have spoken to, there is a lot of torrid lovemaking going on in extramarital beds. Even when women are married to men who satisfy them sexually, they find a special extra charge to the lovemaking in their affairs. Why is illicit sex so great?

For one group of women, it is because sex is so bad in the marriage. For women in situations like this, it's a rebirth.

The Affair Is a Sexual Reawakening

Some women respond so strongly to their lovers because the other man has taught them to be sensual again and they revel in their newfound eroticism.

One woman said, "My sexual life with my husband was practically nil. We have nominal sex five to nine times a year, and sometimes he loses his erection before he enters me. I could count on one hand the number of climaxes I have had with him, although I have faked many. I began to think I was cold. It took four times with my lover before I had a climax. When I did I just cried, knowing that I was not abnormal and that I had not lost all sexual feelings."

A teacher on the West Coast admitted, "My lover helped me play out many of my sexual fantasies, which my husband feels foolish doing. I was able to be my 'true self,' which is a sexy, exciting, and innovative woman—qualities my husband plays down. My lover made me feel alive and exciting again."

The Woman Feels Sexually Charged by Her Lover's Response

After routine, lukewarm responses or coldness at home, turning a man on, giving *him* intense pleasure, makes the sexually neglected wife feel supersexy and erotically powerful.

A woman in her late thirties said of the man with whom she started an affair, "He thinks I'm a good lover—my husband calls me oversexed and falls asleep before I come down from making love. My lover turns on to me. With my husband I feel like a wet mop or piece of furniture."

"Jim made me feel appreciated, sexy, attractive, and loved," said another woman, "something I hadn't felt in years with my husband. He has such a sensual way of looking at me and making me feel so special. That turns me on. The lovemaking is incredible."

The Lover Takes More Pains to Please

He knows he is there mainly for that purpose, and most men in illicit affairs take their role as pleasurers seriously, often spending more time and effort on lovemaking than the average husband. Indeed, a married lover may expend more sexual energy with his married mistress than he does with his legitimate wife.

A school administrator in her forties said, "My lover is everything my husband never was in bed. My lover is fantastic. Our lovemaking sessions last for hours. He is oh so gentle and so strong at the same time. After two years I still get turned on just by looking at him."

Of course, not every unfaithful wife's passion with her extramarital boyfriend is based on a comparison to her husband as a lover. There are many more answers to why sex can and so often does reach such incredible heights in illicit liaisons.

Your Lover Escapes Any Identification with a Parent

Since you are not living in a domestic situation with the other man, you avoid this identification as a restrictive, disapproving figure which so often inhibits you in bed or dampens sexual interest with a husband. As result, in your outlaw romance you may lose your sexual inhibitions and feel freer to experiment, to live out fantasies, to experience your full potential for passion. An important barrier to ecstasy is bypassed in your affair.

The Sex Is New

Your marriage has gone through the honeymoon phase when you and your husband couldn't keep your hands off each other. The initial high passion that exists in many marriages rarely lasts beyond the first two or three years. Sex can still be good, but with living together and habituation it becomes less urgent and somewhat less frequent, going from, let's say, sex every day or four or five times a week to twice a week. With your lover you remain in the extended honeymoon phase of highest passion in the relationship, since you don't live together and see each other only for limited amounts of time.

There Is Ongoing Romance

In marriage, courtship often stops, routines set in, everyday matters take over, and compliments, spontaneous hugs, kisses, and little affectionate gestures are forgotten. Lovers, however, are in a constant state of romance. They bask in open admiration of one another. There is a lot of holding, kissing, complimenting. Romance, as it was originally invented by the troubadours of the Middle Ages, involved love for someone a knight couldn't have—a married woman. So in a sense you are living out romance in its original form in an illicit affair. Women adore romance, and boy does it make them sexy! The atmosphere of romance that surrounds an illicit affair is one of its greatest turn-ons for wives.

Yearning Never Stops

Because you can't see each other all the time, because at least one of you, if not both, belongs to someone else, you never get enough of each other. You yearn for the time when you can be together again, and plot and plan to make it happen. The longings for him, the fantasies of what it is like being with him when you are apart, create pent-up desire that explodes when you are able to join each other once more.

There Is Anxiety

An illicit affair encompasses built-in tension. You are worrying about being caught. You are worrying if it will continue. You are worrying about where your own emotions are taking you. A lot of anxiety can act as a sexual turn-off but, as experiments have shown, a little anxiety can make a person feel real sexy.

In one study published in the *Journal of Abnormal Psychology*, people were purposely placed in anxiety-provoking situations. It was found that the greatest erotic arousal in the subjects was preceded by some degree of anxiety.

Dr. Harold Lief, a leading sex and marital therapist and former head of the Marriage Council of Philadelphia, claims that the anxiety in affairs can be a reason why the lover seems more exciting than the spouse and why people fall in love with the extramarital partner.

It Is Secret and Forbidden

The fact that they are being naughty, doing something they know they shouldn't, can be very exciting to certain people, and if you are one of them it can create an extra erotic charge. Maybe it's just the thought of living on the edge. For some it may be the thrill you get from keeping something secret from a parental figure—your spouse—the same kind of thrill you may have felt as a small child when you hid something from your mother or father.

Some therapists believe the sexiness of doing something secret comes from the time when you were a little child and wondered what your parents were doing behind the closed doors of their bedroom. Sexuality, for you, became connected with something hidden and wondered about. A love affair conducted in secret puts you behind those closed doors symbolically, and the excitement this produces can be very powerful and alluring because it is based on very early, primitive, and *forbidden* sexual feelings.

You Have Already Broken the Social Code

By committing adultery you have defied society's rules. As an outlaw in a state disassociated from family, community, and investment in the future, you may give up your sense of what is "proper" and feel freer to experiment, practice new things, be aggressive. There is often a breakdown of old inhibitions that may have restrained you sexually before or in your marriage. Many women, for example, learn to like oral sex or to use sex toys or to act out fantasies with their lovers for the first time, or just feel more able to "let go" and be really responsive or wild in bed.

An Affair Is an Oasis

When you and your lover meet, it is time out from ordinary life. There are no worries about bills or kids, no chores like shopping, cleaning, or taking out the garbage. For the moment you forget about job worries, petty and major aggravations. It is just the two of you hidden away from the rest of the world, free to concentrate on only one thing—pleasuring each other. Such a carefree atmosphere is conducive to the freer flowing of passion.

An Affair Is a Sexual Institution

Marriage basically is not. Marriage may encompass sex, but it is basically about a lot of other things—raising a family, supporting the social structure, economics, perpetuating the species. Because sex is at the core of what an affair is, it makes sex the most important matter to be dealt with each time you meet, a good atmosphere for passion to flow. In contrast, sex in marriage is sometimes the last thing on your list—something you get around to at the end of the day when everything else is taken care of and you may be exhausted—not a good atmosphere for passion to flow.

You Prepare Yourself for Sex

Your liaison has been preceded by thinking of sex. During the time you are apart, you've been having delicious thoughts about your lover. You carefully groom yourself for this event. Your hair is freshly done; you are wearing an outfit you know you look good in; your lingerie has been chosen with eye and sex appeal in mind; you perfume yourself knowingly. You put lotion on your body so your skin will feel smooth to his touch.

The act of getting yourself together for a meeting with a lover creates anticipation and receptivity. It has been likened to "grooming," the bodily presentation that went on among our primate forebears to signal readiness for sex. The acts of preparation for a tryst are like titillating foreplay to the grand event—the actual rendezvous. By fussing, primping, anticipating, you are helping set the stage for a mindblowing sexual experience.

You Are Both on Best Behavior

As lovers, you don't see each other when you are cranky or distracted by a kid who's been up all night, or when you are sick and don't feel like talking to anyone. When lovers are together they see each other as people under only optimal circumstances. Lovers are bound together not by contracts or obligations, as in marriage, but simply by the desire to be with one another. So it stands to reason they behave very well with one another when they want an affair to continue. With both being so agreeable, supportive, likable, downright lovable, it is natural that the desire to give and receive pleasure is enhanced.

It Is an Established Relationship

A final reason that sex is so good for women in their affairs is that they are involved in an *ongoing* sexual relationship. Almost all of the 250 letters from wives about their affairs talked about liaisons that had been going on for months and years with the end nowhere in sight. It was not unusual to hear of affairs that had lasted five to fifteen years. Women's sexuality, tied as it is to their emotions, does not do well in quick affairs. Women like established relationships, in which they feel freer to express their full sensuality, and that is what most of them achieve with their lovers.

Who, then, are these lovers that awaken such passion in other men's wives?

Chapter 9

⚜

THE OTHER MAN

Whom does a married woman choose for her lover? Judging from the 250 letters in my files, here are seven of the leading requirements that you have if you are among the majority of women.

WHAT HE IS LIKE

1. ***Your lover must be the opposite of your husband.*** "I got involved with this other man," wrote one woman of thirty-six, "because I found he had a lot of the qualities my husband *used* to have. He is sensitive to my needs, thoughtful, protective, romantic, free of anger, and I felt genuinely cared for and wanted."

The main point of reference, for many women embarked upon an affair, is the man they are married to. Most women respond to attributes that they feel are missing in the husband—qualities that they hunger for. Wives seem upset and angry that their husbands are not living up to their early promise.

Obviously what the woman above is saying is as much about her husband as her lover. Translated, her statement means that her husband is insensitive, unthoughtful, unprotective, unromantic, frequently angry, and makes her feel unappreciated or unloved.

You can create a picture of the husband from the portrait an unfaithful wife draws of her lover. Although there are women who are able to appreciate the differing qualities in each of the men in their lives, it is rare that a lover would be as appealing as he is to *most* wives without this contrast, and in this sense he lives in the shadow of the husband.

2. *He knows how to give compliments.* By word and deed your lover makes you feel noticed, special, attractive, and appreciated. Again this virtue exists in comparison to the failure of husband, who in the view of many an adulterous wife takes her for granted, neglects her, treats her like a domestic convenience, doesn't romance her, or fails to remark on anything positive about her as a person—either her physical attributes or her talents. He may even belittle her, making her feel worthless and unimportant. I was struck by how many wives used the word *nothing* to describe how they felt at home. Marriage seems to make many wives feel anonymous and diminished as women, something the lover's attentions counteract.

Noted one wife in her mid-thirties, speaking of her current lover, "He appreciates my looks as well as my intellect, neither of which my husband seems to notice. He also appreciates any little thing I do for him. My husband only notices when dinner isn't ready when he gets home."

Another wife commented, "Frank made me feel appreciated, sexy, attractive, and loved, something I hadn't felt in years with my husband. Frank isn't a classically handsome man. He's someone you wouldn't look at twice if you passed him on the street, but he makes me feel so special, just by the way he looks at me. That makes me deeply attracted to him."

3. *He makes you feel you are sharing something important with him.* It could be work interests, marital problems, an outlook on life, or emotional support. Most women experience this feeling of sharing with the other man before deciding to become sexually intimate.

Similar marital problems may make a woman feel as if a man is a fellow sufferer—the lovers can ease each other's pain. Someone who creates a sense of fun, playfulness, sexiness, or an upbeat attitude missing at home can appear to be a kindred soul. A person who shares your worries, who is there for you when you need consolation, encouragement, a sounding board, makes you think of him warmly as a real buddy in life.

A wife in her mid-thirties said, "We met in early spring. In the fall he confided his problems with his wife. It happened that we shared the same problems, desires, and concerns about our marriages. It was at this point, seven months after we met, that I realized I had tremendous sexual attraction to this man and told him we needed to be careful. It was then he kissed me for the first time."

A secretary in San Diego said, "We began sharing problems and we became the best of friends. Our work was also going great as a result. All of a sudden we both felt that our friendship was changing into something more. We thought about each other constantly and three months later we wound up in bed."

Today, common work interests are particularly important as a prelude to an affair. A husband may ignore or put down the importance of the wife's job, or he may simply not be interested in what she does, while the woman and her lover often spend day after day in the same workplace. But even if the husband is exemplary in his attitude toward his wife's work, the majority of lovers these days meet on the job and they understand each other's work world better than any spouse can. This creates a tremendous bond and gives the lover a big edge over the husband.

A woman now divorcing her husband for her boss, who is leaving his wife, said, "The closeness between us developed more and more, working together and accomplishing good goals at the office. We were a team." Sharing a job can be an intimate and heady experience, creating unexpected emotional feelings for a myriad of wives.

4. *He listens to you with empathy and understanding.* "He was always thoughtful and ready to hear what I had to say without judgments or preconceived notions," explained a wife of thirty-three, describing what attracted her to her boss.

"He listens and talks and doesn't make me feel dumb. We help each other feel better just talking about our problems," said a wife in her early forties.

I was struck by how often wives mentioned their lovers' ability to listen seriously to what was on their minds. Husbands imagine it's a lover's good looks or sexuality, but in reality most wives are seduced in their extramarital relationships by the ability to communicate—to talk openly to their lovers without fear, and feel they are truly heard. Again one gets the impression from this that many husbands either don't listen, don't want to listen, or discount what wives have to say.

5. *He encourages you in your goals.* A man often marries a woman to be a wife and a mother. Or he is content that her job is less important than his. Other aspirations may upset him. A wife's desire to succeed at nondomestic tasks, or accelerate her career goals, can threaten the status quo and the existing power structure of the marriage in which the husband has been the dominant one. If the wife becomes successful at work, she clearly will have more control in the marital relationship.

A husband, with some resentment, also often regards a wife's job as a rival for her time and attention. The lover, with no such fears or hidden agenda to maintain the status quo, often points out a woman's strengths, encourages her to expand her ambitions, acts as her teacher. In many of the letters in my files the wife, speaking of her extramarital partner, refers to him not only as her friend and lover, but her mentor. She thinks he is on her side, cheering her on, a very strong factor in creating emotional attachment.

"I feel important," wrote one woman, "because he praises me for my gifts and raw talents. He coaches me, encourages me."

A wife in her twenties, involved with another man for more than a year, explained, "My husband never cared for my opinions and feelings. He discouraged my tastes, hobbies, and abilities. Then here I find a guy who has the same tastes as I have and who tries to encourage me to achieve higher goals in life." Now in love with this other man, she ended with "I have no idea where this will all end, but it is very painful."

6. *He is married.* Unfaithful wives differ from philandering husbands. Most husbands seduce single women. The office affairs survey confirmed the findings of other studies: The overwhelming majority of wives get involved with someone else's husband. This may be because, at least at the beginning of their affairs, women feel that a married man is safer, less likely to pose a threat to their own marriages. However, this premise often proves false as the wife, despite her best intentions to keep it light, finds herself increasingly involved emotionally. Very often, according to the women whose stories I heard, she ends up ruing her choice, saying that it's a mistake to get involved with a married man because you will always be number two in his life.

7. *He is persistent.* Among wives' lovers there are a sizable number of men who, along with their other characteristics, have the guts and personality to keep pursuing and trying to interest a woman for a long time, and finally win. These men generally combine flattery with

gentle persistence and patience, and this turns out to be a seductive combination for many women.

Lovers do not need to be handsome or young. Many turn out to be ordinary-looking, less impressive physically than the woman's husband. "The man I am involved with is not particularly attractive physically but he is the most sensitive, caring, romantic man I have ever known," said a forty-six-year-old administrator.

Many are quite a bit older, often decades older than the husband. They don't have to be as well off either. The husband is often more successful. While women look for financial security and stability when searching for a husband, they often concentrate more on what a man can offer them emotionally if he is a potential lover.

THE LOVER'S MOTIVATIONS

What moves a man to become the bed partner of a married woman? The motivations of these men seem to fall into three basic categories:

1. *The husband has complaints against his wife.* Perhaps she has lost interest in sex; perhaps they don't get along for one reason or another; perhaps he feels she gives the kids or her career too much attention and him too little. For this kind of husband the affair results from a grudge against the spouse as much as an attraction to the new partner (as it does for many wives). And for him, as well as a wife in the same position, it may be a source of comfort.

2. *The man simply wants to have an affair.* These are men with no major problems at home. Very often they have had other extramarital liaisons. Either periodically or continuously they play around. The junior or major Don Juans who have multiple affairs in their married lives are numerous. Some are honest, but others use the excuses of the first category—complaints against the wife—to mask their basic urge to stray. Many married women believe the stories about the wife's faults and fail to realize that the lover may simply be a playaround. Others get at least part of the picture but don't seem to care, often rationalizing his extramarital history by feeling that what they have together is "special."

A woman in her mid-thirties whose affair had lasted five years, and who wanted it to go on forever, said of her lover, "He has had many affairs. He says his wife is cold. I don't know if she was always cold or became cold because she found out about the other women."

Some of these men, as in this case, can continue an affair for a long time. They are content just to have another woman on the side. It makes them feel more manly or less trapped in the marriage, or dilutes the intimacy with the wife that may make them vulnerable or uncomfortable. Others—the worst kind—are only after a quick conquest. When this happens to a woman who enters the liaison sincerely, the results can be devastating.

A thirty-five-year-old wife, the mother of three children, married for fifteen years, said, "Three years ago I made a horrendous mistake. I became another notch on the gun of the town Lothario. When I realized I was being used as his latest fool, I attempted suicide."

Another type in this group is the man who has been married a long time or is in a midlife crisis. He has no major complaints against his wife. He has not cheated before. He simply wants to pep up his sex life with a new romance or add spice to his very routine life. Research shows that men of this kind become happier in their domestic situation because of the affair. They are less restless or bored. Unfaithful wives may actually be helping their lovers' marriages along, a thought that would upset many of them if they knew.

3. *The man works closely with a woman, often as her superior.* It can't be denied. Day-in and day-out closeness does breed sexuality, and sometimes he is as surprised as she by what develops. These can be agonizing affairs for both. Stories about them start: "We never intended to have an affair," and go on to talk about working together for many hours each day.

In other cases, however, and there are many of these, when a man is a woman's boss he may take advantage of his position to create a sexual opportunity. Many working wives' affairs are with their bosses. It is easy for a woman to be more vulnerable to a man's advances when he is her employer. His position makes him feel powerful to her, and this has an erotic edge for women. Her job depends on his goodwill as well. He can also maneuver the woman into seductive situations.

This woman's description of the start of her affair with her boss illustrates just how a superior's position at work can affect a female employee: "One day I was alone in the office. He came in, pulled my head back, kissed me and said, 'Come up to my office.' I guess I was really stunned and curious at the same time. When I did go up and sit down in front of his desk and looked at him behind it, I had a sense of how imposing and powerful he was, and that was a turn-on. He simply looked at me and said, 'I want to make love to you.' We made plans to meet the following week."

One boss knowingly stalked a woman employee in her twenties who had been married for only six months: "We started the affair when I had to go somewhere downtown after work. He said he was going to the same place and would show me how to get there. We ended up having a few drinks and talking most of the evening. Nothing happened that night but we confronted each other with our feelings the next day at work. From then on we've been seeing each other."

Another boss was much more crude and blatant, according to this thirty-eight-year-old wife: "I had a car accident while on the job. My boss had to take me back to the scene of the accident. When it was all over he asked me when we were going out. I was taken aback. He later admitted he had this planned for two years and he knew in his mind he would eventually have me. However, on this day he told me he had to discuss some business with me and asked me to meet him in a particular office at a certain time. In the back of my mind I thought something might be up but I wasn't sure. Anyway, when I got to the office he was already there waiting with his dick hanging out of his pants. It was so big and beautiful—I had never seen anything like it before. I told him I couldn't make love to him because it wouldn't fit. He said he would make it fit and walked out. That's how the affair began. The relationship lasted for four years." It ended with bitterness when this wife found out her lover was playing around with other women. He left her because of her emotional recriminations.

Another woman described a relationship with her boss that also left her feeling used, angry, and upset: "My boss's wife had just left him. He kept after me to go out with him. It started with a drink after work. I kept refusing to sleep with him. He kept insisting, saying how much he really cared for me and that he didn't want anybody else. Well, I gave in. We had an affair for about two months. Then one day he walked in after I had been with him the night before and he barely looked at me. After that it was all downhill. He dumped me. It was upsetting to be in the same office with him day after day. It was extremely painful to be in the same room with an ex-lover who ignores you. I'm really mad for giving in to him. We had been good friends for several years. Now we don't even have friendship. He is no longer with our company and I'm glad."

UNATTACHED LOVERS

Single men who get involved with married women are in the extreme minority, but they certainly exist. Among them are also exploitive bosses and Don Juans who like to conquer attractive women whether married or not. Others are nonmonogamists who have regular girlfriends and, like some married men, enjoy an extra relationship. Some are men who are afraid of too much closeness or commitment, so an affair with an unavailable married woman suits them. Others simply give in to an attraction.

If the affair escalates, they find themselves in trouble when they are sincere. They don't like having to sneak around with the woman. They don't like the limitations on the time they can see her. On the other hand, the woman may be troubled by the fact that a single man may want to date more-available women while still sleeping with her. "It's very hard when you're married and he's single," declared a woman in her forties. "He has his own life. You have no control over it, but wish you did."

The woman involved with a "free" man may grapple more with the thought of leaving her own marriage for him than a woman whose lover is also married and not about to leave his wife.

Overwhelmingly, however, the lovers of married women are not single. They are married men.

WHAT THEY WANT

Whatever their original motivation, most of these husbands want the affair to stay within bounds. They thrive on the diversion, the excitement of illicit, forbidden sex, the variety the affair provides. For some there is relief from troubles at home. For all there is a tremendous boost to the ego. They feel stronger, more virile, more masculine with an outside love. If the woman is much younger it may make them feel young again themselves, an extra ego boost. Most adore the romance and some are even willing to let themselves play at "love."

In an affair that lasts a long time—and affairs with married women tend to—a man often seems ready to offer friendship, guidance, and a shoulder to lean on, to which the woman generally responds with gratitude, admiration, and increasing affection. This reassures a woman that she is valued as a person and is not merely his sex object—an important distinction for wives in affairs.

Some lovers in these limited, closeted, clandestine relationships are also able to reveal themselves emotionally. If there is openness, it makes you feel that you have achieved with him what women, in general, hanker after—intimate communication with a man. This may make your passion boil as much as the lovemaking.

Often the man is giving more personal attention to his extramarital partner and revealing more to her than to his wife, with whom life is more complicated.

In your affair it is just the two of you locked away by yourselves. The marriage includes children, in-laws, diversions, duties, chores, grudges, vulnerabilities, power games—all of which may interfere with soul-baring intimacies, and with paying ongoing attention to the laudable personal characteristics of a spouse.

What the married man involved with a married woman *doesn't* want is for the relationship to become too serious. It is the rare man who desires anything that will really threaten his own marriage. He may really be a good friend, he may or may not allow himself to say "I love you" or "You mean a lot to me" to his lover, but, if he does say he cares, he still isn't committing himself to anything.

A wife of twenty-seven wrote, "I know he loves me, but no matter how much he loves me and I love him, that cannot replace the love he feels for his children. He lives for his boys. I would marry him tomorrow if I could, but it's an impossibility."

Most men, even when they have some affection for the other woman, are able to keep an affair from taking over their emotional lives. This is in direct contrast to women, who tend to become consumed. In letter after letter, case history after case history, wives confessed that their heads were totally occupied by their lovers.

"I'm in a dream world and don't care about anything else except seeing him and talking to him," said one wife in her thirties.

For the man in question it is generally not the same grand, all-encompassing passion. Most often the affair that throws a woman into an emotional tizzy is, for the man, more of a casual "something on the side," even when there is some affection involved. Men generally regard an affair as an addition to marriage, not a relationship to think about as a possible replacement. However, even when they don't really want it to happen, many women start to fantasize about possible marriage to the lover as the relationship heats up.

In one way or another most men let the woman know the restrictions of the relationship, either from the very beginning or in response to her deepening involvement—an emotional investment that may flatter the lover but, at the same time, cause some discomfort. "I have a lot of hopes from this affair. Some even scare my lover. This is definitely not just a fling," said a thirty-two-year-old wife who works in a retail store.

Numerous examples of the way men warn their partners that the affair is just an affair come from the letters in my files:

- "My boss and I fell in love five years ago. He is in a terrible marriage which is filled with threats and intimidation. He, however, does not leave. He tells me he fears the repercussions. I am distraught over this. He, however, is content with our relationship because he says it brings him peace."

- "Philip has a small child and told me right away that his son was the most important thing to him and that he couldn't promise me anything."

- "I love him very deeply but I don't think he'll ever leave his wife. He says it's because of the kids."

- "He made it very clear he has a good marriage and terrific kids."

- "I know he cares for me, but he always said divorce is not an option for him because the thought of his children not being with him every day is unthinkable."

- "He has said he is not going to get a divorce, which I believe."

- "I know that my love will not leave his family for me—he's told me that. He says he could never hurt them like that, and he couldn't take the public humiliation."

- "I was ready to leave everything for him, but he isn't ready to leave his wife and house for me."

The fear of losing or hurting their children seems to be the favorite excuse men use when making it clear that there are limits to what an extramarital partner should expect. Sometimes it's true; sometimes it's just an excuse.

One man even went so far as to claim that terror of losing his grandchildren kept him bound to his marriage—he obviously could no longer cite his very grown-up children as deterrents. The woman involved with him, however, believed him.

WOMEN WHO DENY REALITY

I think that many unfaithful wives are rather naïve about their lovers and what is really happening with them.

To begin with, in the time it takes for the relationship to become sexual, there is often some self-deception going on. It is important for the wife to think that she and the man are only friends. Women don't want to be merely sex toys. They want to be desired as whole people and, as a result, they may prefer to shut out the possibility that he has sex on his mind—or that she does. They don't entertain the possibility that this person who is encouraging them, listening to them sympathetically, commiserating with them, has perhaps another motivation in the back of his mind.

As for themselves, some women are aware of instant sexual chemistry, but for many it is only *after* the affair is consummated that they can admit, "Looking back on it, I think there was an attraction from the very beginning."

In this way, by thinking that it grew out of a wonderful, irresistible friendship without ulterior motives, women are better able to justify their physical infidelity when it occurs. He values her; she values him. It wasn't "just sex."

Then, when the actual sexual part of the affair is under way, the woman wants to believe the best about her lover and the seriousness of the affair. She may deliberately ignore or underplay the fact that, although it is her first, he may have had affairs before. To dwell on it would be to question his sincerity or seriousness, something she doesn't want to do.

Wives also frequently refuse to believe what they are told directly by their lovers. He is being honest but you don't want to accept the truth.

Here are some examples of wives grappling with reality and its denial:

- "In the beginning he let me know this would be purely sexual. I feel it's more, that he really cares. I've met his wife at business affairs. It's beyond me how they got together, but he says he loves her."

- "I have approached my lover on the subject of commitment, and he said if our present marriages were both dissolved he could not promise me that he would marry me. That hurts me deeply." The conflict between what this woman wants to hear and what she actually does, between her fantasy and reality, is evident in the next mixed-up sentence: "In spite of the fact there is no actual commitment, having sexual relations with this other person makes me believe there is a nonverbal commitment, which I doubt there really is on his part." She gets it right, however, and says it for a lot of women, in the last sentence of her letter: "When it comes to our relationship I think with my heart, not my head."

Sometimes you are helped down the wrong path by self-serving lovers who simply lie to you: "I was married fourteen years when my affair with my boss started. My marriage was going nowhere. So was his. I went through four and a half years of broken promises on his part and broken dreams on mine. He was always telling me to wait, it was coming—his divorce. It sure did. Three months after his divorce and three years after mine, I caught him with another woman he had started seeing nine months before. After all those years of loving him, he fired me."

A lot of wives give in to premature fantasies: They instantly make more of an affair than it can possibly be at a very early stage.

One woman who was involved with a co-worker for five months said she first started up with him because her marriage was bad and she didn't love her husband; her lover was also unhappily married, and he was sweet to her. "I knew him for six months. He was flirting with me," she remembered. "Then one day he told me couldn't stand it if he couldn't touch me. That made me very excited. I made the first move by kissing him and he responded with a fiery passion. I'll never forget that first kiss."

She added, "I don't want to break up his marriage. He has two children and I don't want to hurt them. I thought one kiss would end my wondering what it would feel like, but it only made the sparks turn into a flame. I can't turn back now because I've fallen in love with this sweet, adorable man."

What makes this woman's protestation of love and her ruminations about not wanting to break up his marriage unrealistic and out of touch with the facts is that, according to her own statement: "We've only been alone once since the affair started."

Chapter 10

HOW AFFAIRS PROGRESS

Most married women start their affairs very slowly. It isn't like sex in the singles world, which occurs after three, four, or five dates. An extramarital adventure is a serious matter for women—and a serious transgression of what they think they believe in. They don't rush into it lightly.

Although, of course, there are some wives who fly quickly into a lover's arms, the vast majority of women whose stories I heard spent a long time getting to know the men who eventually became their extramarital sex partners. The torrid part of the affair was generally preceded by a lengthy period of bantering and flirting or exchanged confidences that suddenly, one day, took on a more emotional meaning.

The catalyst that turned the fun and friendship into a sexual relationship for many women was a change in the emotional climate of the woman's marriage. In her eyes, something started to go wrong; or, if it was wrong already, it looked worse to her (perhaps in contrast to what was happening with this new man).

But even without any problems at home, the chances for an ultimate seduction are good when you and a man dance around each other for a long period of time.

"We spent six months getting to know each other. After a few months the attraction grew and the teasing and flirting became more intense, the looks much longer and deeper. We never intended to have an affair or fall deeply in love," said a thirty-three-year old woman who is disturbed now by how much she cares for the other man.

A friendly, confiding, often laughter-filled or flirtatious relationship with a man may continue not only for months but over a period of *years*. Amazingly common were stories of one year, even three, four, five, or more, before intercourse took place.

"Steven and I became friends shortly after I started working in his department. We were honestly very good friends for over a year. We went to lunch a lot and chatted at the office. He was nice and we liked each other's company.

"My marriage was in trouble—my husband was having his second affair, which I was unaware of at the time—and suddenly I found myself very attracted to Steven and dreaming of being with him. Something occurred at work that triggered my emotions for Steven. He felt the same way. We knew that something was happening between us, so he asked me to meet him after work. We met and confessed our feelings and attraction and agreed to have an affair. Our love grew and so did the relationship. Steven and I aren't the 'affair' type. We never meant to get involved and neither of us would ever have another affair. We feel somehow we were destined to be together."

Another woman recounted, "We worked together for three years before anything happened. We got along great and kidded and teased one another constantly. I think we have always been attracted to one another, although we just admitted it last fall. We finally got together when both of our marriages hit rocky points. Right after our first baby was born I became very unhappy with my husband. His attitude toward our life had changed with the addition of our child. My lover's wife became disinterested in sex after the birth of their second child. This led to our attraction building—we discovered that we both were dissatisfied at home and the normal flirting took on a new dimension. Finally, one Saturday while working together, we ended up kissing, and that started our affair."

TIME TOGETHER

Once an affair is under way, according to the letters in my files, the average unfaithful wife spends less than five hours a week alone with her lover. Some women manage to get together with their lovers once or twice a week, but for a surprising number of wives, sexual rendezvous are far fewer than that.

Extramarital involvements can get by with very little actual physical contact, even though the sex may be fantastic when it does occur. It is as if the idea of the affair and the emotions or fantasies it produces are as important as sleeping together for certain women and men. It makes them feel important, sexy, desirable, excited, perhaps naughty, or less hemmed in by demands of ordinary life, no matter how little they actually sleep together.

Letters and case histories reveal illicit partners who make love once every couple of months or even only twice a year, although the lovers may talk to each other on the phone or in person more often or, in some cases, see each other at work each day.

"Our sexual encounters are few and far between, but our secret embraces and private talks are more frequent," wrote a forty-seven-year-old secretary involved with her boss for the past eight months.

"Ours started as a casual friendship," explained a woman in her thirties. "I knew him about two years. He would come into the office to see my boss. We would kid around, talk about television and movies. After a while, I couldn't wait to get in to work in the morning to see if he was there. I don't get many compliments from my husband. I don't feel I'm attractive to him. This other man made me feel pretty. He would say something nice like 'You smell good today,' or 'You look nice,' but never made any advances towards me. A close friendship grew. A group of us at work would go to lunch once in a while and I would look forward to seeing him then. He has a great sense of humor, he's gentle, he listens to what I have to say.

"Last Christmas, after our group's usual lunch, he leaned over and kissed me and said he loves me. I couldn't lie. I said the same thing. We've made love twice in the nine months since we confessed our love. It's very difficult to plan time alone."

Despite the infrequency of lovemaking this woman admitted, "My free time is spent thinking of this guy. I hope we will last a lifetime."

A wife in her forties, involved with a boss eleven years younger, said, "We keep our times together down to once a month, but we go to lunch once a week when we can at least touch and talk for a while. He writes me wonderful notes about once a week, and usually by the time we can be together we are starved for each other."

A thirty-six-year-old woman explained, "I had traveled five years in my job and not one man turned my head, but then I bumped into this crazy guy and it just happened. We are together now three times a year since we are located in different regions." Despite the fact that this is basically a long-distance love, this woman admits to a deep emotional attachment to her lover.

A statistician in her late forties ruminated, "Right now I would settle for more time alone with this man, since we get together so little. I would even settle for one week alone with him every three months, but, as it is right now, I only get one half hour alone with him every three months." She sees him on business trips since he lives out of town. Again, despite the sparse physical contact, she says, "I love him deeply."

A marketing executive in her late forties, involved with her boss, knew him for *nine years*(!) before this happened:

"We were on a business trip, having a drink, and he very tentatively leaned forward to kiss me. I kissed him back! When we travel on business we sometimes are able to be alone. This happens once every six to eight weeks. It is enough to make us both feel desirable and desired again." Her emotions are not as involved as those of the women above: "I went into this wanting some attention and some good sex and have gotten both."

A woman in her thirties, who would like to stop the affair if she could because "what's right is right and what's wrong is wrong," said, "We have tried to end it several times. We now accept the fact that we want to see each other even if it's just one or two times a year. We write each other at the office. And he calls two or three times a week."

I suspect that husbands with unattached women as their partners make love more regularly than wives whose liaisons are with married men. It's a question of logistics. A single woman has her own living quarters and a married man can meet her there twice a week, for example, or as often as they both want. However, a married man trysting with a married woman has to go to places like motels, which, unless he has a lot of discretionary income, can be expensive. Or he has to borrow an apartment, which is often embarrassing or inconvenient and unreliable.

As a result, when two married lovers do get together they have to be resourceful, and they are, according to the results of the office affairs survey.

Where They Make Love

Although the preponderance of women's affairs today are with co-workers or bosses, there is less hanky-panky in the actual office than is imagined. A small minority of wives admit to making love after hours in places of business. One cited the back room of her office. Another woman told me about carrying on with her lover in his private office with the door locked while fellow workers were still milling around outside. But the majority make other arrangements.

In addition to hotels and motels in and out of town and at conventions, lovers steal time together in parking garages, on beaches, in parks, in the woods, on boats, and in country cabins and beach houses. They escape to nearby towns. Parked cars in secluded spots are big with married lovers, who may rival teenagers in the use of motor vehicles for trysts.

An automobile is where the sexual part of the affair sometimes starts, as was the case for this woman in Texas: "I have been married for fifteen years. For about a year my husband stopped paying attention to me and stopped going anywhere with me. I was very lonely and starved for affection. I was made supervisor over the second shift. This man and I worked quite close together. He began to tell me how pretty I was and made me feel good about myself. He asked if he could call me sometime. I said, 'Sure.' Then one night he needed a ride home, so I gave him one. We made love in the car."

Home Alone

Despite the danger, married women invite their lovers into their own homes when they know their husbands are going to be away, generally during a lunch hour. Or they go to the lover's house when he thinks his wife will be gone. Love instead of lunch is a common occurrence when two lovers are married. For some the peril of making love on home turf is the name of the game—they get a special thrill from it. For others, adultery in the marital bed is an extra secret hostile blow to a spouse they feel deserves it. For many, it is desperation. It is a risk you are willing to take just to be able to be alone with your lover.

One husband remembers coming home early from work on a summer day and walking in on his wife with her boyfriend in his bedroom. "It is bad enough knowing your wife is cheating on you," he says, "but the betrayal is particularly devastating when it is in your own home, in your own bed." His marriage did not survive the discovery.

Socializing Together

Some women like to include their lovers in their domestic social lives, inviting them to parties, for example.

In one case that is where the first move that finally led to an affair actually took place—in a woman's own home with her husband in a different room: "Five years ago my lover was interviewed by my boss. While he waited I got him coffee. He still remembers what I wore that fateful day. He joined the company and we came into contact many times throughout the day. I knew he was attracted to me, and he later confessed that he half believed that he took the job because of that attraction. He was married with three children. His family couldn't join him for many months while he looked for suitable housing. I enjoyed his attention but I was happily married. I invited him to a large house party we had during the holidays because he was away from his family. I found myself gravitating toward him that night. We finally ended up kissing in the game room."

In other instances, the adulterous couples and their spouses are together more often: "There are times we travel together with our spouses. We enjoy each other's company and the secret part of our relationship is tucked away for a while," explained a wife in the Midwest.

Another women wrote, "Both of us have to attend dinners and parties with our spouses. The four of us chat nicely and no one would ever suspect we are lovers."

For the adulterous couple there can be excitement in sharing their secret in the presence of spouses. It is also a way of seeing the lover in circumstances more normal than the usual clandestine ones.

No matter how women choose to conduct their love affairs, however, there are predictable phases that the illicit relationship will go through.

THE STAGES OF AN AFFAIR

Part One: The Tease

The first stage of the affair is before sex takes place, when there is an increasing sense of closeness to and interest in the man. This part of the relationship, as I have already explained, is often lengthy and can take months or years. It is in this initial stage of titillation that the first shift in focus away from the marriage and toward the lover occurs. The woman starts to feel that she can't wait to get in to work to see or perhaps hear from this man. She thinks about him more and more. She dresses and makes herself up more carefully, knowing she will see him.

In addition, she feels better and better about herself. Her ego is being stroked by the fact that this man is taking what she has to say seriously, if she is still defining this as "friendship." Or she may be excited and pleased that he finds her attractive, if he is complimenting her and she is aware that he is interested in her as a woman. Her spirits may be lifted by the kidding around, the fun they are having: "We would find ourselves stopping in the middle of dictation sessions to talk. We laughed a lot together."

He may try to find times and places where they can be alone, inviting her to lunch, offering to drive her home, taking walks with her, sitting next to her at office functions. This, of course, increases a sense of intimacy between them.

Over time, as the relationship progresses during this pre-intercourse stage, the woman becomes more aware of a growing attraction. She often thinks of it with a mixture of pleasure and a sense of danger. She may be moved to talk about it with the man—which, whether she realizes it or not, is often the very signal he has been waiting for, because he has been monitoring the situation.

Encouraged, he kisses her, confesses feelings toward her, or suggests that they act on the mutual attraction. Some men simply sense the growing feelings of the woman without her saying anything and initiate the sexual part, generally by a sudden embrace. Or perhaps by an invitation like this, which could lead to only one conclusion:

"My marriage had started to fall apart. He was there to talk to. He was very understanding and supportive. The affair started when I went home with him supposedly only for lunch, after months of his asking." You can guess what happened.

THE FIRST MOVE

Whichever way the sexual gesture is made, softened by the months of friendship, excitement, flirtation, and growing attraction, the wife responds. Often she has thought about what she would do ahead of time, so when she gives in it is no surprise to her. The initial stage is over. Adultery has begun.

Of course, not every affair starts in the way I have described. Some begin with more overt sexual expressions by the man and progress to intercourse much faster. Some start with a crazy chemical attraction that the woman is quite conscious of from the minute she lays eyes on him. Some women have strong generalized fantasies about an affair and are ripe for it when the right man comes along:

"I'm thirty-five years old and have been married for sixteen years. Lately I find my fantasy world is taking over. I envision myself having affairs with men. I'm not unhappy in my marriage, although we both work long hours. I have a full career and two children I love. But lately I'm having these fantasies three or four times a day."

Sometimes the lovers, before deciding to go all the way, have been necking for a while: "We started wanting to touch each other (hand on the shoulder, hand brushing the other's hand). I found myself happy to go to work and sad to leave. Then, kisses in the office. We went on for months just having 'groping' and 'long kissing' sessions. Then he told me he couldn't stand it any longer—we had to go to bed with each other. We met out of town. I was not disappointed. It was fireworks and shooting stars. It still is, twenty-one years later."

And, of course, a few more-aggressive women hurry things along by offering the first kiss, gesture, or suggestion.

Nevertheless, although there are various routes to bed, what I have described here, in broad outline, is stage one of the majority of wives' affairs, according to the letters and case histories in my files.

Part Two: Euphoria

The first weeks and months of a new, sexy, extramarital love affair are incredibly exciting, exhilarating, wonderful for the mind and spirit of the woman. She feels renewed—more attractive, livelier, sexier than she has felt in a long time. She hugs her forbidden relationship secretly and inwardly revels in the delight of feeling wanted, pretty, and pursued.

She feels buoyantly self-confident—validated as a woman and a worth-while person. The hidden goal of a sexual affair is precisely this for most women, and it has been achieved.

Whatever other motivations existed for the affair, she thinks she has found a solution: He brings her comfort, revenge, better sex, the romance or flattering attention she missed in her marriage. The pleasure has not yet been heavily tainted by pain, although guilt over the transgression may lead to attempts, by certain women, to break it off in the first months, attempts that often fail because the joy the lover brings is at least as great as the remorse. Other women fluctuate between feeling some guilt and none at all.

A woman in her thirties, the mother of two, admitted, "There are plenty of times I feel guilty and times I don't. Why, if someone makes my world a little brighter among all life's ups and downs, can't I smile?"

Still others feel little or no guilt ever, and they may wonder at the fact that it is so easy for them, even though they don't really like the lying involved. Generally the women who fail to suffer from guilt feel justified in philandering because of their husbands' behavior.

INTIMATE TALK

One of the most intense pleasures women feel during this part and the rest of an affair is the ease with which they can communicate with their lovers. The truth is that many women feel freer to say whatever they want to the other man—freer than they did in relationships before marriage when they were looking for a husband, freer than in marriage. Typical was a statement by a wife in her early twenties: "I was able to tell him everything, even things I had never told my husband."

Why are women so open with their lovers? Because, in this stage of first euphoria, they aren't trying to win the man's approval as a possible mate. They know the relationship is limited by the circumstances. It is what it is. They are what they are.

Another factor that makes women feel more able to reveal themselves to a lover is the same one that allows them to "let go" sexually with him (see Chapter 8): They are in an outlaw situation anyway, so what do they have to lose? And, importantly, the lover escapes the kind of identification as a parental figure that makes husbands seem disapproving and inhibits wives with them.

So wives are open and honest with their lovers. They delight in being heard. Their private conversations on the telephone, over lunches, in stolen moments alone at the office, are treasured as much as the times when they can make love.

THE HEART TAKES OVER

Somewhere, frequently between the third and sixth months of the affair, if it has persisted, a wife's emotions start to cause trouble. They may have been involved before she even slept with the other man. Some women, after months of friendship and growing attraction, think that they have fallen in love, which makes them feel justified in having sex with the man. But if it wasn't experienced as love before, after a few months of sleeping with him most women feel at least somewhat "in love" with the extramarital partner. The women who didn't experience this were a small minority, according to my letters and case histories. When love takes over, it generally catapults the woman into the third stage of an affair.

Part Three: Obsession, Conflict, and Agony

What may have started, in the woman's mind, as a romp is now a serious connection to her lover and, if she is like the majority of women, she realizes she is in deeper than she expected to be.

"Originally I thought I would have an affair to keep from divorcing my husband, because financially that is impossible, but I fell in love with my lover," said a thirty-three-year-old wife. "Hope against hope, I still dream that someday he'll want to be with me enough to try and work out some solution."

Another woman in her thirties confessed, "I thought I could remain detached and just enjoy the friendship and sexual fulfillment I receive from this affair. But I could not. I have fallen deeply in love with him. Enough to leave my marriage if there could be a future for us. But at this time in my partner's life he cannot walk out of his marriage. And that desperately hurts."

By stage three, most lovers have already told the woman in one way or another not to expect much more from the relationship. Many wives originally made an agreement with their lover that it would remain casual. However, since women's emotions are joined to their bodies, few can keep to the contract.

"Even if an understanding is formed at the start that it is only for fun," said a woman in her early twenties, "it just doesn't hold where matters of the heart are concerned." She, of course, fell in love with her partner, to her own dismay.

DOES HE LOVE ME?

Most wives, to whom the affair has become a deadly serious matter by this stage, need to feel that the extramarital partner loves them. You can take comfort from this even if anything else seems impossible, from your standpoint or his. Love also keeps intact the important ego boost supplied by the lover.

"I broke up with him several times," said a thirty-two-year-old woman about her relationship with a man who won't leave his wife, although she divorced her husband. "I always go back. I don't believe he doesn't love his wife, but I do believe he loves me. I thought I was after fun and games when this started and that we would be helping each other in our marriages, but it ended up a real different story."

"I would like the reassurance of hearing *if* he loves me. I think if he told me he loved me it would be okay. I was told by him that if he had one friend in the world it would be me, but is that the same thing as being loved?" agonized a woman in her forties.

HE'S IN YOUR HEAD

Obsessed by the relationship by stage three, the majority of women have their lovers constantly with them in their minds. "I know it's wrong but he's all I think about," said one.

Wives count the days till they can be together with him. At home they are often lonely or miserable, missing the lover. "I enjoy going to work only because he is there. When he is on vacation or a business trip I feel lost," said one woman.

Wives with lovers hate Saturday and Sunday, or are at least ambivalent about days at home, because they lose contact. "I miss him *terribly* on weekends; that's why we have our Mondays together," confessed a thirty-five-year-old wife who added, "I started this just for excitement and to see what it would be like with someone else. But I fell in love and I *can't* lose him."

Vacations with the family are also spoiled by yearnings for the lover left behind. On home turf, when wives go out with their husbands they take along a third person—the lover in their heads. In general, wives in affairs are restless and distracted creatures.

Mental obsession with another man may drive guilt out of their minds, or at least not make it the prime issue. The wife concentrates more on the situation with the lover, her feelings for him, what should she do about it, what he feels about her.

However, for some wives, constant preoccupation with the lover adds to self-reproach: "The guilt is terrible if you have a conscience," explained a twenty-nine-year-old wife.

A wife in Cleveland admitted, "I feel terrible about it, but he's always on my mind. I love him very much. He says he cares for me but doesn't say he loves me. It's driving me crazy."

PROBLEMS AT HOME

Sometimes guilty feelings and intense preoccupation make wives testy with their spouses. For the guilt ridden, outbursts may be due to irritability caused by frayed nerves, or they can be an unconscious tactic to elicit anger from a spouse, which in turn makes you feel more justified to be cheating.

One man remembers that his wife suddenly started blowing up at him a lot. It was uncharacteristic and it confused him, until he learned months later that she had been having an affair with a fellow teacher.

If they aren't angry, unfaithful wives may seem remote at home. Their heads are elsewhere and the husband feels it even if he doesn't understand the cause.

Sex may be suffering as well. Many women—not all—have trouble sleeping with their husbands when they have a lover, and they make excuses not to. Studies reveal that unfaithful wives have more of a problem continuing with marital sex than husbands, who are often excited and sexually pepped up by the idea of having two women. Some men like to go directly from their lovers' arms to their wives' beds, something far fewer women can tolerate.

The wife may have an easier time continuing to sleep with her husband if she still likes him on some level or if sexual interludes with her lover are infrequent, as is the case for this woman in her thirties: "I have a husband who is fun to be with and, after twelve years, we still have sex two or three times a week. Yet we have grown different these past twelve years. I fell in love with a co-worker and would love to marry him. However, he has told me he can't leave because of his children." Involved with her for more than a year, the lover had to move to a different city, and they now meet there one or two times a year.

FEELINGS ABOUT HIS WIFE

In this intense third period, when the affair has taken over their mental and emotional lives, many women deny to themselves that the man's relationship with his wife may be more sexually or emotionally satisfying than he lets on. On the other hand, some women feel consciously jealous of the lover's wife, comparing her unfavorably to themselves.

"His marriage is not crumbling, but I know his wife personally and she is a very negative person. As this man's job grows in scope and responsibility, she feels more and more threatened and does not support him as I do at work," said a secretary who had been having an affair with her boss for two years.

Another woman in her thirties said, "He was the perfect 'family man.' From what I saw, his wife sat home with their daughter, did not work, had diamonds, fur coats, a Jaguar, a very nice home in a fancy neighborhood, anything she wanted. I guess I sound very bitter and jealous because I was and still am."

For some women like this one, the lover's wife becomes the enemy by stage three: She is the one who has his top priority, or his worldly goods, or his commitment. Feeling that she is doomed to second place in her lover's life, the woman grieves.

"It hurts to know that you have to share this man you love with someone else," wrote a wife of twenty-four whose affair with a married co-worker had gone on for a year and a half.

Women may struggle with jealousy about the wife and console themselves with the fact that they are superior to her or are loved anyway. But they have to accept her presence no matter how they feel. However, wives generally draw the line at other women. They expect extramarital monogamy from their lovers.

OTHER WOMEN

If you find out that your lover has another girlfriend, it damn near kills you. The sense of being special, your increased self-esteem—the benefits of the affair—come crashing down. There is additional and incredible pain.

Not only must the wife deal with the fact that she has betrayed her husband, but also the fact that her lover has, in her eyes, betrayed her. This often means the end of the relationship. (If it doesn't, it means the end of your self-respect.)

A wife who had met her single lover as her marriage was crumbling said, "I had a whirlwind romance with this guy at work who was everything my husband wasn't. My new 'Romeo' took me on romantic excursions everywhere, but a year and a half later I found out he was cheating on me. He tried telling me this other woman was just a friend, but as soon as I dumped him, they were engaged."

HEARTACHES

On the whole, even when a lover remains faithful, by stage three of the relationship conflict and painful emotions seem to be the rule, rather than the exception. It's particularly true when the wife is in love (as most women are), whether she wants to marry her lover or not.

"Take it from me," said a wife in her late twenties, "it's all heartache and misery when you have an affair with a married man. Don't get me wrong, there are always those special times together. But the misery and heartache are bigger players in your life than those special times, and if I had it to do over again it would have never happened."

"An affair brings excitement and pleasure," remarked a wife in Michigan, "but also sorrow and pain. It's like a roller coaster ride."

The phrase *roller coaster* kept reappearing in letters as a metaphor for the extreme ups and downs plus perilous excitement experienced during an extramarital relationship. "I've never had so many highs and lows. It's been great and it's been awful," said a twenty-four-year-old bookkeeper.

An executive secretary in her forties explained, "When I'm with him it's like being in heaven. But a day or two after I've seen him, I'm an emotional wreck because our time together is limited. It's also hard to act normal at home. Then you start to wonder if you're going to get a phone call telling you something—like it's all over. In a way I wish I never had started seeing this person."

"I don't regret the affair because I needed the feeling of being wanted again. Not just in bed, but in other ways. I don't want the affair to end and I don't want to let go of my husband either. I know I'm doing wrong, but I'm too involved. I would tell other women not to start an affair because it's hard to get out of it," wrote a woman of twenty-three.

A MESSED-UP LIFE

Here, in her own words, is the agonized, dramatic story of a woman whose whole life and marriage of nine months was torn apart by the emotionally charged conflict that enveloped her when she fell in love with a man at work:

Over the summer John and I had developed a working friendship. One day I heard him mention that he was so busy he had no time for lunch. I slipped a candy bar onto his desk so he wouldn't be hungry. John mentioned the candy to me and I confessed that I had left it.

Shortly afterward John asked me if I was going to watch the company baseball game. He urged me to go and I did. It didn't matter, I thought. We were just friends.

At the end of the baseball season the company sponsored a party for players and fans. John kept wanting to know if I was going. I said yes. I also made plans to stay at my old roommate's apartment in town rather than go home to the suburbs where we lived. John and I decided to have a drink before I went to my girlfriend's. Before the first drink he gave me a kiss. I wanted that kiss so bad I didn't even think about my marriage.

John and I realized if we gave in to our desires we would have a rough time ahead. After all, I was married. John confessed that he was attracted to me all summer. That night we walked and kissed and realized our lives would never be the same again. Over the next few months we would go to lunch, meet after work, spend the night together after the company bowling league game. We were in love but torn. I had a husband, he had a girlfriend. We would be together for months, then feel guilty and stop talking for a month. We would always end up back together.

My home life was a mess. My inner conflict drove me to create more and more problems with my husband. Finally, I could not stand the hurt I was causing—my husband was a nice guy, how could I hurt him? I felt the only way out was to have my husband's baby. In that way the affair would have to end.

My husband was glad I wanted to sleep with him again. He was delighted when I got pregnant. I was torn between happiness and a desire to be with John. I would ride the train home and think of him. I would look out the window and think, *My life is now more of a mess. I'm pregnant and I wish it was John's baby, not my husband's.* It came to the point where I wished I would lose the baby—an awful, painful thought. That thought became a reality. Two months into the pregnancy I had a miscarriage.

The affair resumed. The turmoil at home and inside me resumed. It was as if I were two different people leading one life.

John pushed me for a divorce. I couldn't do it, and soon after he proposed to his girlfriend. My world crashed. I had just become an officer in the firm I worked for. It should have been great for me, but instead I was on the verge of tears. The affair was over, I thought.

I decided to repair my marriage and give my husband what he wanted—a baby. In the middle of trying to get pregnant, John had lunch with me and expressed his love for me and offered to call off his engagement. I didn't know what to do.

Soon I learned that I had gotten pregnant before that lunch. I figured then that this would end the affair and I would be happy again.

After five months of pregnancy I could not take working with John anymore. I loved him but couldn't have him. He wanted to marry me and offered to raise the baby as his own. I could not separate my husband from his future child. I quit work.

John would call me at home. We'd chat but never let our guard down.

My son is now ten months old. John is married. He calls every few months and we talk but we never express our love for each other. His marriage is at best okay. Mine is okay with thoughts of divorce. I still love John. I love my son. I don't love my husband. I'm trapped. I'm thinking of calling John.

CRAZINESS

A few women go a little crazy during stage three, particularly a wife who in some way has given up on her marriage and wants to live with her lover, or who has been propelled by the affair into divorcing her husband and is frustrated by her lover's refusal to leave his wife.

In one instance, a woman who met her lover while she was still married found her affair became a crazymaking matter after her husband died unexpectedly: "I adored him. I wanted him to be with me forever. After confronting him and learning he would never consider divorce, I went a little wacko. I found myself in front of his house one night with a rock and a note attached to it in my hand, watching his wife through a window. I got a grip on myself and set the rock down, but the next day he found my rock and related to me that he had heard a loud sound outside the night before. I then told him about my nocturnal visit. He freaked out."

Even without such extreme behavior, most wives, flooded with a mixture of pleasure and pain, find themselves struggling with a strong, often tortured dependency on the affair. Many can't give it up even if they think they should.

PUSH AND PULL

Although wives may find their self-esteem improved by another man's attentions, an extramarital affair is really not a liberating experience for the majority of women. Wives tend to become emotional slaves to a relationship over which they feel they have little control and which, indeed, often ends up controlling them.

A thirty-five-year-old bookkeeper who separated from her husband after starting her affair said, "He loves me very much, but he has a son who means the world to him. He always tells me he can't bear the thought of losing me. I have tried to break it off several times, only to end up in his arms crying. I do love him. I guess the bad thing is that I feel in my heart he will never leave his wife and boy. I keep hanging in, knowing that what we have is very special. I am not sure how much longer I will."

"Wow, I never had a lover so wonderful," said a woman in her thirties. "I fell in love or maybe was possessed by him. I now lead a double life. It's scary and exciting. The stress is terrible. I think many infections I've had recently are a result of it. Lots of times I've wanted to leave and go back to the way I was before I met him, but he always talks me out of it. I'm really very confused about my feelings for him and my husband. It's been four years. If my husband found out he would be terribly hurt. He is also very much in love with me, but he's a poor lover compared to the other man. It's very hard to stay sane."

A wife of thirty-three said, "It's been on and off for four months now. We decide it can't go anywhere and that we just have to remain friends, but sooner or later we end up back together. Sometimes I'll be having a lot of trouble at home and I just want to run to Brad, but he is either unavailable or too busy and I'll get angry at him. The emotional part is definitely hard for me to handle."

A woman who left her marriage a month after starting an affair with a co-worker said, "I have tried ending it because I didn't think it was going anywhere. I tried four times but let myself get talked out of it."

A woman of thirty-four told of her struggles: "My self-esteem is again at an all-time low. He won't leave his wife but he begs me to continue our relationship and says he loves me. I have again fallen in love with my husband but I have not been successful in breaking the relationship with my boss. I can't seem to let go. My hope right now is that I will have the strength to be able to end it."

Another woman confided, "My marriage was not great at the time we met, but it was not bad. I have very different feelings about the affair. Sometimes I wish we could marry—our sex is great, we communicate very well and are very close. At times I would say, yes, this has enhanced my life, but there is so much anguish, a lot of confusion, and over-whelming emotion when it is time to part. However, I love him very deeply and he says he loves me, but I don't think he'll leave his wife, 'because of the kids.' Sometimes I don't know what to think. I have tried to tell myself that this is not healthy, but I continue to want to see him."

Part Four: Making Peace

In order for an affair to last a long time—and many do—the wife has to calm the turmoil, at least somewhat, by making some sort of peace with the relationship's limitations.

You have to come to terms with any or all of these facts:

- that it will go nowhere
- that he is never going to leave his wife, or you don't intend to end your marriage

- that the pleasure received is equal to the pain, or at least is worth the moments of agony
- *or* that you are unable to end it no matter how you feel, so you'll take what you can from it

The peace you make may be an uneasy one, with regrets and some longing built in. It often has a bittersweet quality, and may be more like resignation than peace. But the fourth stage of an affair is the one in which the wife has come to accept, on some level, the boundaries of the situation.

BACK IN CONTROL

The widow who went "a little wacko" with the rock outside her lover's home told where she was presently, ten years into the affair with this same man. Now forty-nine, she was married again to another man, and was currently living with her second husband.

> After that experience with the rock, I distanced myself from my lover for a period of time, got control, and started to see the relationship in a new way. I knew he would never leave his family. I accepted that fact and dated others. I tried to stop seeing him many, many times throughout the years, but because we work closely together, day after day, my resolve was always broken by the sheer force of our chemistry.
>
> Five years later I met a very nice man who was crazy about me. He courted me with gusto. I fell in love with him. After struggling to stay away from my lover for over a year, one afternoon after he had invited me to have a friendly game of golf with him, I gave in to my pent-up and tumultuous desire and attraction, in the high grass—like a dog in heat—and once again we became lovers.
>
> This time I finally got control of my feelings. We are really good people, highly respected with good jobs and friends. I am married and now we both have good marriages. We simply have no desire to end our relationship. I know he loves me in a way he never loved anyone. He has never had any other relationship outside his marriage.
>
> We are very close, love each other—but not enough to hurt others for our selfishness. Loving him and working with him make my heart

sing, my days brighter. I look forward to seeing him every day and any stolen moments during the week. I love being "in love"; he stirs my very core, makes me feel young, desirable, and sexy. He says the same about me. Why can't we continue as long as we are extremely discreet? My husband and I are very happily married. If I had never met my lover before meeting him, I would never entertain the thought of having an affair.

Another woman said, "It took me a year to put my relationship with my lover in the proper perspective. He asked nothing of me. I gave freely. He made it clear he had a good marriage and terrific kids. You have to keep your head on straight and not expect the impossible. Nothing was offered except friendship and comfort and sex if I wanted it. I still have to remind myself of these things occasionally now."

"It's been over a year," wrote an administrator in Chicago. "I've experienced everything from passionate sex to the ultimate 'other woman' hurt—hurt that cuts clear through my heart.

"So where do I go from here? I want love, passion, romance, companionship—but that's a fantasy. I go day to day and enjoy what I am experiencing. Yes, I would ultimately like to marry this man—but that's a fantasy, too."

BYPASSING THE WORST

Some women go straight into stage four, without passing through emotional hell first. From the beginning they know what the affair is and isn't. They enjoy what they can receive from their illicit relationships without too much self-reproach or regret. These women are in the minority but, in the end, they are the ones who handle their affairs best.

A woman who was married for more than twenty years when she met her lover said, "At the time I met Lester there was little or no feeling left in my marriage. My affair with him began three years ago. The man let me know where he was coming from and left the choice up to me. I knew from the outset where things would or wouldn't go. I accept things as they are and will always do so. I do not want to lose someone I love and who loves me, holds me, cares about me, and shares—yes, shares—his life with me. The last three years of my life have helped change me into a better woman. I now have self-confidence. I will be happy for as long as possible. As far as I'm concerned, things need not change."

A wife who sees her lover two or three times a year explained her attitude: "I was faced with family problems at home with my stepchildren far beyond my own control and did not realize until after I started it that I needed an affair to sustain me.

"I have no hopes for the affair other than friendship, companionship, lots of good times, and good lovemaking. Never have I been disappointed. He and I both decided we would never allow our relationship to break up our marriages. We both work to keep it that way and understand we are each other's port in the storm."

A similar statement came from a woman married for twenty-two years: "At the time I started the affair I was sexually deprived and my lover was in the same position. We decided to give each other the intimacy and passion we both missed very much. I expect nothing from him. We share a wonderful bond and we are good friends and lovers. The sex is incredible. We have no inhibitions with one another. We are open and very loving. This is all I want—to keep my life the way it is—and so does he. We are honest and each of us gives a lot of enjoyment to the other. We keep our affair and our lives very separate. I think we will continue on for as long as we both want to."

A thirty-six-year-old wife in Montana said, "I don't want my affair to end anytime soon. Both of us are married and have no plans to change that situation. I care very deeply for my husband, and he for his wife. An affair is not for everyone. At times it's very hard. It's not proper or honorable, but, again, I feel that life is too short and can be taken away at any time, so enjoy yourself. You have to go in with your eyes wide open and know that you will always be second in his life and that you will live a secret life, that you can never be open about it or discuss it with anyone."

Another woman who still experiences some difficulties, but has achieved a basic acceptance of the situation anyway, confessed, "This has been an extreme roller coaster. You need a lot of patience and control of your emotions. When we are together, we are in our own little world! However secure I feel during those times, it's the time we can't be together that becomes difficult. As a woman I need reassurances. And when I need it the most is the time he's unavailable. This dual role as wife and lover is difficult, but I suppose if you want something bad enough you will learn to cope. We do not expect anything from each other but 'us.' Neither one of us wants to end our marriage. We would just like to keep an ongoing affair. We both realize this is an explosive situation because of both our positions in the community. I suppose we'll deal with the situation if we're found out, but for now we are happy."

Some women, such as this one, simply surrender to the lover and his wishes from the very beginning: "I'll play any part in his life he wants me to play as long as I'm a part of it. I love him with all my heart, soul, mind, and body."

FEAR

Through all the stages of the affair, whether they have mentally accommodated to its restrictions or not, the majority of wives are always quite aware of the danger of adultery. In the back of their minds is the possibility of being found out.

A thirty-four-year-old woman, in a liaison with her much older boss who has had several illicit relationships before, said, "Having an affair isn't easy. You're sneaking around all the time, you're telling one lie to cover another—all the while hoping you don't get caught. I don't like to do these things to my husband—I love him. In his own way he's good to me and is a good father. Sometimes I panic when I think about him finding out. I know he'd divorce me. But at the same time, I'm not ready to break off my affair with my lover either—I love him also."

For a few, like the following woman, it isn't only the fear of being divorced or hurting their spouses; it's the terror of physical harm: "My husband is dangerous. He has shown many times he is vindictive, and I absolutely believe he is capable of shooting either me alone or my lover as well, if he discovers our affair. He has guns. His first wife left him for another man. His mother abused him. He has revealed he has a disturbed mind when dealing with difficult women. In a fit of passion, who knows what would happen? My lover is fully aware of this. Yet he can't or won't let go. We agree that one of us would have to move away from the area to end it."

By itself, however, the lingering sense of danger or fear of discovery is rarely what ends an affair for women. They struggle on, bearing their uneasy burden.

"I still love my husband and I never want to hurt him. I know this would hurt him and I hope to God he never finds out. I also know I cannot stop this affair," declared a wife in Wisconsin.

A woman married twenty-eight years said, "I would lose the respect of my family and my husband if our affair was known, yet I continue to see this man whenever I can, even though I know it's a threat and hopeless."

Part Five: Endings

Women don't easily end their affairs no matter what is going on between the lovers, no matter how worried they are about the consequences.

Although there are exceptions—some of which I detail in this chapter—it seems, judging by the attitude of the majority of unfaithful wives whose stories I heard, that women largely leave the ending of their affairs up to the man in question. In spite of conflict and pain, wives find it hard to give up a lover on their own. Many eventually employ therapists to help them end their affairs. But the sentiment expressed by this woman is quite common: "I keep trying to prepare myself for our separation, but I'm not willing to let him go. I'll keep him and the risks until he says 'no more.' "

Letter after letter from unfaithful wives contained warnings to other women that it is much harder to get out of an affair than get into one. Women develop real, entangling bonds with their illicit partners, bonds of friendship as well as passion and love. The woman often regards the other man as her most intimate ally in life, and it is true that married lovers often exchange confidences about children, work, feelings, spouses.

THE SICK PART

However, the bond you feel also often has an unhealthy component. Your lover provides you with a fix, whether it is for your self-esteem or to feel passionate or pretty, and this may operate like drug or alcohol dependency, gluing you to the affair. Sometimes you can't let go even when you know it isn't good for you, for example when he's driving you crazy, not giving you enough or not treating you well, as in this case of a wife of sixty-two involved with a man of fifty-eight:

"It all started eight and a half years ago. I met this man on my job. He made the first move and kissed me. I was in shock. He is a married man with five grown kids and ten grandchildren. I have been married

147

for forty-two years. We got involved and now I truly love this man. He tells me he loves me but I think he lies. He makes dates and promises and breaks many of them. I get so upset with him. At times he treats me good, then he treats me like dirt. I don't know where I stand or what to do about him. My friend and I have not had sex for quite a while. He only wants to go to breakfast or lunch and seems not to have time at night for me like he used to. In the beginning it was wonderful, but for the past year it has been lousy and I am upset. His pet sayings are 'Hang in there,' 'We'll see,' and 'Have patience.' I do love him and don't know what to do." Of course this badly treated woman is hanging in there long beyond the time when she should have stopped the relationship.

When you have reconciled yourself to living one day at a time, or when you simply *can't* give him up, your illicit relationship can go on for a very long time. Lovers all over the world secretly meet for years and years. One woman told of a relationship that was going into its third decade.

WHY LOVERS SPLIT

When an affair did end it was often for these reasons:

Demands by you or your partner escalated and the other couldn't take it. Often this happens because a lover refuses to accept the limitations of the situation and creates intense pressure for the partner to leave home.

A woman who knew the end was near said, "I must admit that our relationship of over five years is waning. I wish it were not so, but I can no longer accept not being number one, and this has reduced us to something less than the passionate, carefree lovers we were for so long. Am I angry because of it? Yes! He is wealthy and handsome and sexy and the best friend I ever had. He stuck by me through times of serious health problems; he gave me tremendous personal strength. He rewarded my successes and held my hand when things were not so great. Is it any wonder that I resent not being his wife?

"He used to say he was staying because of the children. I found comfort in that as I ticked off the chronological passing of their ages. Last May he admitted to me that he was never going to leave his wife."

The one being pressured, of course, was the partner who pulled out. Most frequently it was the man. However, in a few cases, women found their lovers too impossible in one way or another, and they took the initiative in breaking off the relationship.

A hospital admissions clerk in her forties told her story:

At the time I met this man, my husband and I were having problems. It was a second marriage for both of us and my two children lived with us. My husband is fourteen years older than I am and we had very different ideas about what children should be allowed to do. I felt I was being torn in two directions. My husband is also a workaholic and spent very little time with me.

I became friendly with this man at work. We talked a lot and were very comfortable with each other. He was thoughtful and gave me a lot of emotional support. I grew to love him and he loved me. I had great hopes that we would have a future together. I felt much closer to him than my husband.

It was wonderful at first, but things began to change. He became very possessive and jealous. If I talked to any of the other men I worked with, he accused me of being involved with them. If he couldn't reach me on the telephone, he thought I was out with another man. He would say terrible things to me and I would end up in tears. We always made up because I was so attached to him, but I began to feel very bad about myself. It got so I was miserable most of the time. I finally broke the relationship off.

A wife of twenty-four recounted, "We would meet at least once a week; a couple of times it was two nights. He always said it was more than just a physical relationship and that he cared for me. We both ended up caring a lot about each other, but he started to want complete control of the relationship and I couldn't deal with that. I tried talking about it with him but he never wanted to. Finally, I ended it. I would have liked for it to have gone on if we could have reached some kind of understanding, but he wasn't willing. Now we don't speak to each other, although I've tried."

The relationship became too involved for your lover's comfort, even when no explicit demands were made. Often the end came because you were too much in love with the man and he became afraid you were going to do something foolish, as was true for this woman in her twenties:

"He is the first man to ever break my heart. It is the only time I felt actual physical pain from a lost love. He is seventeen years older than I am and he said all along that it wouldn't work out. When he finally ended it for the hundredth and last time, it was a loving, caring, heart-breaking good-bye.

"I think he sensed that I was getting ready to leave my husband. He told me to make a happy life with my husband and kids. His last words were 'If it was a bad experience, you leave and move on; if it was a good experience, you cherish it and move on.' I'll always cherish it!"

A wife in New York said, "Two years ago I started a casual affair with my husband's married friend. The relationship was fulfilling because it gave us both what we were missing in our married lives—sexual satisfaction. Everything was fine until I started to really fall in love with him and made him my priority over and above anything else, including my husband. We would meet every day and made love whenever we could. I made a decision to leave my husband because of the guilt. It never happened because my lover stopped me from filing for a divorce. He finally admitted that he can't leave his wife and he can't be responsible for wrecking my married life. I tried to forget him and concentrated on reviving my old relationship with my husband, to no avail. The relationship is dead and all I think of is my married ex-lover."

Your lover cheated on you. In this case a woman's emotions boiled over, alienating her lover:

"The relationship lasted for four years. He ended it because I started to get too emotional. He doesn't like emotional women. I got emotional because I suspected he was having other affairs besides the one with me and I can't deal with that. I'm a one-on-one person whether both of us are married or not."

A woman of twenty-five said, "The affair is over. I don't love Victor anymore. He hurt me emotionally. He started having an affair with one of my girlfriends at work. I bore the humiliation of them making goo-goo eyes at each other, sending gifts and flowers, and bringing each other meals at work for nearly a year. I think it was to punish myself for what I had done to my husband and marriage. Finally I got fed up enough to quit and get a job somewhere else, away from Victor.

"Consequently, Victor quit and got a job working at my new place of employment. I wouldn't even speak to him for two months. Then one night, at break time, he came outside with me and we ended up kissing. I quit the next day. As far as I know he is still with my ex-girlfriend. How could she put up with a man like that?"

Your lover turned out to be an all-round rat. After the initial courtship period your lover stopped treating you so well, and the situation turned tortured and ugly.

A wife in her forties admitted, "The only lover I ever permitted myself in my long marriage is a man who has, I finally discovered, a disconnected heart. I have been emotionally abused by him too much and too often, going repeatedly through cycles of intense pleasure to intense pain, into disillusionment, blaming, and then desperate attempts to make up. I also suspect he has had other lovers along with me, even though he denies it. I ended it and employed a female therapist to guide me through my grieving and to help me restrain myself from contacting him."

The guilt proved too much for one of you. Sometimes it was the woman who called a halt, but although women in affairs are generally guiltier than men, it doesn't necessarily make them end the affair. They suffer with it and continue. In these two cases it was the man's guilt that finally rang the death knell for the relationship.

"A year after our affair started, the situation became complicated and upsetting," explained a woman in Santa Fe. "Whenever Sid started to feel too close, he would back off for a few weeks. He wouldn't call me and we wouldn't see each other after work until he felt in control once more. Then it would begin again. The on-and-off pattern upset me and at times made me angry. I didn't understand because I loved him and felt he was deserting me. He carried the guilt for both of us. He felt guilty about his family and mine and became moody at home and at work.

"He finally ended our relationship just short of our second anniversary. That was five months ago. I miss him terribly and still haven't gotten over him."

An office manager of thirty-five said, "Towards the middle of June he told me he couldn't do this anymore, he felt guilty, he thought that anything that went wrong was a sign to him that he was being punished for what he was doing. He kept mentioning that he couldn't forget what his deceased mother told him: 'Once you make your bed, you must lie in it.' So he ended it and there I was, in my opinion dead. Life was over, life had no meaning. I didn't know if I was coming or going. All I did was cry all the time. And that son of a bitch went on like nothing ever happened. He said he knew it was hard but I would get over it. He said that there was nothing to do but act like nothing ever happened, and just work together each day and leave at night to go home like nothing ever happened. All through this my husband never suspected a thing. You cannot imagine how sorry I am now for what I did to him, a man who never hurt me in any way."

One of you changed jobs. Another frequent reason for the end of an affair between co-workers is when one leaves the place where they both were employed and they subsequently drift apart.

Sometimes the desertion is one-sided, as was the case for this wife involved in an affair with a man she had known for four years previously: "I moved to a different job," she said. "We didn't say good-bye. He just said to me, 'Where there's a will, there's a way,' and that he loves me. It's been six months now and he hasn't called and I haven't seen him. What I feel right now is pain."

A move to another part of the country also brought about the demise of affairs, although many lovers continued to meet once or twice a year anyway, and kept up some contact by phone or letter.

Your marital status, or his, changed. Sometimes affairs start when a person has just separated from a spouse. Often they end for the same reason.

This wife's liaison began when her employer's marriage fell apart: "My boss and I have worked together alone for nine years. For the majority of the time, the relationship was strictly professional. When he separated from his wife six months ago, he leaned on me a great deal both professionally and personally. A strong bond and friendship developed. Our mutual desire was evident and we became lovers approximately two months ago."

Although this couple realized that their short affair had to end soon because "neither wants to divorce the present spouse to be with the other," more often the stories I heard were about extramarital relationships that had gone on for much longer, with much more emotional involvement. Only when divorce entered the picture did they suddenly change in character.

Very often the same woman who hung around for a long time while she was married takes a clearer look at the situation once her husband is out of the equation. Finally facing up to the fact that her lover is never going to leave his wife for her, even though she left her husband for him, the woman weighs her future and decides that she can't tie herself to a married man. So she moves on.

Sometimes, as in the case of this separated wife, it is with the encouragement of her lover: "Our affair has died down now that he doesn't work with me anymore and I've moved. I see him maybe once a month now, but he calls me twice a week. He encourages me to go out and date and get on with my life. He doesn't want me to stop living for him. I intend to go back to being friends with Hal and get on with a life of my own, but I'll always love him and miss him and wish I could have had more with him."

A separated woman of thirty-four said:

Jack has tried to leave his wife four times and he has never made it out. She is fighting for him and I feel he still loves her in some way. He loves both of us and basically is sitting on the fence to see which clicks as being right. Logically speaking, he looks at his big home, cars, three kids, and a wife who wants him to stay and says, "Look what I built up in the last twelve years—why walk away?" Yet I know he truly loves me as well. I love him so much and I wanted to believe the hope he gave me about leaving his wife and marriage for me someday. I should never have let him talk about such things.

I know now that I need to get my key back from him and tell him not to call. But we both know it won't work while I still work with him, so I am actively looking for another job. I guess I realize that life goes on without him. He has a whole other existence that doesn't include me. He says he loves me too much to keep hurting me. Besides, I want to get married again. I don't want to waste ten years with him, and one day wake up old and bitter with nothing to show for my devotion. The wife will always have the honor, respect, and benefits of being married to your lover. You get old, lonely, and used. I feel ending this affair on a positive note will at least keep the door open for me if he ever does leave his wife. This is so hard to do, but I know I must. I am getting out.

Another woman, a bookkeeper of thirty-five, admitted, "I have an attraction for younger men, and the man I had my three-year affair with was five years my junior, well built, and very good-looking. We started meeting just for coffee and eventually started meeting for sex. He was very inexperienced even though he was married twice, and I enjoyed being his 'teacher.'

"At this time I have been divorced for eight months and ended the affair because a married man can't offer a single woman the time she needs. There are enough great men out there without wasting your years on unavailable men."

Of course, some women who ended their marriages during their affairs find they are as helpless to end the relationship with the lover as when they were married.

This thirty-four-year-old woman, now divorced, said, "I've tried to cope in various ways. I tried not to have sex with him until he left her. I gave in after two months. I've tried dating other men (ten altogether) and I'm not enjoying that. Lastly, I told him that maybe we shouldn't see each other for a while until he quit dragging things on and on. We both were so stressed over the thought of not seeing each other, we were back in less than a week with franticness."

A twenty-seven-year-old woman in the South told her story: "It all started when we met at church. We were both very lonely and unhappy in our marriages. I was always at home alone and he was always away trying to find business trips to go on just to get away from his wife. One day at a social gathering we started talking and one thing led to another. I told him to give me a call sometime and we would continue our discussion. He did, and after a couple of weeks of phone calls we finally decided that we both wanted to meet at some secluded place. We did and that was two and a half years ago. We've both fallen very much in love. I am now divorced, but he says he can't until his kids are out of school. That will be another three years. I suppose that will make him feel like he has done his family duty and has raised his children. I honestly believe he will do this, but I just don't know if I can hold out that long."

It isn't always only the woman's divorce that threatens the rupture of an illicit relationship. It may also be the man's. After he finally splits from his wife, he decides he prefers his freedom. For you it may have been a real love affair that you hoped would end in marriage. For him it was a transition affair—a way to get out of his marriage.

A woman in Boston described her relationship and its unexpected outcome:

My affair with my boss started three and a half years ago when everything seemed to be going wrong. I wasn't happy with my marriage, and my stepchildren were growing into their teenage years and didn't need me as much as they had when they were younger. I have been their mother for twelve years. The intimacy in my marriage was gone and my self-esteem was at an all-time low.

Going to work every day was a joy because someone needed me. I worked very closely with my boss as his receptionist. The first nine months I worked in the office we maintained a professional relationship, but I could feel the attraction growing stronger every day. One night a group of us from the office went to a birthday party for a co-worker at a local bar. My boss and I had danced a few fast dances together and then the slow dances started. Just the touch of his hand on my neck drove me wild. That night our affair started.

We pledged eternal love to each other over the next few months, which eventually turned into years. We planned where we would live and how we would live our lives together after our divorces were final. He promised me everything.

Two years into the relationship, I left my husband and children and filed for divorce. I had a lot of financial problems living by myself but I was determined that I would make a go of it because he loved me. Our times together soon became stressful and farther apart. I came to the realization that he would not leave his wife. He has a good bit of money with his income and his wife's combined, and he couldn't part with the "toys" he had obtained with his wealth. To divorce her and marry me would be one step down the financial ladder. I went back to my husband for financial reasons.

I always thought my friends were crazy when they told me he would never leave. I felt that he truly loved me and wanted to spend the rest of his life with me, as I did with him. The hurt is beyond belief when the reality of the situation finally hits you. I have considered suicide once. I am not the kind of person to ever think of such a thing, but I was so depressed I didn't feel the need to go on with my life. Since then I have been in counseling, hoping with the help of my counselor that I will gain the strength to let go of this relationship.

Sometimes when you *both* get divorced during a hot and heavy affair instead of getting together as you expected, the relationship explodes. This is exactly what happened to a human resources specialist:

At the present time I've taken my children 820 miles in order to get away from my husband and my lover. It hurts more to be away from my lover! I got involved with him at work by just being his friend. I'd been married for twelve years. My husband never told me he loved me, never talked or listened to me. I was very lonely. My lover was having problems with his wife. He spent lunch hours talking about her and how he felt. We became best friends. He didn't even hug or kiss me till well over a year! We were friends for over two years before he told me he was in love with me. Then we became lovers, talked about a future and growing old together.

He left his wife six months ago. I moved out two months ago. As soon as he was served with divorce papers, he asked me to set him up with a girl in my office. It crushed me. He told me I couldn't be in love with him and that I interfered with his life. Prior to that he was sweet and loving. He called me every night to say good night and told me he was proud of me.

My marriage has been dead for years, so my kids and I took off— two states away. My heart is broken. I'm still in love with him.

A woman in her thirties confided:

For about six months we both lived in our respective marriages. I moved out first. He left home about a month later. We never lived together. Weekends and holidays were about the only time he stayed here.

My divorce is nearly final. It is uncontested and reasonably amicable. His has been protracted and difficult. He's dealing with an enormous amount of guilt and pressure from the kids prompted by his wife. I live a sort of Ping-Pong existence. I know what our feelings are for each other. He's told me he wants to marry me. Most of the time I want to marry him, too.

Right now, after one and one half years together, we're not seeing each other. I made the proverbial ultimatum: Finish the divorce and let's get on with our lives or let me get on with mine. I miss him terribly.

I hope he misses me. It's very sad to see him at work. He doesn't talk to me and won't even look at me most of the time.

It rarely happens, but some women, like this one, are smart enough to take a closer look at their lovers as mate material after they have left their husbands: "My affair has lasted five years now. I love this man very much, but the age difference is the problem. I am now thirty-one, he is sixty. When I reach my prime he'll be ready for the walker. I once had a dream of marrying him, but I guess I woke up and smelled the coffee."

Your affair was discovered. When one or both of the spouses find out what has been going on, it may abruptly end the idyll.

A woman involved with a single man said, "I was over at his apartment one afternoon and my husband found me there. My lover lived on a busy street and my husband spotted my parked car. I have two children. Everyone was hurt. My boyfriend could not deal with this and he transferred to a different site out of state."

A thirty-year-old wife, married for nine years, admitted, "I am recovering from an affair, and I do mean recovering. My affair lasted four short months. It was a beautiful thing and I feel no guilt for having it. But I do feel cheated. Why? Because he got back with his wife (my husband does not know) and I was left with nothing but memories. He approached me first, he was the one to lead, yet he was also the one to leave. He told me he loved me and I believe he does. His wife found out about us and got a legal separation. In three days he was back home. Up till the time he went back to his wife, he told me he loved me and wanted me. But he also said he could not leave his responsibilities. I *never* asked him to leave her. Now when he sees me, he can't even look at me or speak to me. He says it's because he still cares about me. It isn't fair!"

You decide to fix up your marriage. Sometimes a wife decides it's better to remake her marriage than to continue with her lover.

A young redhead in Oregon said, "I got involved because I was lonely. My husband had no interest in my company (he was using cocaine throughout most of our marriage). I was wishing someone would want me. That someone turned out to be my boss. He treated me nice and complimented me all the time. I felt good about myself when I was with him. I could forget about the pain of my marriage. One day he kissed me and that's when it started. The affair is now over. I gained the strength to say, 'I deserve to be happy,' and told my husband if he used drugs once more I would leave. Since then we've been working on building our marriage. My boss knew and understood the situation. I told him I wanted to give my husband 100 percent of me now and see if our marriage can work."

You and your lover get married. When both lovers leave their spouses and decide to pitch their own tent together, some consider it to be a happy ending. Lovers who wind up together remarried are in the extreme minority, so women shouldn't count on this as the end of their own scenarios. However, once in a while it happens.

Here is one woman in Seattle for whom this appears to be true:

I never intended to have an affair in spite of the fact that my marriage is not ideal. My lover is my former college professor.

My husband hadn't slept with me for four years before I started the affair. He still hasn't, which is one reason the affair is not as emotionally traumatic for either my lover or me as it could be. He is relieved, as I am, that we don't have to share each other physically with anyone else.

With the exception of our sexual relationship, my husband and I get along well. We have two daughters, ten and thirteen, and he is an excellent father and provider. Since I started college he has been extremely supportive.

If I do have any guilt over this affair it is because my husband is a wonderful man who happens to have a low sex drive. He informed me of this fact long before we were married, but our sexual relationship before marriage and before my girls were born was satisfying. I had no reason to suspect that he would lose interest in sex after our second child was born. I did not let myself go and, in fact, look young and attractive for my age, forty. I have tried countless times over the past five years to have my husband agree to counseling or even just to talk about it, but he refuses, saying we'll resume our sexual relationship after I graduate.

In any event, the man with whom I'm involved is caring, sensitive, understanding, and very sexy. We have a strong emotional commitment and spend many hours discussing the affair and its ramifications for everyone concerned. When I get my degree in the spring and get a job, I intend to ask my husband for a divorce. My biggest concern is the impact this will have on my children. My husband will undoubtedly find someone else quickly. He'll be a good catch. I'm sure my lover and I will get married fairly soon after my divorce. He has met my children and they get along well.

Since this woman's boyfriend is single, her chances for marriage are better than for a woman whose extramarital partner has to extricate himself from a marriage.

As illustrated by many of the cases above, a woman often leaves her husband fully expecting her lover to follow with his own separation, and then discovers with great pain, after the die is cast, that he is unable to follow through.

However, that is not the only scenario for emotional disaster.

Quite frequently you split, and he splits; you start living together and you feel your dream has come true. Then he suddenly goes back to his wife, leaving you high, dry, and distraught.

When your lover, whom you thought you had captured, runs back home, the ensuing hurt, bewilderment, anger, and blow to the ego are devastating, and it often takes women a long time to get over the experience.

Wives seem more willing to accept an unfaithful husband back than the other way around. It is important to remember that the chances of being able to return to your marriage are smaller than his, if the affair falls apart after you've already left home.

However, even if your lover stays, and even if you marry him, a completely happy ending is not always ensured. Sometimes there is, indeed, marital bliss with a more compatible marriage partner, but sometimes there are also some mixed feelings or downright regret, as expressed in this lament from a saddened woman:

"Three years ago I had an affair. I left my husband. In the process I lost my children, my home, and my business. I've been married to the other man now for a year and a half, but I long for my old life. It was an impetuous thing to do, and even though I love my present husband I can't stop thinking about getting back with my ex. Because of the children I see him and speak to him frequently. He has not remarried and claims he never will, even though he has a steady girlfriend. I am thirty-five and we were together for eleven years. I don't know what to do. It would hurt my present husband terribly if he knew this. I'm sure he would become violent."

Another woman, who is now living with her lover, admitted, "We both have two children. I feel as if I sacrificed a lot of things to find my happiness. My younger child chose to stay with his father. I'll never get over that. It's further complicated by the fact that my lover's separated wife works at the same institution I do and I know well that I carry the 'other woman' label."

The other thing that may mar the happiness of a relationship that started as an extramarital affair is the specter of future infidelity.

Particularly for a man with a history of previous infidelity, another triangle may be in the cards in a new marriage. Once he is remarried, he may again need the reassurance supplied by a new conquest, or once more he may feel the need to escape from the intimacy of the marital relationship, or the feeling of being trapped that takes over once commitment is established. And so he escapes into another affair.

Or, if he comes from a family in which there were extramarital adventures, he may be driven to repeat this pattern compulsively again and again in his own life. Of course, all of this may be true for you as well. However, Annette Lawson found that women who marry their extramarital partners tend to recommit firmly to the idea of monogamy in their new marriages, while husbands who have cheated do not.

I don't mean to imply that happy endings and happy remarriages don't occur. Of course they do. However, leaving one man for another is a high-risk game. But then again, so is the entire affair, haunted as it is by the terrifying thought of your husband's finding out. What happens when he does?

Chapter 11

※

OUT IN THE OPEN

How do husbands find out? Your spouse can have his suspicions aroused, or even uncover the whole secret affair, by the following—a cautionary list if you are trying to cover your tracks, or a rundown of what to watch for if you are wondering whether your wife is straying.

FIFTEEN CLUES THAT CAN GIVE YOU AWAY

1. ***Your habits have changed.*** You work longer hours, staying late at your place of business more often than you used to, or going to more company-affiliated events like bowling team matches or baseball games. Or you may tell your husband that you are spending the evening with friends or relatives, or at a community or church activity, more frequently than in the past. These stolen times, of course, are the moments you and your lover get together.

2. ***You seem more distracted at home.*** As I have explained in other parts of this book, the majority of unfaithful wives become mentally consumed by their extramarital relationships and may appear to their husbands to be lost in thought or preoccupied, less thoughtful or attentive in general.

3. *You have a new wardrobe of sexy lingerie.* Seductive underwear is a staple of romantic affairs. Fresh bras and panties or teddies suddenly appear and are worn on those nights when, for one reason or another, you are coming home late. Or they are seen going into your suitcase when you are going to out-of-town conventions or on business trips where, of course, you will meet your lover.

4. *You come home with fresh makeup on from a late evening out.* If you had spent hours working or cheering on a company team, your makeup would not be as dewy fresh and perfect as it is when, after making love to your partner, you have reapplied it before returning home.

5. *Your sex habits have changed.* You are less interested in making love to your husband than you used to be. Some wives, who feel they are cheating on their lovers if they have sex with their husbands, make excuses in order not to have sex at all, or as infrequently as possible.

It is much rarer for women than men, but, in a few cases, a wife may get so sexually hopped up by her affair that she becomes more interested in sex than she used to be, or more adventurous about positions and acts, putting to use things she has learned to enjoy with her lover.

6. *Your conversation is peppered with references to your boss or some other male friend at the office.* Often, at least at the beginning of a romance, before it has turned into a sexual affair, you talk openly about the man with whom you have a deepening friendship. This may tip a husband off that something is going on, since he knows that when men get close to a female they generally want to have sex with her. Suspicions may become particularly aroused if, after you start sleeping with the other man, you abruptly clam up about him.

7. *Your children are acting up.* Your mental distraction may be felt by your children even before your husband. Children are acutely sensitive—they know it when a parent's energies go outside the home. Puzzled as to the cause, often blaming themselves for having done something wrong, children may revert to behavior like bedwetting or thumb sucking, or they may become cranky or start to have nightmares. If they are teenagers, they may get themselves into trouble by sneaking out at night, having sexual adventures themselves, or perhaps even drinking alcohol or experimenting with drugs. This is an often an unconscious attempt to bring the parent's attention back into the home.

8. *You are irritable with your husband or given to sudden outbursts.* As I have explained before, many wives, in order to expiate the guilt they feel for having an affair, lash out at the husband, provoking

some rage in return, which then makes them feel justified in cheating on such an angry, unreasonable man.

9. *He feels confused.* Your husband just senses something different or strange about you, and the subtle or not-so-subtle changes in your behavior puzzle him even if he doesn't say anything to you directly about what he is feeling.

10. *You are paying more attention to your appearance.* You finally lose those extra pounds, dress more carefully when going to work, make sure to blow-dry your hair, and use your best makeup to go to the office—to impress the other man, of course.

11. *There are fresh sheets on the bed more often.* Many wives invite their lovers home when their husbands are at work and the kids at school. They generally change the sheets after lovemaking to obliterate any signs of what they have been up to.

12. *You leave a clue around.* One wife sentimentally kept the notes her lover liked to send her, and her husband found one. Another spouse came upon the Valentine's Day card his wife was preparing to give her lover. Still another kept finding matches from a bar in the glove compartment of his wife's car and confronted her. Another came upon a diaphragm in the bathroom when he and his wife had not made love in weeks.

13. *You are discovered together.* Your husband comes home unexpectedly at lunchtime and comes upon the two of you in the bedroom. You are seen leaving a motel together. Your mate tries to reach you at your hotel when you are out of town on business and your lover answers the phone, or you are not in your room at any hour of the day or night.

14. *Your lover's wife tells him.* You may not be the one who has been careless. It may be your partner in illicit love who has done something to tip his wife off to your relationship. Many outraged wives in situations like this call the husband of the married girlfriend and spill the beans. Sometimes the tip-off comes from a fellow worker, a neighbor, or a relative who has heard about it or seen you with your lover and thinks your husband should know what's going on.

15. *You stop trying to change things that were bothering you before.* If you felt you weren't getting enough sex, you stop attempting to entice your husband. If you were complaining that he didn't communicate enough, you stop trying to open him up. If he drank too much or had other bad habits, you stop railing at him about them. After finding

some satisfaction and fulfillment with the other man, you give up on your husband and stop bothering him about things that you were carrying on about before.

WHAT ELSE CLUES REVEAL

From reading some of the above clues, you can not only alert yourself to things that arouse suspicion but also see why experts feel that affairs are very destructive to marriages.

Your husband feels disoriented and left out, if not actually suspicious. You are expending less energy on him, the family, and your home. Inevitably, your marriage loses intimacy as distance is created because your thoughts and emotions are on someone else.

You may have originally entered an affair with the idea that you were trying to save your marriage by getting satisfaction elsewhere, but, as this thirty-six-year-old wife in Idaho found out, problems don't get solved in this way:

"My lover ended our affair six months ago just short of our third year together. I have now been married twenty years and nothing has improved. We have no relationship, no communication, and nothing in common." This woman warned other wives, "If you care about your lover, it will have an effect on your spouse and your marriage."

Instead of getting better, whatever problem propelled you into infidelity generally gets worse.

Wives find, once their attention is on a lover, that any lack of communication with the husband grows greater. Or, for the first time, you are the one who is withholding. Now you have whole blocks of important things you can't talk to him about. And he, sensing your dwindling interest, may withdraw and become even less communicative than he was before.

If you are getting good sex elsewhere, by comparison lovemaking with your husband may seem even worse; or once you feel the passion you do with your lover, you may become more and more unwilling to settle for anything less at home.

If you are having open, honest, and intimate conversations with your lover, your relationship with your husband may now seem even less satisfactory, routine, or shallow.

If you feel a sense of ongoing excitement from your affair, your home life may seem more boring than it did before.

If you are in love with your extramarital partner, you may feel out of love with your husband.

In women's lives, it is very hard for a marriage to compete with an affair. The affair is Technicolor; the marriage becomes black-and-white or just plain dingy gray.

You have to realize, then, that an extramarital relationship can destroy, or at least permanently dent, whatever it is that you have had with your husband in the past.

A woman in Missouri lamented, "I am now separated from my husband due to a relationship I have with an older man at work. I completely tuned out my husband because of this man."

In Annette Lawson's study, 40 percent of the women felt that their affairs had worsened or finished off their marriages.

Studies by Gurgul and by Shirley Glass and Thomas Wright show that affairs make men more content with long-standing marriages, while discontent increases for wives.

This is true both for women who had major gripes about their husbands before they committed adultery, and for those who thought their marriages were good, or good enough, before another man entered the picture.

Whether because of greater unhappiness, unendurable guilt, the increasing distance between mates in a marriage, or discovery of the affair, there is always the danger of divorce—a possibility that is much greater for women than men who cheat. Kinsey concluded that men were twice as likely as women to blame a spouse's affair for the dissolution of a marriage.

In Annette Lawson's study, more adulterous wives than husbands ended up separated from their spouses. The male reaction (coupled with the extent of female emotional involvement in affairs) is obviously much more lethal to the future well-being of the couple.

WHY MEN REACT WITH SO MUCH FURY

To begin with, women are in one sense more prepared. Infidelity has been well publicized as a male habit and, as a result, although you may still feel his fling as an intense betrayal, you expect it more simply because your husband is a man.

You are also more apt to forgive (if not forget) adultery if your husband abandons the other woman. You consider the children, your economic situation, your own diminished prospects if you are an older wife. You have been taught as a woman in our society to conciliate, and so you often do, even in the face of infidelity.

On the other hand, women are still expected to be faithful in our society. Studies show that men are less likely than women to be suspicious—so when a wife commits adultery it comes as more of a shock to the husband and, as things now stand, it is considered more of a sin by everyone.

A husband feels dishonored, humiliated in the eyes of the world by a wife's infidelity. Cuckolds are traditionally objects of derision by other men. Their injured manhood is the subject of sly laughter, and since men are so competitive with one another, they feel this as unbearable.

Also, on a subliminal level, a man may look upon his wife as his property, and so he reacts with rage that his territory has been violated. In addition, men's competition with one another is especially acute in the area of sex. They are frightened, as well as unmanned and enraged, by the thought that another male—your lover—might be better in bed or have a superior sexual organ. Typically, you as a female may worry that the other woman is prettier or younger, but your husband's greatest worry as a male is that he has been shown up as an inferior bed partner by another man.

Finally, he can't regard your transgression as a fling just for sex. He knows how women get involved emotionally, so he thinks your affair is more serious than any extramarital adventure on his part might be.

All of this can lead to extreme emotions and out-of-control reactions when a husband finds out that his wife has been cheating. Studies show sexual jealousy to be the leading cause of marital violence by males. Some wronged husbands try to beat up or kill the other man—but more turn the attack upon the wife. The newspapers are periodically filled with grisly tales of a jealous husband brutally battering or gunning down his adulterous wife—often with her lover.

In Homer's *Odyssey*, when the hero Odysseus returned home from his long travels, he simply killed all his wife's suitors. In many cultures murdering a wife for adultery is considered acceptable, while a wife's killing her unfaithful husband is not.

Although, in recent times, there seems to be some increase in the number of men who can somehow weather a wife's infidelity, allowing the marriage to continue, if you are found out you still stand a much greater chance of total marital disaster than if it were the other way around.

In addition to the other reasons I've cited for this—humiliation, rage at the other man—the question of whom a husband blames comes into the picture. When a wife is faced with her husband's adultery, she often agonizes about what is wrong with *her* or her marriage, and somehow blames herself for her husband's transgressions. A husband will rarely take that tack. He'll blame you and the other man, and opt for action instead of introspection. "More often than not, he will move to end the marriage," says Dr. Shirley Glass a psychologist who studies gender differences in adultery. She is in agreement with most other experts, who find that men fall apart more than women and are less forgiving.

If your husband has an atypical, rather mild reaction to your infidelity, I would wonder why.

HIDDEN REASONS WHEN HUSBANDS ARE LENIENT

Some men take the news more tolerantly than others because they have been playing around, too. If so, your adultery may make your husband feel relieved. Or, in the interest of fair play, he may feel less entitled to express his anger completely, even though inwardly he may be jealous and upset.

The reverse may be true as well. If you are a philandering wife who catches your husband in a sexual relationship with another woman, you may respond less strongly than you would if you were still monogamous.

A forty-eight-year-old statistician, who had been having a long-term affair with a professional colleague, explained her reaction when she returned home one day to find her husband in their bed with someone else: "I think it would have been real life-shattering, a horrible experience, walking in on them, if I hadn't been having my own affair. I thought to myself, *He may be going a little bit further with it by bringing someone into our house, but well, you know, he's not doing any worse than I am.* It was traumatic for me, but I didn't do anything extreme."

Sometimes your husband's reaction may be tempered by the thought that your infidelity is a sexual opportunity for him. Now he can feel freer to live out his own desire for a sexual adventure.

Men who have despaired of ever being able to fulfill a spouse's emotional or sexual needs may be more tolerant as well. They are willing to let a wife go elsewhere to find what she's been complaining about missing. They just want her to stop bothering them.

Some of these husbands may actually encourage a wife to take a lover. One woman whose sexual desires were greater than her husband's remembers how, at one point, he kept urging her to take vacations without him at places known to have a lot of men and women looking for partners. She got his signal and started what turned out to be a series of affairs with other men—relationships she was able to conduct quite easily because her husband always accepted without question whatever excuse she offered, no matter how flimsy, for being gone the evening or even the whole night.

Other husbands may encourage a wife's infidelity because they are excited by the idea of her sleeping with another man. This can be a disguised form of homosexual interest in other men. In extreme cases, men like to watch the sexual proceedings from a hidden place, getting a sexual kick in this manner.

One architect remembers meeting a married woman and taking her to bed. In the middle of lovemaking, he became aware of her husband emerging from a hiding place behind the draperies and walking across the room to the night table beside the bed. The husband picked up a watch lying there, put it on, and calmly left through the bedroom door.

Sometimes a man who has been philandering himself wants an open marriage and therefore gives his wife permission to play around. This is a tricky business, however, and the consequences can be unexpected, as in this case:

A lawyer who had been having a series of flings finally had a talk with his wife, told her of his adventures, and made an agreement with her that she could do the same. She took him at his word and started an affair with a married man she and her husband knew.

The wife of this man found out, called her rival, and set up an appointment to discuss the matter. But the lawyer's wife became frightened of the confrontation, and instead of being home at the appointed time for their discussion she abandoned her apartment, leaving a note on the door for her lover's wife to find when she arrived.

However, it was a hot summer day, and the lawyer decided to leave work early. He came home early and discovered the note on the door left by his wife. Reading it he got the picture, and when his wife arrived home he confronted her. She admitted her extramarital entanglement and felt safe in doing so because her husband had encouraged it. He seemed reasonable, admitting that he understood why she could have been attracted to the other man—he was good-looking and successful. On that note the couple went to sleep. However, when they awoke the next morning, the first words out of her husband's mouth were "What shall we tell the children about the divorce?"

Stories in my files also tell of wives in open marriages who fell in love with a lover—something the husband could not tolerate.

Occasionally a mate's reaction to infidelity may also be tempered by the wife's choice of an extramarital partner. Some husbands are less upset if you are involved with a man of superior social status or someone with impressive wealth. A celebrity or billionaire or a leading politician in your area may be regarded as almost an asset. A good example of this is the husband of one of Lord Byron's mistresses. He hung a portrait of his renowned rival in a prominent place in his own home. The husbands of married mistresses at royal courts often let their wives' affairs go on without interference, and sometimes even profited from the liaisons.

When TV celebrity Ed McMahon was faced with evidence that his wife was cheating, it was even more unforgivable to him, I am sure, because her lover was much lower on the social ladder.

In cases like this, when the wife chooses a man of lower social stature, the husband feels doubly humiliated, cheapened by his wife's choice.

YEARNING TO TELL ALL

Some women are seized with the desire to confess. Why do they want to?

Sometimes the motivation is anger. You really wish to hurt your husband for some past or ongoing sin. Or you are so mad at him for ignoring you, belittling you, making you feel unwanted and undesirable, that you have to let him know that some other man finds you attractive and worthwhile even if he doesn't.

Some women simply want to end a marriage in which they are miserable and unfulfilled.

Sometimes you have become so confused and crazed from trying to juggle your lover and your home life, or feel so bad about all the sneaking around, that you feel you must unburden yourself. Studies show that women are much more bothered than men by the deceit involved in adultery. By confessing, the woman essentially is out to make herself feel better.

Some women desire to make a clean breast of the matter. They want to get rid of the guilt or put their marriages on a better footing after they have ended their affairs.

SHOULD YOU CONFESS?

Wanting to confess does not necessarily make it a good idea, unless you really want out of the marriage. There are times, however, when I think it *is* necessary to tell the truth:

1. When your husband already suspects and has been asking you if you are having an affair. If he feels it in his bones, has found a clue, or has seen signs, it is unfair to continue to stonewall him. Denying his perceptions and instincts can drive him crazy.
2. When he has confessed his affair to you in an attempt to put the marriage together again. Once more, it is unfair to keep your affair secret when he has voluntarily brought his out into the open. This may be a good chance to open up a discussion about what has been wrong between you.
3. If you are really attempting, as a couple, to make your relationship better by going into marriage therapy together.

I have interviewed women for this book who thought they genuinely wanted to improve their marriages. In an effort to do so, they were going into counseling with their husbands, but they had absolutely no intention of either divulging their secret in therapy or, in some cases, ending their affairs. By keeping your affair a secret you are not allowing the therapist to do his or her job completely, and you are leaving one important matter between you and your husband unattended to.

The best way to admit to an affair is when both of you are seeing one marital therapist. The therapist will help with damage control and guide you as a couple through the crisis precipitated by your confession.

However, if you confess to an affair, you must also be willing to give it up. Not to do so will negate your confession—you will go back to keeping future meetings or other contacts with your lover secret, and thus increase the distance between yourself and your spouse when you want to decrease it. If your husband suspects—and he will—keeping your lover will also escalate the crisis between you.

The decision to go into counseling together should be based on your desire to address the whole marriage, rather than just for the sake of a confession. If you think you can continue your affair but deal effectively with your marriage otherwise, in or out of therapy, you are deluding yourself about your desire to make your marriage work.

There is no other way. You must stop your affair if you are serious about better times or reconciliation with your husband.

WHEN TO KEEP YOUR MOUTH SHUT

If you are sure your husband has no inkling of what has been going on, your affair is truly over, and you aren't in therapy (or he won't go for couple counseling), but you want to put your energy back into the marriage, I don't recommend a confession. The results can be too devastating to your marriage and your husband.

If you are still troubled by an affair in the distant past, even a one- or two-night stand, and you would like to tell your husband about it because you truly love him—don't. Again, you may precipitate a crisis that is hard to contain.

If you are tempted to tell your husband about your affair because the guilt you bear is eating you up—don't, if he has no idea of your betrayal. A confession to make *yourself* feel better will only make *him* feel incredibly bad. You've made a mistake and you have to deal with the guilt by yourself, instead of shifting the problem to your husband. One way to do this is to revise the way you think about the affair. Instead of saying to yourself, *I am a bad person for having done this*, think of it as a mistake you made. Even basically good people make bad mistakes.

Finally, you have to judge the man you are married to. Some men are prone to violence, and to confess would be to provoke a dangerous attack.

Others are so fragile, so emotionally vulnerable—so lacking in self-esteem—that the devastation you wreak would be too costly to their delicate egos.

Others are of such an unforgiving nature, or are prone to so much anger, that the relationship would not stand a chance after a confession from you.

It is, therefore, important to think about what kind of man you are married to, and whether you are prepared to face the possible end of your marriage, when evaluating the risks of telling all.

It is also important to think more about what kind of a man your husband really is, what kind of marriage you have, and who your lover is when assessing just how much the other man means to you. You may think you love him, but do you really? Let's find out.

Chapter 12

※

IS IT TRUE LOVE, IS IT A
BETTER LOVE?

So you think you are in love with the other man. You are certainly not alone. Sooner or later, most unfaithful wives have that secretly happy, giddy, but troubling feeling.

Although you may not want to hear this, very often what you are experiencing is the illusion of love, not the genuine article.

How can you tell whether it is real love or just an unreasonable facsimile? By looking at some of the most common reasons why women who claim to be in love are making a mistake. Consider whether any or all of the following apply to you. Be honest with yourself.

MISTAKES WOMEN MAKE

1. *Subliminally, you may need to push yourself into an "in love" state in order to feel right about having sex with another man.* Psychologist Shirley Glass, writing in the *Journal of Sex Research* in August 1992, concluded from the responses of 155 females that contemporary women still regard love as the strongest (and, in many cases, the only) excuse for extramarital involvement. Seventy-seven percent of them consid-

ered it a justification for infidelity. Emotional intimacy, which women tend to translate into love, was rated second on the list of things that made an extramarital relationship morally acceptable. Least approval went to sexual reasons for adultery. This makes it quite clear that for an overwhelming majority of today's females, love makes adultery okay, but lust, or even just liking, by itself does not, so you may just *have* to feel in love when you are having an affair.

2. ***Sex makes you feel in love.*** It can work the other way around, as well. As explained in other parts of this book (see pages 41–43) female biological and social programming works to create emotional bonds with a partner once a sexual liaison is established. It may not be just the charm of the man in question. This tends to happen with any man you continue to have sex with, even if you didn't feel in love to begin with.

3. ***You confuse excitement with love.*** Your soaring spirits, the intrigue, the contrast of the affair with the predictable routines and less than heady obligations of marriage, may make you feel as if you have a new lease on life. The emotional uproar and feeling of being radiantly alive generated by an affair are so seductive, so gratifying, and, for some, so much like a throwback to their teenage years that they think, *This must be love.* Being on a high again may be fun, but it doesn't necessarily spell enduring love.

4. ***You mistake gratitude for love.*** Your lover makes you feel wanted, prettier, smarter, sexier, or more sure of yourself. Especially when this is in contrast to a husband who has neglected, belittled, or ignored you, it may make you think, without examining the relationship in depth, that the new man is someone to love simply because he makes you feel so good about yourself.

5. ***The prolonged romance makes you feel as if you are in love.*** In an affair, you never go beyond the highly romantic phase of a relationship. You are still in many ways continually courting each other, trying to please each other, complimenting each other, meeting in romantic, hidden circumstances, no matter how long the affair continues. This may make you feel that love exists, but it may also be merely the romantic trappings that are seducing you emotionally.

6. ***You never see him enough.*** Because your time together is limited, because you desire to be with him more but can't be, it creates a constant state of wanting that can be confused with love.

7. ***Uncertainty makes you feel it is love.*** You aren't sure he loves you or loves you enough; you don't know what is going to happen to

the two of you. The unsettling nature of the relationship may make you want to nail it down into something more committed. You need emotional security and stability, but you may mistake your longing for it for love.

8. ***Needing to win a competition makes you feel it is love.*** You know you are not his highest priority and it kills you, makes you want him with even greater intensity. The need for him to put you at the top of his list, before his wife, may drive you into feeling you must have this man. The heat of competition with a spouse can give rise to very intense, primitive emotions that may be mistaken for love.

9. ***You are idealizing your lover.*** Since, by its very nature, an affair is secret and sequestered, the relationship hasn't been tried out in real life. Since you have seen your lover only under very limited circumstances, your picture of him may be more perfect than he is in reality, creating a feeling of love for him.

You don't know how you and he would be together or how he would react by himself if there were, for example, money troubles, job reversals, if you had to be together when you're very tired or cranky. You have no idea how he would be with your friends or family. You don't know if you and he would have the same needs for closeness or space, or if sex would thrive or wither under conditions of continued intimacy and commitment.

Pay heed to this letter written by an adulterous wife: "Our affair (while both were still married) was idyllic. We both brought the best of ourselves to the brief time we had together. I viewed us as compatible because everything was so wonderful. After our splits took place, reality set in: kids, ex-spouses, extended families, work, alimony, soccer, religion, laundry, etc. We find now that we are hopelessly at odds over a number of things. . . . It ain't all it's cracked up to be."

10. ***You have a need to be rescued.*** Your marriage was basically on the rocks. You may have tried but couldn't get your husband to change. You may be married to an uncaring, insensitive man, or someone who isn't interested in sex anymore, or a workaholic, an alcoholic, or a druggie. You may have been afraid or financially unable to strike out on your own. You secretly longed for someone or something to get you out of your unfulfilling marriage. Then along came your lover, who seemed the opposite of whatever was wrong with your husband, and you started thinking of him as the answer to your prayers. Your need to be rescued may be behind feelings of love more than the man himself.

11. ***The triangle you find yourself in (you, your lover, your husband) has raised powerful love issues from the past.*** In any triangle you are reliving the Oedipal period in your childhood—the time around the age of five or six when children fall in love with the parent of the opposite sex. As a little girl you yearned for your father, had sexual feelings for him, feared reprisal for those feelings from your mother, and finally realized, if you developed normally, that you couldn't have the parental object of your strong libidinal desires.

These old, very strong yearnings and conflicts around the issue of forbidden love are unconsciously relived in your present-day triangle, perhaps giving it an intensity it wouldn't merit on its own.

12. ***You have the need to merge.*** You want to become one with another person and take falling head-over-heels in love as the route to this symbiotic union.

People who have a basic, primitive urge to merge generally don't have a clear idea of who they are as individuals. They take their identity from the other person. When love fails, as in faulty marriages, people who need to merge with a partner to feel whole are left floundering, unsure of who they are, and empty.

They may try to merge once again in an extramarital relationship by falling desperately in love, imagining the other person is so much like them, and obsessing about the lover.

WHAT IS TRUE LOVE?

Here is what real love, rather than the myth and illusion of it, is all about.

- True love takes a while to develop. It doesn't happen instantly. Immediate chemistry and attraction is one thing, true love another. Attraction can grow into real love, but only as the relationship is tested over time.

- True love is based on a knowledge of the other person that unfolds in a variety of circumstances.

- You love that person for his inner being as much as for his looks, wealth, power, or position in the world.

- True love is not based on complete idealization of the other person. It is founded on some knowledge and acceptance of bad points as well as wonderful ones, weaknesses as well as strengths.

- True love allows you to tolerate some ambivalent or even some passing hostile thoughts about the object of your affections. People who can fall in love but can't stay in love often turn off completely when something negative arises in the relationship.

- True love is a mutual thing. It isn't one person withholding, the other pursuing. It isn't one doing all the catering, the other all the receiving. It is based on a genuine desire to do your best to fulfill each other.

- True love is based on respect. You treat the other person with consideration and dignity and he does the same for you.

- True love is based on honesty and having the other's interests in mind as well as your own. You don't lead the other person on and mislead him or her just to hold on. You don't, for example, tell a partner to hang in there or wait until the kids are grown when you really have no intention of ever leaving home.

- In true love you don't use the other person—for example, to advance your career, to make a spouse jealous, to express hostility toward a mate, or for sexual pleasure alone.

- True love is lived in reality, not largely in fantasy. If you meet only once every few months, the relationship is mostly in your head. If it is conducted for the most part on the telephone, it is mostly in your head as well. If you constantly think romantically about someone no longer in your life and feel it's an alive love, you are living in a dream. Your thoughts may be lovely, but it ain't true love.

- True love doesn't exclude problems arising between you. Nor in true love do you believe, *If we love each other everything will automatically work out.* Problems have to be anticipated, recognized, dealt with, and resolved, and that takes work by both of you rather than expecting trouble to go away just because you feel love for one another.

- True love does not give us the ability to read each other's minds. *If he (or she) really loves me, he should know what I want without my having to tell him,* is how a lot of people feel. This is not the way love works. In true love, communication counts. It adds to love, it doesn't spoil it, to have to tell. In true love, you aren't afraid to speak up about your needs and desires, and you don't feel that something is wrong, that he doesn't love you, if your partner does not automatically know what is on your mind.

- In true love, two do not become one. You have individual differences, separate likes, desires, and interests. You respect each other's differences and make room for them in the relationship.
- In true love partners are able to reveal themselves—to tell the other person about fears, hopes, and doubts as well as positive things—without being afraid that confessions will be used against them.
- There isn't only one person in this world who is meant to be your true love. There are others with whom true love is possible.

Only you can determine how many of the factors above apply to your relationship with your lover (or your husband). If you don't know whether some of the characteristics of love are present in your affair, it may be because you really don't know the other man well enough, no matter how long the affair has gone on.

WHAT ARE HIS WIFE'S GRIPES?

Perhaps you already realize that this chapter is meant to make you look more realistically at your extramarital affair and your partner in it.

To further your evaluation of your lover along more realistic lines, there is one other pertinent question you should ask yourself: What are his wife's complaints (if she has any) about your lover? She has lived with him and there may be more truth to her gripes than he acknowledges.

One woman, after two years of feeling totally in love with the other man, was on the verge of a divorce from her husband as a result. At this point, she suddenly began to realize that the complaint of her lover's wife—that he was irresponsible with money—had a basis in fact. It was only when this woman began thinking about her lover more realistically, as she considered marriage to him, that she was able to pierce through the haze of romance to glimpse his real character and the problems that would affect her if she were hooked up to this man.

If you are seriously considering marrying the other man, or are placing your marriage in jeopardy because you love him, you also have to think about the reactions of your children, because they will affect your own sense of well-being and your future happiness. I have heard story after story of women who left their marriages for another man and alienated their children in the process. Many refused to live with the mother after the divorce, preferring to stay with the father even when he wasn't fighting for this right. Others hated the man who replaced their father and acted with great hostility toward him.

WHAT ARE YOUR PROBLEMS WITH YOUR MARRIAGE?

I urge you to reassess your marriage as well, when you ponder whether you really love the other man or if he loves you. This is an important thing to do, since so many extramarital affairs start because a woman feels something has gone wrong at home.

Bad Marriages, "Good" Affairs

Of course, there are marriages that are genuinely bad. You have a husband who abuses you either mentally or physically, or you have a husband who is an alcoholic or drug addict. There are husbands who don't regard wives as people with needs of their own. Everything has to be their way and they bully you into complying.

There are husbands who refuse to communicate with you no matter how hard you try, no matter how much you ask them to. There are husbands who are cold and never show any kind of affection even after you have told them a million times that you are withering without it.

There are husbands who refuse to have sex with you, and refuse to go into joint therapy to address problems that keep arising between you.

There are husbands who are bad fathers, abusive with your children. There are husbands with whom you are genuinely incompatible in a myriad of important basic ways.

In these kinds of marriages, a love affair is often a way for a wife to gain more assurance about her power to attract again. Her lover allows her to see her own positive qualities, which she may have forgotten. The lover, if he is supportive, may give her the confidence she needs to end a marriage that is already emotionally over, or to at least have something that is more loving or nourishing in her life.

But in many other cases, a wife may blame her husband for her unhappiness when, in reality, she may have had more to do with what went amiss in the marriage than she is aware of. Here are some questions to ask yourself to find out if you had a hand in your own fate.

How Wives Unconsciously Create Their Own Unhappiness

Is my relationship with my husband an emotional repeat of a relationship from the past? It is very, very, very common, as marriage therapists know, for husbands and wives to re-create within a marriage some drama from childhood. For example, you may have grown up with a father who was distant and uncommunicative or cold and undemonstrative, and this left you, as a child, frustrated and yearning for his attention and demonstrations of love. Today, as a wife, you may find yourself having those same troubling feelings of unfulfillment with your husband—he doesn't pay enough attention to you, he is cold or withdrawn. Whatever they were, you accuse your husband of the same lacks that you originally felt with your father (or your mother).

You either project your parent's traits onto your husband and see him in a way that may not be entirely based in reality, or you actually may have unconsciously chosen him originally because you would be able to repeat with him the kind of relationship you were used to. Either way, you had a lot more to do with the unhappiness you feel in your marriage than you are aware of. And you stand a great chance of repeating this same pattern with another man, no matter how different he appears to be originally.

You may also get some insight into your husband's behavior by wondering if he is projecting traits from one of his parents onto you and feeling angry, hostile, or distant as a result. For example, a man with a very domineering, critical, or suffocating mother (or father) may begin to see his wife in the same light. If she tries to bring up the least little thing she thinks is wrong, he has the same old feelings he originally had with his difficult-to-please parent. Eventually these old feelings completely color his view of his spouse.

Am I able to tolerate some bad feelings along with good ones? The minute some ambivalent or negative emotions crop up in the marriage, many people feel that the partner is really terrible, love has disappeared, and the marriage is going downhill. This isn't true at all. There are always negative feelings, even hate, that go along with positive feelings in any ongoing relationship. The ability to tolerate good along with bad, to sometimes see things or someone else as gray rather than all black or all white, is considered by mental health professionals to be a prerequisite for achieving long-lasting love.

If you are one of the people who divide others into all-good and all-bad camps, consider the possibility that you may have turned your lover into the bearer of all positive qualities and made your husband in your mind the repository of all bad ones. Neither, of course, is altogether true.

Why do I feel bored or restless in my marriage? You may be seeking the excitement of an affair for the wrong reason. Dr. Otto Kernberg, an eminent psychiatrist, is one of the many mental health professionals who feel that boredom is often a cover-up for anger or hostility in marriage. When you feel mad at your husband and suppress it, refusing to express or deal with it, it gets turned into the feeling that everything is muted—and thus boring—between you.

Is there something that really annoys you but that you haven't raised or resolved with your husband? Recognizing and dealing openly with your anger will do more to remove this kind of boredom in your domestic life than turning to another man for thrills.

Of course, there are couples who do lead a life that is too centered on responsibilities, leaving little or no time for leisure or enjoyment, but boredom of this type can be conquered by paying more attention to a joint social life and creating more opportunities for playtime with your husband, rather than searching for excitement with someone else. You can't wait for your husband to change your patterns. You have to take initiative for zipping things up by becoming more active—for example, getting baby-sitters, buying tickets to shows, making reservations at romantic restaurants, trying a new sport or hobby together.

Am I playing a part in keeping the unhappiness in my marriage going? (See pages 91–93.) Although you blame your misery entirely on your husband, very often you, the dissatisfied wife, have been a conspirator in maintaining it. You work hard, unconsciously, to keep your unhappiness going.

An example is Helen, who complains that she is overburdened. She

181

has a full-time job and takes care of the kids and household chores without much help from her husband. Periodically, her anger boils over, and she accuses her husband of not doing his share.

Although it is true that these days her husband, Gene, only occasionally tries to help with the kids and the housework, this wasn't always the case. Originally, he tried a lot. But every time he did something, like vacuum the rugs, remove the dishes from the dishwasher, bathe the kids, or take them to the playground, he found himself attacked by Helen. She complained that he left some lint on the rug, didn't put the dishes in the right place, didn't wash the kids' hair right, brought the children home too late, too early, or too dirty. Nothing he did was ever done well enough in Helen's eyes.

Criticisms of his efforts made Gene feel stupid and angry. It has finally gotten to the point where Gene is reluctant to even try to meet Helen's high standards.

What Helen doesn't realize is the part she plays in discouraging her husband from helping out at home.

Of course there is a hidden reason for this. Helen likes to be in control and have everything her way. She really wants to run the show and actually prefers not getting help to having things done in some other manner.

Helen helped create the situation that makes her feel so unhappy with her husband, whom she calls lazy and selfish. She blames her unhappiness all on him, and recently found comfort in the arms of another man where all her obligations and sense of being overburdened could be forgotten.

It would be wise to try to think about what you may have done or are doing to perpetuate your dissatisfactions as a wife. Do you act helpless with your husband and invite his treatment of you as a child? Do you keep yearning for him to be romantic with you but discourage his kisses or hugs when you are busy, or dress only in the sloppiest clothes at home instead of creating a situation for romance to flower—wearing pretty, seductive clothes, creating occasional candlelit dinners served in the dining room instead of microwave dishes in the kitchen, planning nights out where you go dancing cheek to cheek instead of always sitting in a movie house watching shoot-outs on your evenings out?

You sometimes have to change your ways, as well as have your husband change his, to make things better between you.

Am I perpetuating in my own marriage a pattern from my parents' relationship? Children who have grown up in homes where adultery took place are sometimes compelled, unconsciously, to do the same thing in their own marriages. It pays to question whether any infidelity on your parents' part may be playing into the adultery you are now committing in your own marriage.

Women who grew up in homes where the mother was the victim of a husband's brutality or alcoholism may repeat this pattern in their own marriages as well.

Am I re-creating a triangle from the past? Were your mother and father always vying for your love? Did you grow up in the center of a triangle that you are now repeating by having two people—your lover and your husband—as rivals for your affections? Is this really the lure of your lover versus your husband?

Am I comparing my marriage to the "in love" state I feel for my lover? Of course, the marriage looks worse—less fulfilling, less intoxicating by comparison—but it may be a good enough marriage when judged from other angles. Please think about this.

Now it is time to ask yourself some questions about your own personality. Who you are psychologically may play more of a part in your marital unhappiness than you realize.

Do I have an unrealistic expectation of perpetual romance? There are plenty of romance junkies in our culture, created by magazines, books, and movies portraying love as romance—being swept away, seeing a person across a crowded room, feeling overpowering longing or passion that never wavers or changes.

There is little in our culture that more accurately portrays enduring love with its everyday chores, its ups and downs, its disillusionments as well as its pleasures. Romance junkies feel something is wrong with their marriages once the period of high romance ends—even though there really isn't anything terribly wrong. There are many wives who enter love affairs for this reason—they feel something is missing in the marriage and think they have found love again when another man starts romancing them. Your need of perpetual romance and your inability to accept the inevitable simmering down in a long-term relationship may make you feel more unhappy in your marriage than the situation warrants.

Am I lacking in self-esteem? An inordinately large number of women find lovers in order to validate their own worth and desirability. They may blame a spouse for making them feel bad about themselves, and a husband may have contributed his part; however, a person with true self-regard would maintain a positive image of herself no matter what happened in her marriage. True self-esteem comes from within rather than from another person.

If your ego is so depleted that you require continual shoring up, you may need a more-than-average amount of praise and demonstrations of love. If you don't get it from your husband, you feel unhappy with him.

He may actually admire you but fail to voice it, assuming you know how he feels. He fails to recognize that he is dealing with someone whose self-doubts make her need a lot of reassurance.

If your self-esteem is very, very poor, no matter what your husband gives, it isn't enough. You have a need to see yourself validated in the eyes of new men to feel desirable.

It pays to mull this over and ask yourself: How much of a part does poor self-esteem play in my love life?

Do I have an unconscious fear of too much intimacy? Do you sometimes feel crowded by your husband? Do you wish he wouldn't keep asking you questions about how you are feeling or reacting to something, or that he would stop bringing up emotional issues that make you want to escape? Although there are more husbands than wives who try to dodge intimacy, there are also women who need less closeness than their husbands. They may feel suffocated by their mates at times.

Experts recognize that affairs always create a certain amount of distance between spouses and, for some people, that is actually the purpose of the affair—to create more space in the marriage in order to feel more comfortable. Could this be operating in your life?

Did I marry my husband for security, his authority, or his power and now expect him to have qualities he never had? Many women select a husband because he has a good career, comes from a higher social class, or will give them a lifestyle they want, without wondering if he will be, for example, tender, affectionate, communicative, sensitive. When he turns out not to have qualities that they begin to hanker after once their original goals are achieved, they blame him—even though he is exactly as he was when they courted and married. They feel their unhappiness is his fault when, indeed, it isn't. He was what they chose and needed most at that time, and may still need.

A calmer, more intellectual (rather than emotional) reevaluation of what you have with your lover, versus what you have with your husband, could keep you from acting impetuously or destructively. Your heart has been working overtime. Now it's time to let your head take over. You may come to different conclusions about your love affair, or your husband, as a result of some honest introspection.

But even if you don't, you will not suffer from thinking along the lines I have suggested. You will be more sure that your conclusion that you really do have a bad marriage, and that you deserve better as a result, is based on reality rather than a distorted view of the relationship.

You may now be more absolutely convinced that, despite your best efforts, your husband really is abusive, does put you down constantly, really is emotionally or sexually withholding, is a hopeless alcoholic or drug addict, or simply does not have qualities or values that jibe with yours or give you satisfaction in any way.

If this is the case, being found out may be exactly what you want. Unconsciously you needed to be found out in order to end the marriage.

However, some women discover where their heart really lies only after disaster strikes and the affair is discovered. Even if this happens, there are ways to save the situation if it's your marriage you value most and want to preserve.

Chapter 13

❈

FACING THE MUSIC

The worst has happened! Your husband knows all, either because you have told him or he has found out in some other way.

If your affair was uncovered because he found a clue, it is quite possible that this wasn't an accident. Experts agree that clues left around are generally a signal that you wanted him to know. In some cases, wives simply want to end a marriage and choose this way to do it. More often, careless clues are actually a hopeful sign for the marriage. Most wives who drop clues want to send a message to their husbands that some need wasn't being met in the marriage, so they went elsewhere to fulfill it. Women like this are actually trying to rescue their marriages.

Perhaps it wasn't a clue. Maybe he confronted you with his growing suspicions and you confessed. Women are inclined to open up when they are directly asked, while men, as a group, have a tendency to continue denying that they are cheating even when confronted with hard evidence.

Of course, it is possible that someone else told him.

Whichever way it happened, you now have to face the music.

What to Do at First

Dealing with His Reactions

Your spouse is going to be wildly angry. He is going to feel horribly betrayed. He is going to suffer intense pain.

Most likely this will make you very guilty. You are also going to feel afraid. Your life is falling apart.

His outrage and wrathful indignation are justified, and in your heart you know it. So the best thing you can do for him and yourself, during this tumultuous, tortuous first stage after disclosure, is to allow him to let out whatever he is feeling.

There will be a strong tendency on your part to defend yourself and counter his attacks. You may blame your husband for the whole thing: It was his lacks—whatever you thought was wrong in your marriage— that led you to do it. You wouldn't have done it otherwise.

Thus, with shouts and maybe tears you are apt to end up blaming each other. (Although it is not likely to happen at this stage, if you get through this and go on to the healing phase, you will both be able to take some blame rather than dumping the problem entirely on each other.)

However, whatever you need to say is allowed in this rather out-of-control emotional moment. Expect some mean verbal assaults. The purpose now is simply to vent. Because this is so important for your future together, I urge you to try not to squelch your husband or shut him up in any way. Listen to him. Don't shout him down with your counter-accusations. Don't run out of the room screaming, "I'm not going to take any more of this!" If you let him air his emotions, it may allow him to go on to the reconstructive part of the postaffair relationship. This should be your goal if you want to preserve your marriage.

Ranting and raving may continue for several days or even a couple of weeks, but once your husband has discharged his initial shock and anger, the venting should permit him to calm down enough to perhaps be able to look at things from different and more long-term perspectives. He then may be able to ponder a little more realistically what would happen if your marriage ended. Financial considerations and the fate of his children may now enter his mind. He may be more ready to really listen to you than he was initially.

Get an Immediate Plan Going

The single most important thing you have to establish following the first outcries are your mutual plans for the immediate future. Do you both want the marriage to continue or don't you? Your husband may be threatening divorce in the heat of the moment. But he may feel differently in a little while. The same may be true for you. No matter how each of you feels about the need for an instant separation, I urge you not to take any hasty action. You *both* need time to explore what happened and why, before you can reach a somewhat sane conclusion about the future.

Even if your husband is screaming "Divorce!," if you want at least a shot at preserving the marriage, try to get him to agree to one of two things. An immediate visit to a marriage therapist would be the best course of action. You will then have the help of a trained third party to deal with the crisis and sort things out. Men are generally more resistant to therapy than women, so, if he adamantly refuses to do this, then try to get him to agree to at least spend time together with you over the coming weeks, discussing everything connected to the affair and what went on in your marriage that may have led up to it.

You need to get a joint therapeutic program into action. It is preferable to do it with professional help, but if you pursue the following outline it is also possible without it.

Tell Him You Are Sorry

When you see how much anguish you have caused your husband, you probably will be sorry. Even if you feel justified in having your affair, it is helpful to let him know that you are in pain, too, that it hurts you to see how much you have hurt him.

If You Still Care For Him, Tell Him So

No matter how you feel about the other man, if there is still love in your heart for your husband let him know it. Some contrition for what you are putting him through and signs of your caring for him will help set the stage for what follows.

Next Steps

If he agrees to talk before doing anything definitive, or if he has told you he wants to save the marriage, here is what you two must then do.

Make an Agreement to Cooperate, at Least Temporarily

Both of you have to work at this to have it produce results. A unified approach is important right now even if your husband seems tilted toward breaking up because of your affair.

One way to persuade him to adopt such an approach is to tell him that it would be helpful to work together at least for a little while, to make sure you are both doing what you want to and what, in the long run, is best for the family. Explain to him that this includes your children, who undoubtedly are aware of and are upset by what is going on between the two of you, even though they may not be talking about it.

If you can agree to cooperate, during a series of talks, you can then give your children the following crucial message as a mother and father team. Facing them together, tell them: "Mommy and Daddy are having some problems right now, but we are trying to work them out." Do not mention the affair specifically. The important thing is to reassure them: "We both love you and are trying to do what is best for the whole family." I can't stress enough how important it is to impart this to your kids, preferably as a cooperating team.

Set Aside at Least Two One-Hour Sessions a Week for Your Discussions

You must both agree that this time is inviolable and that neither is to make excuses not to be there or to cut the talk short. There should be complete privacy. Turn on the answering machine and agree not to take phone calls until you are through. Or take the phone off the hook. Pick a time of day when you aren't tired—don't select an hour close to bedtime.

A trick that might get things off to a good start: At least for your initial talks, when emotions are running high and are apt to break out in an uncontrollable way, choose a quiet but public place for your discussion. Find a location where you won't have to talk loudly to speak or strain to hear one another, and where there is plenty of space between you and others so you won't have to worry about being overheard. The presence of strangers reduces the chances of a shouting match or that either of you will go out of control.

However, if things do start to get out of hand, adjourn the discussion and agree to meet again on another day.

Learn the Basics of Good Communication

These communication skills will help you both in every stage after an affair—in the venting-of-emotions phase, in this second stage when you will be discussing the affair and what led up to it, and, if you decide to go on together, in the final phase when you will be a committed couple again, trying to heal the blow to your marriage. Good communication habits will also stand you in good stead for the rest of your life together.

Use Language That Defuses

Agree together that putdowns, insults, threats, and sarcastic remarks are out of bounds. The best way to avoid inflammatory statements and to say what is on your mind is to use only sentences that begin with "I." The "I" language is part of effective communication. For example, "I felt unloved, or that you didn't care about me." "I need some romancing before I can feel really sexy." If you use sentences beginning with "you," as most people do, you end up with an accusation that invokes a defensive response; for example, "You are cold and unfeeling," "You only care about yourself." By using the "I" language, however, you state your needs without attacking the other person's ego. This allows you to be heard.

Agree to Be Honest

Problems don't get solved unless you are completely open with one another. Also, the loss of trust is a major issue when a spouse has had an affair. Honesty is the first step in restoring trust and is part of the better communication skills that increase intimacy between partners—intimacy that has been diminished during the affair.

Take Turns Listening

In order to be heard, really heard, you both have to decide that you will not cut each other off. Without this basic agreement you are apt to have a shouting match. If you make a deal to take turns—with one talking while the other only listens—you both get your day in court.

Listen in a Nonjudgmental, Undefensive Way

Listening with an open mind, even when what is said implies criticism of you, is at the heart of a constructive dialogue between you and your husband. You both have to resist the feeling that you always have to defend yourself.

Discuss Discomfort

If you bring up the fact that you both are going to feel uncomfortable during some of your discussions ahead of time, it will help control the impulse in either of you to flee or even lash out when the anxiety level rises.

Talk About Details

People who discover that a mate has been unfaithful often obsess about the affair. Your husband is going to want to know about the other man—who he is, how you met, how long the affair has been going on, how often and where you meet. You have to be truthful and tell him what he wants to know, even though it is embarrassing or painful for you. He will question you about the extent of your involvement. Give honest answers to questions: "Were you emotionally involved?" "Yes."

"Do you love him?" "I am confused, I don't know," or "No, I don't love him," or "I thought I did, but now I don't."

Be Prepared to Discuss Intimate Matters

Some men will want to know if your lover is handsome or rich. Most want to know some of the intimate facts about your lovemaking. Is he a better lover? Does he have a bigger penis? How often can he make love in one session? It is important to empathize with what your husband is feeling that prompts these kinds of questions. It isn't only curiosity, it is his feeling of sexual rejection. He is nursing the possibility that he is a lesser lover than the other man. Basically he is feeling sexually insecure. He is also, by his questions, revealing the competitiveness between men that extends to sexual matters.

If your husband was as good a lover or even a better one (which may be the case, since sex per se is not the goal of most women's affairs), you can honestly reassure him of this fact. But, since this is such a sore spot for men, you might cushion things a bit (but always within the bounds of truth) if sex really was better with your lover. For example, "Sex with you was good but we always did it when we were tired."

If something needs to be fixed in your love life with your husband, now is the time to let him know it in as kind a way as possible, using the "I" language. For example, if you lacked a buildup that was necessary to good sex for you, explain it: "I need to talk and be held before plunging into intercourse." Let him know that he, instead of your lover, could satisfy you in this way.

Talk About What You Got Out of the Affair

It is important not to limit your mutual discussions just to details about the lovemaking or how the romance was conducted. For most women, it is emotional issues that keep them involved with someone else, no matter how wonderful the lovemaking is. Tell your husband about the sense of intimacy, communication, the feeling of being listened to or understood, the increase in self-esteem, the feeling of being important—whatever it is that you feel your lover gives you. This will help you clarify for yourself what unmet needs were satisfied in the affair, and give your husband a clue to what went wrong between you and how he may have contributed to the current crisis.

Discuss Whether You Plan to See Your Lover

Your husband may simply ask you about your intentions, or he may forbid you to see your lover. If you have a desire to continue your marriage, you have to be honest about your plans. You can't go on to the next stage of putting the marriage back together again if you expect to continue your affair. A sore that is still open is not ready to heal. However, most women, once the secret is out, feel they are forced to choose between the lover and the marriage—a correct assumption. And, since surveys indicate that the majority of wives in affairs don't want to end their marriages, more often than not they opt for the marriage. If you are going to give up your lover or already have, you should tell your husband this as soon as possible. Let him know that you are ready, willing, and able to recommit to the marriage and do whatever work is necessary to recover from the crisis your affair has precipitated, and that you hope he will do the same.

Accept Responsibility for Your Actions

No matter what your husband did that led up to it, it was your decision to take a lover. Let him know that you feel accountable for your choice, and that (if you feel this now) it was a mistake. A tip to deal with self-recriminations and guilt: Enlarge your thinking. Infidelity may have been a mistake in judgment, but a mistake does not make you an evil person.

Now that you have heard some dos, here are some don'ts to keep in mind:

Don't Bring Relatives or Friends into It

It will only complicate matters and make things worse to have relatives and friends ganging up on either one of you, taking sides, telling him or telling you what to do. For the moment the best thing you can do is to deal with each other in the ways I am outlining. If you want to bring anyone else in, let it be a trained therapist who won't take sides.

Don't Try to Make Your Kids Your Allies

It is common for the aggrieved party to try to get the kids—especially teenage ones—to side with him or her against the parent who has been unfaithful. Sometimes, however, a wife who feels that her husband has driven her to it will try to make the kids understand that it was his fault, so they should side with her. Or she tries to use the children to beg their father to stay. Take it from the experts—to put your children in such a position is to do them harm that will linger for years after. So agree ahead of time not to try to make your children take sides or use them in any other way, no matter what ultimately happens between the two of you.

Don't Use Your Lover as Your Confidant

Even if you have stopped the physical part of the affair, you may still want to use your lover as your sounding board. You can't do this. It prolongs emotional closeness and bonds between you, draws intimacy away from you and your husband, and will be interpreted by your spouse, if he finds out, as your continuing the affair. Sorry, you have to cut off contact if you want to put your marriage back together.

Don't Be Surprised by Sexual Advances

Your husband may want to have sex with you right after learning about your affair. It is a strange phenomenon but it happens frequently enough. Some men may get excited thinking about you as a sex object again. Others get a perverse thrill from imagining you with another man. Still others use the sex to express their hostility or even ownership of your body. Do not expect tender sex at this time—it is likely to be more as if he is taking you than making love. Also, don't make the mistake of thinking that this is a sign of reconciliation—it may not be.

Don't Offer to Sleep in Another Room

Resist your husband's offer or desire to do the same. Even if you both expressly state that you will keep way over on opposite sides of the bed, it is better to sleep in the same room than to disappear into different parts of the house. Separate rooms emphasize a sense of estrangement. The same bed makes you seem like something of a couple still.

Don't Allow Violence

Your husband may want to beat you up. No matter how wrong you feel about your actions, you cannot allow yourself to be his punching bag. At any time, if he starts becoming violent, get out of the house and harm's way until he has calmed down. Take seriously any threats to kill you and/or your lover if you know your husband to be prone to violence, or if he owns a gun or other dangerous weapon.

Don't Become a Dishrag or Slave to Your Husband

You may have made a mistake, but that doesn't mean that you have to lose your dignity. The idea, as you will discover in the coming sections, is to have your needs (and his) respected and fulfilled in your relationship, not to give up all your needs in favor of his in order to get back into his good graces.

Don't Expect That You Will Stop Thinking About Your Lover

Even if you give him up, you are going to have memories, yearnings, and sadness to deal with. At the same time that you are putting your efforts into trying to fix things up with your husband, you are going to be grieving about your lost partner. You don't have to feel guilty about this or think that you are crazy for missing your lover while you are also trying to reconcile with your husband. Mourning for an important relationship, even an illicit one, is normal. It is something you have to go through. Memories will lessen and grief will gradually disappear with time. Your lover will recede into the past even faster if you begin to see how much better things can be with your husband.

Don't Think Your Marriage Is Saved

If, at this stage, after learning details of your affair, your husband agrees that he wants to stay married to you, the tendency is to breathe a sigh of relief and assume the crisis is over. It isn't. There are marriages that endure but are at least partially, if not completely, dead.

This letter portrays a marriage that goes on but has not been put back together again: "I am twenty-two years old and very unhappy. I have been married to a great man for a little over a year. Recently I had an affair with an older married man. My husband and my lover's wife found out and I confessed everything to both of them. My husband says he still loves me and wants us to be together, but it's been some time since this happened and he still won't talk much to me, and I really can't have sex with him. I want to, but it is so hard when you know you've hurt him so bad. I feel so alone. I try to always make him happy but it seems that nothing is working. I do love him very much. It's crazy because I still think about the other man, who seemed to always care when my husband and I were having problems. I hate to say it, but I sometimes even miss him. I am confused."

This husband and wife haven't really dealt openly or fully with the affair or their marital interactions.

For a healthy, fulfilling marriage in the future, you both have to talk very openly about the affair, your feelings, and your marriage. You must try to uncover and air problems that exist, resolve them, and heal the marriage in the ways I outline.

Before you go on with the healing program, however, I want you, and your husband, to take a little time to answer the following questions to see if you are really ready and able to proceed.

Can You Do the Work That's Necessary to Reconstruct Your Marriage?

1. *Do you both feel there are things you share that bond you as people, apart from a sense of obligation to each other or the fact that*

financially or emotionally it is easier to stay together than live alone? You have to do more than go through the motions of a marriage. There has to be something you feel you share, whether it is a spiritual belief, a sense of humor, your family life together, a perspective on the world, intellectual interests—something that still makes you attractive to one another in some way.

2. *Are you both really committed to the relationship?* If one of you really isn't, or you both aren't, if you both have secret affairs and expect to continue them, if you have a pattern of leading separate lives and expect to continue it, there is no point in trying to make something that doesn't exist out of your relationship.

3. *Are you both willing to change?* There are some alterations that will have to occur in thinking and behavior, and you each should be prepared to do your part.

4. *Are you both willing to look at things from the other's perspective as well as your own?* You can't be concerned only about what you want and how you are feeling. You both need to be able to put yourselves in each other's shoes. In addition to understanding the other's viewpoint intellectually, you have to be ready to try to feel for your spouse—to have empathy for what the other needs and is going through.

5. *Are you both able to admit that you are sometimes wrong?* People who insist they are always right are incapable of compromising and negotiating—two things necessary to reshape themselves and the relationship.

6. *Are you both willing to look inside yourselves?* There are psychological attitudes that may affect your interactions. They need to be uncovered by honest introspection.

7. *Are you willing to talk about painful issues?* They are going to come up.

8. *Are you willing to reveal yourselves?* It will take the willingness and courage to talk about your hopes, dreams, fears, expectations, disappointments, vulnerabilities.

9. *Are you both willing to consider that infidelity may be the result of a mutual problem?* Marriage therapists believe this to be most often the case when infidelity occurs, even if it is not readily apparent. If you can both enlarge your view to see an affair as a symptom of a problem that exists in the relationship, and that perhaps each of you is to blame in certain respects, it improves your chances of a successful reconciliation.

10. ***Do you both have enough control over your impulses to be able to pass up immediate gratification in favor of long-term goals?*** If you can't help giving in to your urges, you will be embroiled in another affair when temptation strikes. Or he will be attacking you or avoiding you because, for the moment, it makes him feel better. Your relationship is not going to get fixed overnight and you both must be able to endure some discomfort along the way in order to enjoy the gratification at the end of the road.

11. ***Are you willing to put time and effort into working at your relationship?*** Change does not occur through magic or just because you want to change. It takes hard, sometimes painful labor, over a long period, and you both have to be willing to give top priority to working at changes no matter how busy you are with other matters.

Chapter 14

❀

GOING FORWARD AS A
COUPLE: HEALING

If you both feel you have what it takes to heal your marriage, or are at least willing to try to learn to have it, you should now be willing to make a pact.

Repeat This Goal to Each Other:

"We want to recommit to each other and put our marriage together again in a better way. We will do whatever we have to, individually and together, to reach this goal."

It is important that both of you hear each other formally commit to this.

Banish Extramarital Activities

If you haven't before, or if you have been ambivalent about it or tempted to return to your lover, or if you have slipped and started seeing him again, now is the time to finally end it. You can't have a happy affair and a really fulfilling marriage at the same time. Seeing another man may have made you feel better, but it never solved any problems that existed with your husband—it merely bypassed them. Let your husband know that you will never take that path again. If you feel tempted to start a relationship with another man, you will talk it over with him rather than act on your attraction. If there are problems, you will confront him with them rather than find the solution with another partner.

For his part, your husband may have been, or is, or will be sorely tempted to have an affair of his own to pay you back. Perhaps he has already gone and done it. He must also pledge not to give in to temptation in the future; if he feels the desire for an extramarital relationship, he must promise that he, too, will talk about it with you rather than give in to an attraction.

Forbid Ongoing Clobbering

You should expect some regressions and an occasional outburst, but you must agree, through discussion, that your husband cannot keep lashing out with unchecked fury and hateful accusations. You both should understand that there is one simple reason for this. Your goal is to put the crisis behind you and heal your marriage. Continual clobbering will seriously interfere with the process.

Create Some Harmless Ways of Venting Anger

For example, when one of you is overwhelmed by hostility and the desire to attack, that person should take a tennis racket and bang it hard on a mattress. Keep doing it until the fury abates. Or wrap a towel around your fist and smash it against the wall in your bathroom until your anger is spent. Dream up your own measures to cool down anger and, as a result, help you deal with your spouse in a less hostile way.

Reverse Negative Thinking

Both of you may feel that your extramarital liaison was a disaster for the marriage. However, you can change your gloomy attitude. Think, instead, that your affair served a positive purpose. It provided you and your husband with the opportunity to make your marriage better, to correct whatever was wrong before, to deal openly and constructively with problems that had not been aired previously.

Through reframing your thoughts, you can also change the characterization of yourself as a lying cheat. Instead, a more positive way of looking at your actions is that you were a woman in search of a solution to a problem you had—even if the solution you chose was a bad and hurtful one.

Finally, instead of continuing to think of yourselves as victims of a horrible situation, you and your husband can think of yourselves as people who are taking charge and doing something about it.

Commit Yourselves to Change

In order to get your marriage back on track, you both are going to have to change. This will involve some conscious or unconscious terror. Change represents the unknown and people are afraid of it. It is often easier to hold on to old patterns simply because they are familiar, even if they are creating unhappiness, than to try out new ways of thinking or behaving.

When you commit yourselves to change, you are also opening yourselves up to the discomfort you both will be experiencing as a result. However, if your relationship is to survive and improve after your affair, you must be willing to weather this.

Talk to Each Other More Effectively

This means giving up old habits that didn't serve you well—for example, patterns of avoidance: never bringing up issues that are bothering you, withdrawing or giving your mate the silent treatment when you are hurt or angry, assuming your partner can read your mind.

An example: Betty started an affair after feeling angry at her husband for a long time. She claimed he didn't understand her or what she was feeling most of the time. Betty thought her husband, Stan, should know what was on her mind without her having to tell him. For her, if he didn't know automatically, it meant he didn't love her. Betty had to learn to explain openly to Stan what she was thinking and wanting. Stan had to learn to ask Betty what she was feeling. These changes apply in reverse as well, with Betty asking Stan what he was feeling and Stan telling his wife what was on his mind.

Patterns based on silence about issues between husbands and wives always preserve the status quo in a relationship. If you don't confront problems and try to solve them, they don't go away. They just go underground and things remain the same.

Another common pattern of ineffective communication is repetitive criticisms or whining and complaining that have become so familiar they are automatically tuned out by your partner. Although you are openly complaining, you aren't being heard because of the way you do it.

You have to learn to talk to each other not with whines or through harping but openly and clearly. Not just about the infidelity itself but about your entire relationship and the problems in it. Affairs don't occur in a vacuum.

Continue Your Agreed-Upon Schedule of Talks

It is important that at least twice a week you still get together with the attitude that this is a sacred commitment of time. During this period of greater cooperation, I would add some talks in a setting that has good memories for you as a couple—for example, a place where you had a romantic picnic, or a beach where you once made love.

Observe These Rules

Write down the following and look at it before each of your discussions: "We agree during the time of our talks that we will not argue, humiliate, judge or blame each other. Things we learn here will not be used now or later to attack or harm one another."

Get Rid of Anger Before Discussions

If either of you finds a mood of anger gathering beforehand, use the techniques you have decided upon previously to disperse your wrath. For example, go into a room by yourself and shout out the most hateful things you can think of. Or whack a pillow with your fist. However you do it, make sure you release your hostility so you can act reasonably together.

Be Specific About the Problems in Your Marriage

It isn't good enough to make general statements like "I feel unhappy." You have to pin it down more. Why do you feel unhappy?

If you discover you are having trouble opening up face-to-face with one another, try writing down your thoughts individually and then exchanging papers. Some couples have found telephone calls helpful. You can talk directly by phone but do not have to look each other in the eye. Written or phone conversations can break the ice enough to lead into one-on-one talks.

Whichever way you do it, you have to tell each other what you think is wrong between you. What you told your husband you got out of your affair can be a springboard. If you felt your lover made you feel important, examine together what may have made you feel unimportant. Was your husband ignoring you, taking you for granted, or putting you down? Or does he think you feel hurt and neglected anytime he wants to do something by himself?

Does he spend too much time at work? Do you spend all your free time with the kids? Have you stopped doing fun things together? Is there a lack of leisure activities in your married life? Have you forgotten about romantic gestures over time?

Be Explicit About What Could Make Things Better

Your individual complaints have to be followed by positive suggestions. You have to be clear about what each of you wants from the other in order to improve your marriage. Think it over before you get together to talk about it.

It can be helpful to take turns telling each other about your idea of a perfect evening after work together.

Here is an example of the way this can work to clarify things between you:

Nell was annoyed and hurt that every night, when Bill came home from work, he never talked to her. He just ate his dinner, played with the kids before their bedtime, then turned his attention to the television set. When Nell imagined out loud how she would prefer it, she thought of Bill coming home, giving her a hug and kiss, asking her how her day had been, and, after the kids had been tucked into bed, talking to her sometimes rather than planting himself in front of the tube.

Bill understood for the first time how slighted Nell had felt by his behavior, how unimportant to him she had felt. He began to see that when Nell revealed how her lover had made her feel noticed and important by his compliments, attention, and conversations with her, it was in reaction to his own inattention. He was angry about it, but he saw more clearly why she had turned to another man.

Bill really loved Nell and now he became determined to show her how much. He began to make sure that each night when he came home he gave Nell the big kiss and hug she yearned for. He talked with her at night about his day, her day, how each of them was feeling. He did this no matter how tired he was. When he felt just too exhausted from some trouble at work, he told her about it.

By telling your partner exactly what you want, you give your spouse the chance to try to meet your needs.

Make Sure You Have Understood

When one is finished talking, the other should ask questions if something needs to be cleared up.

Before ending your discussions you should repeat back to each other your understanding of what has been said. If you have been misunderstood, clarify the issue before you adjourn.

Unearth Hidden Expectations

Frequently, behind the trouble a couple is having there are expectations that the other partner is unaware of. Let me give you an example:

When Arthur married Beverly he expected her to be the same kind of wife his mother had been to his Dad. His mother had been a traditional housewife. She stayed home, catered to her husband, took care of all the housework herself, and had home-cooked meals on the table every night of the week.

Beverly, unlike Arthur's mother, was a working wife. She had a demanding job selling advertising space for a local newspaper.

Because she worked, Beverly expected Arthur to pitch in at home. He did, but reluctantly. Most things ended up being done by Beverly. Because the housework was done less often and less thoroughly than had been the case in his mother's meticulous home, Arthur was dissatisfied.

As a result, he was always criticizing Beverly. She was sloppy, careless—a slob.

When meals weren't ready he became petulant and distant with his wife.

Beverly felt constantly attacked by her husband, and unappreciated. She thought he expected too much from her. When she met a man at work who complimented her instead of criticizing, who made her feel bright and capable instead of bungling and bad, she had an affair with him. It was such a relief from the negative things that were being thrown at her at home. It was only after the affair came out into the open, and she and Arthur started therapy to heal their marriage, that Beverly got some idea of what was behind her husband's critical attitude. She simply had not acted as he expected her to, based on his mother's model.

When his hidden expectations came to light, Arthur was able to see that what he wanted from his busy working wife was unreasonable and based on an image from the past. He stopped criticizing Beverly, whom he loved; he pitched in more willingly, and he and Beverly now live a much more harmonious and contented life together. She has no further need of another man to make her feel appreciated.

Sometimes the hidden expectations that mar happiness are expectations that have changed during a marriage. Originally, for example, Susan chose Joe because he was a good provider, a steady, hardworking man she could count on, a man who would be a good father to her children.

All was well in her life, centered on the home, until the children entered school and Susan went back to work. She worked her way up to a management position in a corporation. Her professional success was exciting, her own feeling about herself expanded, and now Joe seemed very boring to Susan. He was still the same reliable, quiet man she had married, but she wanted him to go out more, to dress more elegantly, and to take her to more sophisticated restaurants. She wanted to do more interesting things with her husband. Susan never told Joe what she wanted of him, however. Instead she nursed her discontent silently and found a man at work who was, she felt, more her type now.

When her affair came to light, Susan and Joe went to a couple therapist. There Susan explained what had happened—that, although she appreciated his good qualities, Joe had not changed to suit her new needs.

This was the first time Joe had heard that Susan wanted him to change. He made an effort to supply Susan with what she needed—a more active social life with him, more exciting outings. They are now beginning to work things out together. Susan has given up her lover.

Make sure you tell each other what you expect, and examine whether it is realistic or based on experiences from the past. If what you need has changed over the course of the marriage, let your mate in on the secret.

Talk About Your Family Histories

There are various ways family backgrounds can play into marriages.

Sometimes there is a family history of playing around that unknowingly compelled you to try it out yourself—a mother or father, for example, who had affairs. An understanding of this can make your husband feel more sympathetic toward your leap into adultery.

Talking about your family background can also reveal hang-ups rooted in the past that led you into an affair. For example, a critical, disapproving, or uncaring parent could have made you feel so insecure about your desirability that you needed to seek reassurance in the conquest of another man. Or something in your husband's background caused him to drink, or to feel so unmanly that, to compensate, he acted in the bullying, macho way that turned you off and pushed you into an affair.

Sometimes what is revealed is that you have assigned traits to a partner that really belonged to a parent. How you see your mate is a projection, rather than a realistic view. For example, you see your husband as an overpowering, controlling man because your father was that way. Every time your husband makes even a mild suggestion, you interpret it as an attempt to dominate you completely. This makes you feel you don't love him anymore, so you seek love with someone else.

Once you see from discussing family backgrounds that there is an overlay from the past distorting how you view one another, you can begin to relate more as the people you really are than as echoes of those in your past.

Not only do discussions about family backgrounds provide new knowledge about each partner's behavior and feelings, but they also often create sympathy for one another. Intimate sharing of this kind results in the couple's feeling much closer.

What Do You Each Need to Feel Loved?

Many affairs are an attempt to obtain from your lover the form of love you crave but are not getting from your mate. You may need hugs, kisses, handholding—lots of physical demonstrations of affection. Your husband may need you to *tell* him that he is appreciated. It is important to listen attentively to each other when you describe what you need to feel loved. Then you each have to remember the things your partner needs, respect rather than ignore or belittle them, and try to fulfill them.

Explore Needs for Closeness as Well as Space

We all have different needs for closeness and distance in a relationship. When intimacy boundaries are out of sync between a husband and wife, it causes trouble. One wants more closeness or space than the other can presently tolerate.

In our culture, the need for intimacy is applauded. The need for some space—which is also legitimate—is considered something shameful. As a consequence, how much time you want to be alone or pursue separate interests is almost never discussed between partners. For a few women, an escape from closeness at home is the reason for an affair; for more, it is the lack of closeness with husbands that sends them straying.

Talking about how much closeness and separateness you each feel comfortable with will reveal whether an incompatibility exists, and can lead you to work out compromises so that an affair will not be an answer in the future.

Uncover the Patterns in Your Interactions

One of the best ways to see what patterns exist is to look at your arguments. A theme that keeps resurfacing is a clue. Are your fights about a power struggle, with each one trying to be superior to the other? Is one partner always giving in, the other always demanding? Do your fights reveal a lack of trust or respect? Maybe instead of arguments there are never any fights about anything. You both sweep issues under the rug, always deny any negative feelings. This can result in your relationship's losing its vitality. Life together becomes boring. A hunt for patterns you share can reveal destructive interactions that mar happiness, lead to affairs, and need to be changed.

Find Out What Kind of Equilibrium Was Maintained by the Affair

Sometimes infidelity safeguards a collusion between partners to keep a specific mode of interaction going. Often collusions involve set roles. For example, you were the responsible partner—he was the charming, irresponsible one who drank or used drugs or spent money unwisely. Perhaps you had grown tired of your role, but instead of telling your husband that and working toward change in the relationship, you had an affair with a more responsible, competent man. Your affair helped you avoid raising issues that would have disturbed the status quo in your marriage. You could both continue in your same old roles and equilibrium was maintained.

Another example of maintaining the status quo: You had a marriage in which there was a lot of distance. You both worked long hours and had a busy social life. You had very little time when you were actually alone together. Then came the age of retirement. Suddenly you were home together a lot, and you felt uncomfortable with the new arrangement. An affair with a neighbor got you out of the house and prevented you from feeling so suffocated by your newfound intimacy. Your husband ignored the signs and never questioned you about your whereabouts. Thus your affair restored your old interaction with one another—there was enough distance between you to make you feel comfortable.

Think about it together. Is there something that your affair helped keep the same between you?

Exchange Places

Switch roles. Your husband pretends to be you; you pretend to be him. Based on what you know and have found out about each other, try to express earnestly how your partner feels about things. Each should talk about the affair, about love and sex, about your life together, from the other's point of view. This exercise will help you feel, on a gut level, the other's positions, hurts, emotions. It creates empathy for your partner.

Talk About Differing Sexual Needs

If one wants more sex than the other, if one likes oral sex and the other doesn't, if you prefer to make love at night and he likes to do it in the morning, you have to talk about it openly. If there are differences, you have to define them so you can begin to do something about them.

Chapter 15

✹

HEALING: THE

FINAL PHASE

At this point you and your husband should have grasped how to communicate more meaningfully than in the past; you know more about problems between you and the hidden motivations that exist in every relationship. You both understand more about why the affair took place from many perspectives. I hope this has made you feel closer. Devote a little time now to bringing back to mind the good things between you.

Think About What Is Right

Speak of things you admire about each other, such as intelligence, gentleness, sweetness, wit, a sense of style. If you appreciate the fact that your partner is someone who can always be counted on, a great parent, or a wonderful organizer, now is the time to bring it out. Tell each other, too, about the things you enjoy doing with one another—walking arm in arm, sitting by the fire, swimming on the beach, traveling—enumerate the goodies in your life.

Reminisce About the Good Times

Pull out the family album. Go over it together. Remember your honeymoon, vacations, when the babies were born, all the fun, warm times when you were happy with one another. Try to visit places with good memories for both of you.

Remember What You Still Share

This exercise will help you focus on the fact that you still have certain bonds. Take a pencil and paper. Individually, draw up a list of what you feel you share. Then exchange lists and see where you agree.

Make Believe That You Must Say Good-bye Forever

Write farewell letters pretending that you will never see one another again. Say what you want your spouse to know. You both may be surprised by the warmth that emerges.

Now you are ready to face the final, tough part of your healing program.

Start Negotiating

You have to give to get—that is what compromise is all about. For example, if you want a kiss and a little conversation every night before dinnertime, and he wants time to be by himself to cool out after work, you should reach a compromise. He can kiss you three nights and be by himself for a while the rest of the week. Or, if you allow him his solitary time before dinner, he will hold you and talk to you after dinner. Neither partner should expect to get something without having to budge an inch.

Begin Changing

From previous discussions you should each have a pretty good idea about what the other wants changed. Now is the time for you and your spouse to tell each other what you are willing to do differently. For example, you are going to stop criticizing your husband so that he can feel and act more warmly toward you. He is going to stop flirting with other women at parties. Whatever you have found to be a sore spot is what you each should be willing to ameliorate in some way.

Show Your Appreciation

Let your partner know you notice and like it when something is being done differently to fulfill your needs. Positive comments will make each of you want to continue the improvements.

Try to Break Out of a Marital Collusion

Here are four signs that a collusion exists: (1) A major unhappiness has existed in the marriage for a long time. (2) You have repeated disagreements over the same issue. It never gets resolved. (3) The relationship seems stale and has no zip. Collusions that keep partners locked into rigid roles often interfere with spontaneity and fun. (4) Your relationship with your spouse is similar to one you had with a parent or sibling early in life. Your partner treats you the same way the parent or sibling did. In collusions each partner tries to mold the other into someone from the past.

If you feel from the description above that you and your partner are locked into strict roles in your interaction, and that this is causing some disharmony, these are the measures you should take:

Have discussions with your partner centering on how you always behave with one another, taking into account what each of you does to make the partner continue to act in a certain fashion—for example, continuing to do things that you know make the other angry.

Once you have some understanding of what your role is vis-à-vis your partner, start to behave in different, less predictable ways. For instance, spouses who are critical should begin to give compliments, mates who are passive should try to act more assertively, partners who have been acting helpless should start doing things for themselves, partners who have been too aloof or independent should let their spouses know how much they are needed.

It is a psychological truth that even if only one partner in a relationship changes his or her behavior, the other, in reaction, starts to act differently, too. Then the collusion that has existed starts to come undone.

The roots of collusions run deep, so you may find this hard to do on your own. If this turns out to be true, consult a licensed marriage therapist who will help you uncover and deal with marital interactions that contribute to your unhappiness.

Solve Intimacy Problems

If you need more closeness than your husband does, or vice versa, start to negotiate. One way to do this is to work out ways in which you can be together but also alone. For example, you can be in the same room but pursue different interests. You read; he listens to music with headphones. Go to a movie complex showing more than one film. Each sees a different movie and you rejoin each other afterward.

It would also be helpful to delve into family backgrounds that may have made intimacy scary for one of you. A person can feel hemmed in by closeness if brought up by a smothering, intrusive mother. Or a partner raised by aloof, distant parents can feel uncomfortable because he or she is not used to closeness. Insight sometimes brings about amelioration. If you know what has made it scary, you may start to become less frightened of intimacy. Or you may be more willing to understand and excuse your partner's intimacy-avoiding actions, and not feel so personally rejected.

Make More Quality Time for Each Other

We live in a world where there are too many demands on our time. Jobs, children, in-laws, friends, social commitments, television, gyms all vie for the hours of our days. We forget, as a result, to make enough time to be together as a couple. Set aside at least two nights a week to be alone without distractions. Make it a rule that there will be no TV watching those evenings. This is time to talk and interact by yourselves. Relationships have to be nourished. Quality time feeds your relationship with your spouse.

DEALING WITH SPECIAL PROBLEMS

Handling Children

Before going on to special problems between you and your husband, I would like to point out that the children in the family are also affected by a parent's infidelity and need some remedial attention as a result.

You may have already noticed some out-of-the-ordinary behavior on the part of your child, even though you have not connected it to your affair. You assumed, as most women (and men) do, that during the time your liaison was a closely guarded secret it could not possibly have harmed the kids, simply because it was hidden.

Unfortunately, this simply isn't true. More and more, experts find that children of all ages, even the littlest ones, have an uncanny ability to sense it when a parent's attention is diverted away from the home and from them.

How do they react to this? They become anxious and often guilt ridden. Your inattention makes them fear that the family is in peril and may disintegrate. They worry about who will take care of them.

In addition, children often blame themselves for your wandering attention. They feel that they must have personally done something wrong to have caused it. They often feel responsible for putting things right again. In their attempt to pull your attention back into the family and keep the home intact, they almost never approach parents directly about their worries and fears. Instead, they act up in one way or another.

Young children may revert to infantile habits of bedwetting or thumb-sucking. They may have nightmares, cling to parents, have temper tantrums, even set fires. If they are well behaved at home they may start having trouble at school. This kind of behavior is an attempt to get you to refocus on them.

Older children may react by becoming sexually promiscuous, drinking, using drugs, or shoplifting.

When an affair comes out in the open, teens, who understand what infidelity is all about, may feel angry or betrayed and act out their anger in antisocial or disruptive ways.

214

WHAT TO DO

If you are having a secret affair it is important to keep your children in mind. Make an extra effort to pay more attention to them so they don't feel you are somehow slipping away.

Once an affair is revealed, children are aware of the ensuing upset between parents even if you try to keep confrontations behind closed doors. They hear the shouting and anger; they sense the tension all around them. If they didn't feel it before, now is the time they will fear that their family is exploding.

Once your husband knows, in addition to handling him, you also have to deal with the children. If possible, your husband should help.

While the two of you are deciding what to do as a couple, go out of your way to reassure the children that although their mother and father are having problems, they are trying to work them out. Tell them that no matter what happens, their parents love them and will always be there to take care of them. Emphasize that the problem is between Mother and Father and is not the children's fault.

Occasionally, a child will stumble onto the fact that a parent is having a secret affair. For example, a child may walk into a room where you are kissing another man, or you may be overheard in a whispered telephone conversation. Teens have been known to walk into a restaurant or park and see a parent holding hands or talking intimately with a strange man.

If a child lets you know that you have been discovered, don't lie. And beware: Experts agree that the worst thing you can do is ask your child to keep the secret from your husband. The child will feel he is carrying an awful burden and is being disloyal to the other parent. A son or daughter will also feel alienated from you. If the parents remain married, the child will worry about the potentially destructive secret he knows and if the parents divorce, the child may blame himself for not telling.

Therefore, the only right thing to do if a child discovers your affair is to tell your husband the truth. Then the two of you should deal with the child together.

Be careful, when talking to children, not to provide them with more details than they can comprehend or want to know.

Although some experts in the past have suggested it, do not ask your child to forgive you. This puts a son or daughter in the role of a parent and gives the child an uncomfortable kind of power in your relationship.

Instead, ask your child to accept you as a person who may have made a mistake or a bad decision, but is still a loving parent.

Re-creating Trust

First, realize that this won't happen overnight. Trust, however, can gradually be restored if you do the following: You must voluntarily tell your husband where you are going and with whom, if you are going out without him. If you plan to work late, be sure to tell him why and leave a phone number where he can reach you. Or ask him to pick you up after you finish at the office. This will keep him from wondering what you are up to.

Scrupulous honesty in all your future dealings with your husband also helps restore a sense of trust.

Finally, broaden your perceptions of the issue of trust. Both of you should draw up a list of the ways that you still can be trusted. For example, if he were sick, he could trust you to look after him. He can trust that you would console him if a close relative or friend died. If he lost his job you would be his ally through hard times. Every time he feels you can never be trusted again, let him look at this trust list.

When He Is Obsessed with the Details of Your Affair

It is my feeling that the obsessive desire to know every last little thing that went on between the spouse and the lover develops more frequently in wives whose husbands have been unfaithful. But sometimes, too, a man whose wife has had an affair becomes just as obsessive. What to do?

First, try to shift the focus from the affair to your marriage. Reassure your husband that your relationship with him is more important to you than anything that happened between you and your lover. If, however, his obsessive curiosity persists, you can try this "inquisition" technique, which some therapists have found works.

Sit down together for the express purpose of discussing the affair. Voluntarily tell him, in as much detail as you can, every minute and intimate thing you remember. Your husband is allowed to ask as many questions for as long as he wants, and you have to answer them. These "inquisitions" can be repeated as often as he wants. Sooner or later, enough will be enough. He will get sick of hearing about all the details again and again and will stop obsessing about what went on.

If You Are Feeling Bad About Yourself

If you feel simply rotten, if you are overwhelmed with negative feelings about yourself because you have hurt your husband or because you have had an affair, here is what you should do:

First, as I suggested before, remind yourself that you may have made a mistake but that doesn't turn you into an absolutely evil person.

Second, take a pad and write down every positive thing you can think of about yourself. For example: "I am a good mother. I am a loyal friend. I am a caring daughter. I work hard at my job and am good at it. I am creative. I am spiritual. I am intelligent."

When you are really down on yourself, pull out your list and read it, or, better yet, read your list of good qualities every morning before you start the day.

Next on your agenda should be putting joy back into your relationship.

RE-CREATING JOY

Compliment Each Other

Remember to keep the positives in mind. Couples are often quick to criticize and slow to compliment after the honeymoon. Let your partner know it when you genuinely admire some quality or some action—even small things.

Create Surprises

To ward off or shake up deadly predictable routines, create a surprise a week for each other. A new sexy nightgown, reservations for an unexpected weekend away, a love note mailed to his or your office, a birthday cake when it's not a birthday, an invitation to a tryst at a posh hotel, one exquisite flower—anything big or small that is unexpected. Such gestures make you more interesting to each other, make you think of and react to your spouse in new ways. Unpredictability, with its built-in tension, can also be sexy. Surprises revitalize relationships.

Reassure Each Other

Each and every day in your postaffair life, you have to let your husband know that you treasure him—that he means so much to you. He needs this kind of reassurance. On the other hand, you need reassurance, too. He has to let you know that he values the relationship he has with you, and that healing your marriage is more important to him than anything you did with the other man.

As a final step toward a renewed and better marriage, you need to revamp your sex life.

Chapter 16

❦

CREATING A NEW AND BETTER SEX LIFE

One of the most immediate problems you will face after the adultery crisis erupts is to make sex comfortable, or even possible again. During sex, or even when the thought of it arises, the ghost of the lover is most likely to emerge in both partners' minds, sometimes prohibiting or ruining the act.

Of course, it is less of a problem, or no problem at all, if you have a husband who wants to make love all the time now because your affair has made you more exciting in his eyes (even if, or perhaps because, he respects you less). Other husbands increase lovemaking because they feel compelled to keep you satisfied at home. They don't want you to go running back to your lover or search elsewhere for sexual fulfillment.

Forget about the reason. If your husband is exhibiting sexual interest, go with it. You will have bypassed a major hurdle on the road to reviving your marriage. Some women are able to respond to their husbands with fervor. Ardor is fueled by relief and happiness at the reconciliation. However, there are others whose own guilt about the infidelity prevents them from either wanting to make love or responding fully to their husbands.

An inability to make love may also be your husband's problem. Perhaps he doesn't want to touch you, either to punish you or because he feels so alienated.

The best cure for sexual aversion on either side is the healing program I've outlined. Honest discussions, airing of feelings and problems, better understanding and communication diminish the wish for revenge. They also create a newfound intimacy that should lead to a desire to seal it in bed.

Generally, it is spouses who haven't undergone either a formal or informal therapeutic program who continue to withhold lovemaking, because they haven't dealt with the anger, hurt, or guilt that is holding them back.

If, however, you and your husband are still having trouble making it together, either seek out a licensed sex therapist (you can find one at the sex clinic of a large local hospital) or try the following.

Bypass Negative Thoughts

This is a technique developed in sex therapy to help people struggling with an aversion to sex with their partners. All advice in this chapter applies to either one of you. When your spouse approaches you, or the idea of having sex enters your mind, monitor the thoughts that float into your head. You will probably discover negative images lurking there. You may think about how much you have hurt him; he may think about you and your lover together or what a rotten thing you did to him. It is negative thoughts like these that are destroying your desire for your partner. In essence, you are turning yourself off, and it is important that you recognize this fact. Once you do, you can learn to control consciously the reactions that are getting in your way.

Train yourself to spot negative thoughts as soon as they arise and immediately squelch them. Think ahead about some quality of your spouse's that you like or some terrific memory of the two of you together. Substitute this prepared positive image the minute one of your negative images starts to surface. Filling your mind with good thoughts rather than bad ones allows your sexuality to flow again.

MAKE YOUR MARRIAGE AN AFFAIR

Once you have resumed sex, you can address, as a team, the whole question of your married erotic life—as it was in the past, and how it will be in the future. Your aim is to make sex better than it was before, and/or to take measures to preserve good sex forever.

Put into your sex life at home some of the things that tend to enhance sex in extramarital affairs.

Restore Romance

For many women the best and most tempting part of an affair is the atmosphere of romance surrounding it. It is also what gives extramarital sex an extra charge for a lot of people. Chances are, if you hankered for it elsewhere, romance had largely gone out of your marriage.

Although women are notorious romance addicts, men in our culture find it just as seductive. To make your sex life more exciting, you both have to work to restore romance in your life together.

Set aside one night a week for a romantic date. Put on a sexy dress and perfume, let him wear his best suit, and go someplace with the right kind of atmosphere for love—a restaurant with candlelight, a roaring fireplace to sit by in winter, an orchestra that plays slow music. Dance close and, yes, dance suggestively. It will lead to good sex afterward.

Take mini-vacations. Country inns are great for feelings of romance; a quick hop to a tropical island can bring out love and lust.

But most effective, in the long run, are ongoing romantic words and gestures. Whisper in each other's ears "I love you" at unexpected moments; pat each other affectionately when you pass by at home. Give each other frequent spontaneous hugs. Women, in particular, complain that husbands are often affectionate only when they want sex. For wives and some husbands, romantic gestures at other times reap erotic rewards later in bed.

Many men find special sexy lingerie at bedtime romantic. Learn what the other considers romantic—then do it!

Introduce Anticipation

Another of the things that can make sex so compelling in an extramarital love affair is anticipation of the grand event. You wonder when you will be with your lover once more and imagine what it will be like. Since anticipation of sex can be a real turn-on, try to bring some of it into your sex life with your mate.

When you are kissing him good-bye before going to work in the morning, whisper what you would like to do to him that night. Or drop a note into his briefcase telling him your naughty intentions. Make a lunch date with your husband, then phone him in the morning to tell him you have made a reservation at a nearby hotel for a sexual matinee. Call him when he has an unhurried moment at work and talk suggestively. This may set his mind going so that he comes on to you like a tiger that night. Of course, your husband can do the same kinds of things to create anticipation for you.

Try New Things

Spouses are often more willing to experiment in their affairs than they are at home. A certain amount of novelty adds zip to love lives and makes sex more interesting and fun. Try out positions that you've never used before. If you need suggestions, consult *The Joy of Sex* by Dr. Alex Comfort, which is filled with tasteful illustrations. New places for lovemaking can be arousing as well—for example, in front of the fireplace, in the car like two teenagers making out, on the floor instead of the bed, on the couch while watching a sexy movie on your VCR.

Experiment with vibrators or other sex toys; apply oil lovingly all over each other's bodies; take sexy pictures of one another with an instant camera.

Create an ongoing program to provide some novelty. Agree to each come up with one sexual surprise a week. Let your imaginations roam! Just thinking about sex with each other in this way can be arousing.

Give Sex a Higher Priority

It certainly is at the top of the list in an affair. In marriage it generally sinks gradually to the bottom—after doing all the chores, after TV, after talking to friends and relatives on the phone. When it is the finale to a busy day, you are either so worn out you prefer to skip it, or you make love when you are most tired and least in the mood. This can create lackluster sex—especially in comparison with the conditions of the affair, which can create spectacular sex.

Set aside prime time for sex so that you make love when you are still fresh, not exhausted. Be sure there is enough time to explore each other in a leisurely way. A lot of time, attention, and planning—generally hours—are given over to lovemaking in affairs. Why not in your marriage?

Put More Play into Sex

This means maybe acting out fantasies together, perhaps some silliness, like a pillow fight that turns into sex, or trying out some minor kink just for fun. The time to stop being such sober citizens is in the bedroom. Many people use their affairs as an escape, an oasis from their duties in normal life. You can use marital sex in this way, too.

Incorporate the Forbidden

Indulging in fantasies and playing with minor kinks also allow you to experience in your marriage something that is often such a turn-on in an affair—doing the forbidden.

Learn More About Each Other's Bodies

You may have been married a long time but never really explored the nuances of each other's sexuality. A good way to do this is to borrow another technique from sex therapy.

Without clothing on, take turns doing the following: One of you lies down on your stomach. Your spouse touches and caresses the entire back half of your body from head to toe. Turn over and allow your partner to do the same over the front of your torso. Hands and fingers should roam over everything, with the exception of genital areas like nipples, penis, vagina. Concentrate on what feels good to you. When your partner touches an area that gives you a thrill, say so out loud, or at least make a recognizable feel-good sound. In this way partners learn to give each other more pleasure.

Do this exercise for about a week. After seven days you can add genital touching, but not to the point of orgasm. Instead, tease. Play with the genitals, go away from them, then return. Always tell your partner what you are enjoying. Finally, after a week of "teasing," you can go on to orgasm. By this time you will have learned a great deal more about your partner's responses.

Deal with Sexual Differences

Playing into many affairs are sexual incompatibilities in marriage that have gone on for years. Although sexual compatibility is often thought to happen through some magic and the right chemistry, it can also be created with the right spirit and the proper steps. But first, you have to acknowledge that a problem exists.

You must talk about it to each other. For example, if you feel your sex drive is higher than your husband's or vice versa, if he likes sex in the morning and you like it at night, start discussing it instead of continuing a pattern of silent advances and refusals, of hurt feelings and open wounds.

Make Sure You Aren't Blaming Sex for Other Problems

Sometimes it is easier to say that sex is the problem than to confront the fact openly that something else in the relationship is out of kilter. For example, you may have lost interest in sex with your husband because he was always criticizing you. Or he stopped wanting to make love to you because he felt you quit paying attention to him once the children were born. You are really angry at your partner and it is the hidden anger that turned you off, not lack of interest per se, although you thought that was what drove you into an affair.

Sometimes, once children are born, or soon after the wedding, you start thinking of your spouse as a parent rather than a sex object, which also dampens desire. It isn't chemistry that's lacking; it's your attitude toward your mate that's at fault.

Did the Spark Ever Really Exist?

Sometimes sex isn't great because one spouse, or both, married the other for reasons that had nothing to do with sexual attraction. For example, you may have married your husband for financial security; he may have chosen you as a wife because he thought you would make a good mother. The excitement of courtship and the wedding may have originally blinded you to the lack of zip that was there from the beginning, but once you settled down into a domestic pattern the realization slowly dawned: "I am not turned on." You may have given yourself to another man to experience passion.

Although this makes pepping up sex at home difficult, it doesn't make it completely impossible. Often couples like and value their mates in other ways and want to stay together even after discovering real passion with another partner.

In circumstances where sexual attraction was not strong from the beginning, you can improve your sex life if you have the goodwill to do so. It may never become as flamboyant as your experience with someone else, but sex can become good enough, if you are willing to settle for this in return for other things that you like with your present mate.

You can create more excitement by doing more interesting things—using a variety of positions, making love at different times of the day, and, in particular, using private or shared fantasies to turn you on. Don't be afraid of having secret fantasies of other people while making love to your spouse, if that is what it takes to make you feel more aroused. As long as it is kept in fantasy, rather than acted out in reality, it's really okay, so don't feel guilty.

Start Sexual Negotiations

Remember that just as in business, you can learn the art of negotiating in sexual matters. The principle is the same—you have to give to get.

Taking turns is an example of this kind of fair trade. For instance, if he likes to make love in the morning and you prefer it at night, do it in the morning sometimes and at night other times. If you enjoy sex more with the lights on but he likes it better in darkness, one time do it in pitch-blackness, the next with a dim lamp or candle.

If you want sex more than he does, you can break the deadlock by realizing that intercourse is not the only way to have sex. He can bring you to climax manually, without any expectation that he has to climax,

too. Another alternative is self-pleasuring with the consent of your partner, even perhaps in his presence (which, incidentally, may sometimes
turn him on).

In reaching solutions to sexual problems you have to be flexible and
not expect everything your way all the time.

Put to Use What You Learned from Your Affair

Some women discover things about their sexual responses they never
knew before. For example, Lucy could never climax with her husband,
whom she had married right out of high school. She thought the blame
was hers. So did her husband. Then she had an affair with Mike. Mike
took great pains to please Lucy. He indulged in lots of foreplay instead
of just putting his penis into her vagina and expecting her to have an
orgasm, as her husband did. Not only was Lucy able to have one climax
when she was with her lover, she discovered she could have many when
Mike stroked her clitoris.

Now she realized that the reason she couldn't have an orgasm during
her marriage was her husband's faulty technique. He had ignored any
kind of stimulation outside of actual intercourse and, as a result, had
been shortchanging his wife.

Linda, on the other hand, discovered that the deep conversation and
handholding that preceded lovemaking with her lover, Dennis, worked
like magic on her sexuality. These were things that never happened at
home anymore, and gradually her sexual response with her husband had
dimmed. Linda knew now that she had to feel intimate and connected
to her partner before she could make love successfully.

Now that Lucy's affair is over and she and her husband have reunited,
she has to tell her husband, or show him by guiding his hand, what she
needs to respond to him.

Linda has to explain her need for *emotional* foreplay to her husband.

Some women, from their affairs, find they have come to like certain
acts, such as oral sex, that they didn't before.

Whatever you have learned from your lover, be grateful for it and,
if you can, put it to use in a marriage you want to save.

In the end a love affair can be viewed as a learning experience, and
not just about sex. You should have found out more about yourself and
your needs, about love, perhaps about safeguarding or endangering a

relationship. Regarding adultery as something to be learned from will help you even if you want to leave your marriage or find it cannot be put back together again.

Interestingly, although divorce may not have been the outcome you desired, one study by Graham Spanier and Randie Margolis found that people who separated after infidelity had a better postmarital adjustment than divorced people who had been faithful. Having learned from their experience that they had skills and qualities valuable in establishing new relationships, they tended to operate with more confidence as singles and dated more frequently than monogamous spouses.

Whichever way it turns out for you—a better marriage or a better divorce—take whatever knowledge you have gleaned from your extra-marital experience with you into the future and make yours a happier, more fulfilling life as a woman.

Chapter 17

❈

FOR TEMPTED WOMEN: IS AN AFFAIR FOR YOU?

This final chapter is for those who haven't given in to temptation yet, but are simply considering an extramarital adventure. Should you or shouldn't you?

Bear in mind everything else I have told you about affairs in this book. Don't forget that affairs, even secret ones, affect your children, and that if you are discovered you may alienate or even lose them.

But, in the end, the best way I can answer the question of whether you should or shouldn't is to let you hear advice from wives who are having affairs. Read what they have to say based on their experiences, then make up your own mind.

"You asked for advice for others. I can only tell you what I told my lover. In spite of the lonely nights without him, the painful times away from him, and being last on his totem pole, I'd do it again in a skinny minute. Knowing and loving him has been the single most important event in my life (except for the birth of my daughter twelve years ago). I surely don't advise women to seek out this kind of a life. It has a real downside, but in all honesty I admit freely and without reservation that I anticipate having him in my life in some form until I die. Even in view of the substantial amount of pain I've felt, it was and is an experience I never regret."

"If you have an affair, be prepared to fall in love. Be prepared for guilt when you must tell your partner. And be prepared for the fact that many lives are affected and many people hurt. You'll have that with you forever. Even if you live happily ever after with your new love, you must live with the guilt of those you hurt and left behind."

"I don't know what advice to give other women except to say that this arrangement, having two men, certainly works for me."

"Affairs are very complicated. An affair can and will destroy not only a marriage but you yourself. End your present relationship, get a grip on your own feelings before you start a new situation."

"The advice I would give is to make sure you really know what you want. If someone told me two years ago something like this would happen, I would have said they were crazy. Now I know that you can become immensely attracted to someone and really cannot help what follows!"

"I don't advise any woman to have an affair. I would think of the two families you would devastate if the relationship became known. That's the scary part. Also I would remember that all important occasions and holidays can seem very lonely without your lover. No gifts are ever exchanged. Finally, it's probably not love but physical attraction."

"What would I tell anyone contemplating an affair? My affair has caused me so much pain, and if it's discovered God only knows what will happen. But the little bit of time I spend with him makes the agony more than worthwhile. I know I should stop. Hell, I should never have started, but what is done is done. Once you've tasted the forbidden fruit of passion you can never be the same again. Be sure you can handle the emotional aspects of an illicit relationship without feeling the need to confess. Think about what will happen if you're found out—not just to you but to your lover, your family and friends, and everyone involved. Having an affair is a serious thing and can have deadly consequences. Just be sure you are prepared to accept those consequences. The best way to deal with an affair is by not beginning it, but, of course, no one ever listens to that kind of advice."

"As long as it's not hurting anyone and you're having a good time—go for it. I did and I love it!"

"Affairs are not for every woman. You should consider it carefully before getting involved. It some cases an affair can help your marriage, but in some cases it can end it. If you have an affair with a co-worker or boss, move carefully and with great caution. It can be awkward at times and you will always feel you have to be on your toes so that fellow workers won't pick up on the relationship. Sex can also complicate a friendship and a working relationship."

"Examine your own feelings about the moral dimension very carefully and either make peace with it or don't do it. It also helps to keep a perspective and a sense of humor."

"My advice to other women: Be sensible and totally discreet. No calls at home, nothing at all at home!"

"I feel I can handle this extra emotional situation but it might strain some marriages. My advice would be, if you can't handle your marriage like you usually do, get out of the extracurricular relationship."

"Be prepared for disappointments but enjoy what you can while you can."

"This affair has opened my eyes to how much we are driven by our desires. Our need for love never ends. I hated to think that, as young as I am, I could never feel again the anticipation and excitement that new love brings. I have found it again, but at what price? At this point I'm not sure I care. I only know that this is what makes life worth living. But if you have an affair, be prepared to lose a lot—your spouse, possibly your children, your job."

"Don't get in it, or get out while you still are able and are in one piece, body and mind. He ruined my life."

"This is my best advice. Ask yourself if it's worth the pain of a possible divorce, the possible 'other woman' label, and the knowledge that your co-workers are watching the thing develop. If the end result is worth it, then stay with it and hold your head high; if not, get out fast."

"I would tell other women to wake up and smell the coffee. Life is too short to live on empty hopes and dreams. If I was to turn back time, I would *never* have an affair again."

"Don't get involved with a married man with children and make sure you don't have any strings attached either. I love the other man, but at the same time I don't know if I could leave my husband. It's confusing."

"Go for it. You receive things outside of your marriage that you may never receive in it; that is, contentment, fulfillment, the feeling of being wanted and a worthy person. Just do not get caught, unless you want to. Good luck!"

"If you feel you need to have an out-of-marriage affair, go ahead and do it. Just practice safe sex and keep your head on straight. Just because you like the sex and companionship doesn't mean you have to get emotionally involved. Watch out for infatuation. It will get you every time."

"My advice would be not to get involved. Every woman feels that her situation is different and that the guy will leave his wife, but that doesn't always happen."

"I have been in therapy for a year now and I am still struggling. If I had it to do over again I'm not sure I would have had the affair. My advice to others is think very carefully and clearly, because this *definitely* could change your life. The stakes are high."

"Enjoy it for however long it lasts. Let him make you feel as wonderful as you make him feel. Enjoy! Enjoy! Enjoy!"

"You are always the other woman at the end of his other priorities. Everything and everyone else comes first. You'll find that this hurts."

"My advice to other women is, don't allow yourself to be in such a weak emotional state that you take the risk of possibly destroying your marriage, hurting a person you care for, and leaving yourself with a small part of emptiness if the affair ends."

"I would tell women that when you are unhappy in your marriage and lose hope that anything will ever change, then an affair can be very tempting and serve a useful purpose. It makes you feel like you're flying for a while after years of feeling down. It makes you feel wanted after years of thinking of yourself as undesirable. It doesn't last, because an affair with someone who is also married is just an affair. But even though my relationship with my lover was time-limited it was, for me, a lifeline. It gave me something to hang on to so that I could finally put an end to my marriage. An affair doesn't solve problems in a marriage, but it can help you decide to split when you see that there is the possibility of living more fully again."

"If a woman can accept what an affair may or may not do to her life, then go for it. I can say I have never been happier."

"Find yourself first. A man won't be the answer to your problems. Learn to love yourself. You don't live for anyone else."

"You'll need a lot of patience and control of your emotions. It's the time you can't be together that becomes difficult. The time you need him most is the time he's unavailable."

"I would tell a woman contemplating an affair, don't have one with someone you work with, at least not when you have daily contact. Sooner or later the relationship will end. Think about how you would feel if you run into your ex-lover after it's over. Also, as best you can, you need to lay down some ground rules. Understand why you and the other person are getting involved with each other in the first place."

"An affair is exciting, but it's no fun waiting for phone calls and not being able to spend more than an hour or two with each other. Holidays are the pits. You are without him and he's with his wife. It's more painful than anything else to be in love with someone you can't have. I would never again be involved with a married man. There are too many others that can be hurt—your family, his family. We've been lucky but also very careful not to get caught. But lives can be ruined. My advice is don't do it."

"If you can't resist him or break it off, be absolutely discreet. Tell no one. Stay reasonable, maintain a normal sex life with your husband, and be everything you are capable of being with him."

"If you can handle the limitations of the experience, it could be one of the best of your life. It has been for me."

"Don't get emotionally involved with a lover if you are already married. That would be a fatal mistake. Rather, go for the physical side of the relationship if that is what you need, as it was in my case."

"It's hard for me to give advice to someone because I don't know what to do about my own situation. I love my husband. He treats me very well. I don't have a good enough reason to cheat; some other women might. I would just urge anyone to be sure of what they are doing when they get married and not to complicate things more after they are married. It hurts too much."

"It can be a bright spot in a lifeless time in your life. But the risk of hurting your husband and kids may be devastating. Remember, there's always that threat."

"Don't have an affair at all, regardless of who it is with. It could lead to love for one or both of you, and because of your situations you might be unable to be with each other. It can cause heartache for both of you."

"Life is too short to spend it unhappily. Reach out and grasp any happiness you can get. Try to be careful and you will have it made. I personally have no regrets."

"Do I recommend an affair? Absolutely not. I paid a terrible price for this affair, especially now that I realize how wonderful life is when you're with someone you want to be with and enjoy sexually. Once you care for the person it only leads to unhappiness. Only heartless people can become involved in these types of situations."

"No matter how much it hurts when we choose to end this affair, I can safely say it will not be a part of my life I regret. I have learned self-confidence through my lover's kindness and openness, and I shared a part of myself that will always be with him."

"Be very sure before you start an affair that you know what your goals are. Be prepared for criticism, possible ostracism, confrontation with the wronged spouses, even threats. For your own peace of mind, be prepared to let him go. I believe if it's meant to be, he'll be back. If not, I had a year and a half of love never to be forgotten. I have no regrets."

"My advice would be to realize that this is a fantasy that probably won't last, so prepare yourself for the inevitable hurt when it's all over and enjoy the short time you may have together."

"An affair is a very, very risky venture for any person who wants to retain a healthy marriage. It is risky because it draws energy away from you and your spouse. On the other hand, it can also work a small miracle in bringing about self-discovery and development. But you cannot be sure that harm will not come to you later. I don't advise it. It takes a strong person to handle it."

"I do know that if you are not happy at home you will find happiness elsewhere. It's human nature; we all need to feel needed and loved. But I would advise women not to get involved in an affair. If things are bad between you and your husband, either get counseling or get out. I wish I had never started up with this other person."

"I feel this is the greatest love of my life, but it is also very draining. This sort of thing does not happen twice in a lifetime. Although I am happy now I would tell anyone else to run (not walk) to the nearest exit rather than become involved with a married man. It is too emotionally exhausting."

"I don't advise anyone to jump into an affair. It is not an answer to anything. I happen to have a very good relationship at present, but things could change and I do run the risk of losing my spouse of twenty years. Would I do it again knowing what I know now? Probably."

"First, if at all possible, do not get involved in a relationship with your boss unless you have definite plans of other employment. To maintain your job status and an affair at the same time will work for a while, but if things go sour in the relationship it will most certainly affect your job. Second, don't think he will leave his wife even if he says he will."

"If you love your husband, please stay and be faithful. It takes time, but you can be happy together again if you really try. If I had to do it over again, it would never have happened."

"Don't have an affair with a married man. It's an emotional roller coaster. It's just a fling for him, and when the flames die down there's nothing left. The man will find another woman to have an affair with, just as fast as he found you. If you have multiple affairs they will eventually wear you down. Seek professional help. I did and it helps."

"Try to look for and take all the good, because it far outweighs the frustrations. But would I ever get involved with someone else again? No!"

"To any woman considering an affair, I recommend *not* to do it unless your marriage is on the way out anyway. After the excitement is over and the guilt sets in, you cannot live your life on a normal basis. You will never be comfortable or at peace with yourself. Daily turmoil will always be with you and the lying will really take its toll on your nerves."

"Don't get involved with a married man. Don't believe anything they tell you. They will tell you whatever it takes to sleep with you and have you available."

"Be cautious. It's easy to develop a deep emotional attachment to someone you can't really have. Sometimes it hurts deeply. You have to keep your priorities straight."

"There is a lot of fun in having an affair, but sometimes it is hard because you can't see him when you want; he is not there when something wrong or right happens, when you are sad or happy. You really cannot count on him. Think with your head, not with your heart, because otherwise you will be in trouble just like I am. It will be difficult to end it no matter how hard you try. The longer the affair continues, the more difficult it is for you to give him up."

"I know I'll end up getting hurt, but he's my obsession. Don't get involved with anyone unless you know you can handle it—and I am not sure I can."

"You have to go into this type of situation with an open mind—what you share may only be sex when you are both married. You will only have a few stolen moments together each week. No matter how involved you are, it is not easy to break up two marriages at once so you can be together all the time."

"I thought one kiss would end my dreaming about what it would be like, but it only made me want him more. So, ladies, think before you leap. The consequences can cause you more pain than you had before you started the affair."

"Don't get involved. If you're married there's always a way of making it work. You married him for some reason, didn't you?"

"Do not get involved if, in any way, you think of divorce in *his* future. Enjoy the affair at face value. Don't read more into it than might be there."

"It hurts so bad, make sure it is worth it. Remember, if you play with fire, you get burned, but love to the fullest. Enjoy what you have and store your heart full of memories. You can hold on to them forever, and no one can take them away."

Appendix

HOW MUCH DO YOU KNOW ABOUT FEMALE INFIDELITY? A QUIZ

1. Sex is the main reason why a woman has an ongoing affair.

   True _____ False _____

2. How much money a woman makes affects whether she will have an affair.

   True _____ False _____

3. Bored housewives are more likely to have affairs than busy working women.

   True _____ False _____

4. If a woman has had a lot of sexual experience before marriage, she is less likely to want to have an affair when she is a wife.

   True _____ False _____

5. The size of the community she lives in influences whether a woman will have an affair.

   True _____ False _____

6. Partners in affairs have the same attitudes toward extramarital sex.

   True _____ False _____

7. Children aren't affected by a mother's secret affair.

   True _____ False _____

8. A husband's affair is more dangerous to the marriage than a wife's adultery.

   True _____ False _____

9. Wives' affairs last longer than those of husbands.

   True _____ False _____

10. Wives' affairs don't need to include sex.

    True _____ False _____

11. If a cheating wife divorces and remarries, she is as likely to cheat again in her new marriage as a husband in the same circumstances.

    True _____ False _____

ANSWERS

1. *False.* Most wives take outside partners because of some unhappiness in their marriages. Although they may enjoy the sex very much, they continue the affair because of that unhappiness and because of friendship and emotional attachment to the man. Wives rate sex less important than husbands do as a reason for starting and continuing an extramarital liaison.

2. *True.* Studies reveal that higher-income women are more likely to take lovers.

3. *False.* Wives who work meet more men, have more opportunities, and end up having more extramarital relationships than women who stay at home. The old stereotype of the bored housewife as the typical adulteress no longer holds true.

4. *False.* Since Kinsey's original sex surveys, almost all research has revealed a link between premarital sexual experience and

extramarital adventures. The more of the first, the greater the likelihood of the second for wives.

5. *True.* Women who live in large urban areas are more prone to have affairs than those who reside in less populated, rural ones. Urban women's attitude toward extramarital sex is more liberal.

6. *False.* A woman and a man in the same affair may have very different attitudes. Women tend to become more emotionally attached to their lovers than men, and may yearn more for expressions of love. Men, as a group, seem content to have a little sex on the side without the same emotional commitment.

7. *False.* Experts agree that kids are, indeed, affected by a mother's extramarital liaison even when it remains very secret. Children feel the mother's emotional energy and interest diverted elsewhere and they are disturbed by this. They may even blame themselves for it.

8. *False.* A wife's affair is more likely to end a marriage than a husband's adultery. One reason: Wives have heard about cheating husbands all their lives, while husbands believe that women are basically monogamous. The husband is, therefore, more shocked by a wife's infidelity and feels it as a greater sin and disgrace, as does society at large. In judging affairs, the double standard is alive and well.

9. *True.* Studies show that wives have longer—and fewer—affairs than husbands.

10. *True.* Surveys show that close to one quarter of all women's affairs are emotional attachments without intercourse.

11. *False.* One recent study revealed that wives who have cheated in a first marriage recommit to monogamy in a second. Husbands who have had extramarital liaisons are less likely to want to be monogamous when they remarry.

SELECTED BIBLIOGRAPHY

Athanasiou, R., and Sarkin, R. "Premarital Sexual Behavior and Postmarital Adjustment." *Archives of Sexual Behavior* 3, no. 3 (1974): 207–225.

Athanasiou, R.; Shaver, P.; and Tavris, C. "Sex: A Report to *Psychology Today* Readers." *Psychology Today* 4 (July 1970): 39–52.

Atwater, L. "Getting Involved: Women's Transition to First Extramarital Sex." *Alternative Lifestyles*, no. 2 (1979): 33–68.

Bell, Robert R.; Turner, Stanley; and Rosen, Lawrence. "A Multivariate Analysis of Female Extramarital Coitus." *Journal of Marriage and the Family* 37, no. 2 (May 1975): 375–384.

Bernard, Jessie. "Infidelity: Some Moral and Social Issues." In *Beyond Monogamy*, edited by J. R. Smith and L. G. Smith. Baltimore: Johns Hopkins University Press, 1974.

Blumstein, Philip, Ph.D., and Schwartz, Pepper, Ph.D. *American Couples: Money, Work, Sex.* New York: William Morrow and Co., 1983.

Botwin, Carol. *Men Who Can't Be Faithful.* New York: Warner Books, 1988.

———. *Is There Sex After Marriage?* Boston: Little, Brown and Co., 1985.

Cuber, John F., and Harroff, Peggy B. *Sex and the Significant Americans.* Baltimore: Penguin Books, 1966.

Dohrenwend, Barbara S., and Dohrenwend, Bruce P. (eds.). *Stressful Life Events: Their Nature and Effects.* New York: John Wiley and Sons, 1974.

Edwards, John N. "Extramarital Involvment: Fact and Theory." *Journal of Sex Research* 9, no. 3 (August 1973): 210–224.

Edwards, John N., and Booth, Alan. "Sexual Behavior in and out of Marriage:

An Assessment of the Correlates." *Journal of Marriage and the Family* 38, no. 1 (February 1976): 73–81.

Eysenck, H. J. *Sex and Personality*. Austin, Tex.: University of Texas Press, 1977.

———. "Hysterical Personality and Sexual Adjustment, Attitudes and Behavior." *Journal of Sex Research* 7, no. 4 (November 1971): 274–281.

Feldman, Harold. *Development of the Husband-Wife Relationship*. Ithaca, N.Y.: Cornell University Press, 1967.

Fisher, Helen E. *The Sex Contract: The Evolution of Human Behavior*. New York: Quill, 1982.

Glass, S. P., and Wright, T. L. "Justifications for Extramarital Relationships: The Association Between Attitudes, Behaviors and Gender." *Journal of Sex Research* 29, no. 3 (August 1992): 361–387.

———. "Sex Differences in Type of Extramarital Involvement and Marital Dissatisfaction." *Sex Roles* 12, nos. 9/10 (1985): 1101–1120.

———. "The Relationship of Extramarital Sex, Length of Marriage, and Sex Differences on Marital Satisfaction and Romanticism: Athanasiou's Data Reanalyzed." *Journal of Marriage and the Family* 39, no. 4 (November 1977): 691–703.

Heyn, Dalma. *The Erotic Silence of the American Wife*. New York: Random House, 1992.

Hoon, P.; Wincze, J.; and Hoon, F. "A Test of Reciprocal Inhibitions: Are Anxiety and Sexual Arousal Mutually Inhibitory?" *Journal of Abnormal Psychology* 86 (1977): 65–74.

Hunt, Morton. *Sexual Behavior in the 1970's*. New York: Playboy Press, 1974.

———. *The Affair*. New York: World Publishing Co., 1969.

Johnson, R. E. "Some Correlates of Extramarital Coitus." *Journal of Marriage and the Family* 32, no. 2 (August 1970): 449–456.

Kelly, Kathryn, and Musialowski, Donna. "Repeated Exposure to Sexually Explicit Stimuli: Novelty, Sex and Sexual Attitudes." *Archives of Sexual Behavior* 15, no. 6 (December 1986): 488–489.

Kernberg, Otto. "Mature Love: Prerequisites and Characteristics." *Journal of the American Psychoanalytic Association* 22, no. 4 (1974): 743–768.

Kinsey, Alfred C.; Pomeroy, Wardell B.; Martin, Clyde E.; and Gebhard, Paul H. *Sexual Behavior in the Human Female*. New York: Pocket Books, 1965.

Kitson, Gay, and Sussman, Marvin. "Marital Complaints, Demographic Characteristics, and Symptoms of Mental Distress in Divorce." *Journal of Marriage and the Family* 44, no. 1 (February 1982): 87–101.

Lampe, Philip E. (ed.). *Adultery in the United States: Close Encounters of the Sixth (or Seventh) Kind*. Buffalo, N.Y.: Prometheus Books, 1987.

Lawson, Annette. *Adultery: An Analysis of Love and Betrayal*. New York: Basic Books, 1988.

McBroom, Paricia. *The Third Sex: The New Professional Woman*. New York: William Morrow and Co., 1986.

Michael, R. P., and Zumpe, D. "Potency in Male Rhesus Monkeys: Effects of Continuously Receptive Females." *Science* 200 (1978): 451–453.

Neubeck, Gerhard (ed.). *Extramarital Relations*. Englewood Cliffs, N.J.: Prentice Hall, 1966.

Offit, Avodah K. *The Sexual Self*. New York: Congdon and Weed, 1983.

Person, Ethel S., M.D. *Dreams of Love and Dateful Encounters: The Power of Romantic Passion*. New York: W. W. Norton and Co., 1988.

Pittman, Frank S., M.D. *Private Lies: Infidelity and the Betrayal of Intimacy*. New York: W. W. Norton and Co., 1989.

———. *Turning Points: Treating Families in Transition and Crisis*. New York: W. W. Norton and Co., 1987.

Schnarch, David M., Ph.D. *Constructing the Sexual Crucible: An Integration of Sexual and Marital Therapy*. New York: W. W. Norton and Co., 1991.

Solomon, Marion F. *Narcissism and Intimacy: Love and Marriage in an Age of Confusion*. New York: W. W. Norton and Co., 1989.

Spanier, Graham, and Margolis, Randie. "Marital Separation and Extramarital Behavior." *Journal of Sex Research* 19, no.1 (February 1983): 23–48.

Tavris, Carol, and Sadd, Susan. *The Redbook Report on Female Sexuality*. New York: Delacorte Press, 1977.

Taylor, Richard. *Having Love Affairs*. Buffalo, N.Y.: Prometheus Books, 1990.

Thompson, Anthony P. "Extramarital Sex: A Review of the Research Literature." *Journal of Sex Research* 19, no.7 (February 1983): 1–22.

———. "Emotional and Sexual Components of Extramarital Relations." *Journal of Marriage and the Family* 46, no. 1 (February 1984): 35–42.

Weis, D. L., and Jurich, J. "Size of Community of Residence as a Predictor of Attitudes Toward Extramarital Sexual Relations." *Journal of Marriage and the Family* 47, no. 1 (February 1985): 173–178.

Willi, Jurg, M.D. *Couples in Collusion*. New York: Jason Aronson, 1982.

Wolfe, Linda. *The Cosmo Report*. New York: Arbor House, 1981.

———. *Playing Around: Women and Extramarital Sex*. New York: William Morrow and Co., 1975.

Wyatt, Gail E., Ph.D.; Peters, Stefanie D., Ph.D.; and Guthrie, Donald, Ph.D. "Kinsey Revisited, Part 1: Comparisons of the Sexual Socialization and Sexual Behavior of White Women over 33 Years." *Archives of Sexual Behavior* 17, no. 3 (1988): 201–239.

INDEX